SIR WALTER SCOTT, BART.

Uniform with this Volume

THE LETTERS OF SIR WALTER SCOTT
1787-1832

Edited by
SIR HERBERT GRIERSON

Centenary Edition : Twelve Volumes

The Scotsman : " This edition will hold its own, as a work of research and scholarship, both in its text and in its notes, with the great editions of the Letters of Horace Walpole, Gray, Lamb, Shelley and Keats.

" We owe an immense debt to Sir Herbert Grierson and his assistants for so perfectly executing a work which Sir Herbert's great predecessor in the English Chair once declared to be impossible to accomplish. It is a work which will come to be recognised, not only for its own merits, but as a supplement and corrective of Lockhart."

Sir Walter Scott, Bart.
From the original picture by Sir John Watson Gordon
painted in the year 1830

SIR WALTER SCOTT, Bart.

BY

SIR HERBERT J. C. GRIERSON

PROFESSOR EMERITUS OF ENGLISH
LITERATURE AND RHETORIC AT
THE UNIVERSITY OF EDINBURGH

THE FOLCROFT PRESS INC. /1970

3/72

SIR WALTER SCOTT, Bart.

BY

SIR HERBERT J. C. GRIERSON

PROFESSOR EMERITUS OF ENGLISH
LITERATURE AND RHETORIC AT
THE UNIVERSITY OF EDINBURGH

NEW YORK
COLUMBIA UNIVERSITY PRESS
LONDON: CONSTABLE & CO., LTD.
1938

IN MEMORIAM
M. L. G.
SURREXERUNT FILII EJUS,
ET BEATISSIMAM PRAEDICAVERUNT;
VIR EJUS ET LAUDAVIT EAM.

PREFACE

THE foundation of the present biography was laid in some lectures delivered at Toronto University in 1932 on the Alexander Foundation, and I have to thank that University for this invitation to develop from my study of Scott's *Letters* some sketch of his life and character as that was taking shape in my mind. Much fresh information has come to light since that time, as the Abbotsford Papers, the Constable and Cadell letter-books and correspondence, have been gathered into the National Library of Scotland. I have tried from these to draw the picture as it presented itself to me without concealment or manipulation.

A very great loss for my book was the death, when that work was hardly well begun, of the late Mr. James Glen, W.S., of Glasgow. He had made the study of Sir Walter Scott's life a hobby during many years, and to him is largely due the correcting of the dates of many of Scott's early letters and with it the right dating of important events, such as Scott's last visit to Fettercairn and Miss Belsches. To him also is due the tracing of the rather mysterious affair of the money left in Chancery belonging to Lady Scott's mother. In these inquiries I was, of course, able to help him from the letters which were coming into my hands, at home and in America, and also from another important contribution to the editing of Scott's letters and the attempt to sketch his life. I mean the bound volumes of letters to Sir Walter, prepared by himself and his secretary, George Gordon, some time before his death, and now in the possession of Sir Hugh Walpole, who was good enough to put them at the disposal of myself and my assistants in the work of editing.

But Mr. Glen was not only a researcher and collector of facts and documents concerning Scott. He was an accountant, and had given much time and thought to the problem of Scott's insolvency and the mutual indebtedness of Scott and his publishers. On this subject he wrote me a letter for publication in the first volume of our edition of the *Letters*, to which I would refer my readers. But I have felt very much the not having Mr. Glen at my elbow to check statements about Scott's financial affairs, for I am not an accountant. I have done my best, but when I venture on details, as at p. 146 or in the note on p. 221, I am generally following Mr. Glen as closely as I could.

One advantage we have enjoyed that Lockhart did not, that is access not only to the letters which passed between Scott and his publishers, Constable and Cadell, but to the letters which passed between these gentlemen themselves, and between them and their London agents and other correspondents. For his account of Scott's relation with the Ballantynes and with Constable, Lockhart was largely dependent on Robert Cadell, whose account could hardly be expected to be entirely impartial. If I have formed a somewhat unfavourable impression of Cadell as a hard man of business, the chief or only person who profited in the end by Scott's gigantic activities, I have tried to keep my own comment within the narrowest limits, leaving his words to speak for themselves.

I have taken Constable and Cadell so much for granted throughout that I find I have nowhere given any history of their connections before Scott became the centre of their interest. Constable, whose first great stroke as a publisher, or bookseller as was the usual term, was the *Edinburgh Review* begun in 1802, made his first business contact with Scott in the same year, when Longman and Rees allowed him a share in the copyright of *The Minstrelsy of the Scottish Border*. With them he shared in the publication of *The Lay of the Last Minstrel* (1805). His first partner, Alexander Gibson Hunter (1804-11), seems to have been principally responsible for Constable's quarrel first with Longman and Rees and then, as my story tells, with Scott. In 1811 Constable formed a fresh partnership with Robert Cathcart, who died within a year, and with Robert Cadell who thereafter was the sole partner, and in 1817 became Constable's son-in-law. He was twenty-three when admitted as a partner, having entered Constable's business as a clerk at the age of nineteen. What capital the fresh partnership brought to Constable came chiefly from Cathcart and had to be refunded on his death. Cadell's wife died within a year after his marriage. Cadell's active career as a partner in Constable's publishing ventures begins, it will thus be seen, just before the return of Scott in 1813 to Constable as his adviser, to be soon his principal and ultimately his sole publisher. Cadell is concerned with all the chief events from the publication of Swift's *Works* (1814), *Waverley* (1814), and *The Lord of the Isles* (1815) to the end. My Life of Scott, including the Epilogue, becomes thus practically a Life of Cadell as publisher, for, as the *Dictionary of National Biography* says, he restricted "his operations almost exclusively to the publication of Scott's works", with the results which I have indicated. From the beginning of his connection with Constable as partner the tenor of his letters was the weakness of that firm from its lack of sufficient capital. This, with Scott's rash anticipation of funds, is the explanation of the ultimate failure, not the Ballantynes, though they and the Printing Office helped in the dissipation of Scott's profits.

Where I have cited from the *Letters*, a reader would find it interesting at times to read the whole letter.

To my acknowledgements above I wish to add my thanks to my friend J. C. Smith, C.B.E., LL.D., for his careful reading of my proofs, and to Mr. W. M. Parker, who also read the proofs and has checked for me, when absent in America, my quotations from manuscripts now in the National Library.

H. J. C. GRIERSON

THE LIBRARY
    COLUMBIA UNIVERSITY, NEW YORK
April 4, 1938

CONTENTS

CHAPTER ONE. 1771-1788
Ancestry and Youth - - - - - - 1

CHAPTER TWO. 1788-1797
Early Loves and Interests - - - - - 17

CHAPTER THREE. 1797-1798
Charlotte Carpenter and Marriage - - - 45

CHAPTER FOUR. 1799-1804
Ballads, *Sir Tristrem* and *The Lay of the Last Minstrel* 70

CHAPTER FIVE. 1805-1810
James Ballantyne and Company, Printers, and John Ballantyne and Company, Publishers - - 83

CHAPTER SIX. 1810-1815
Rokeby to *Guy Mannering*—Financial Crisis - - 103

CHAPTER SEVEN. 1815-1816
The Antiquary to *Tales of my Landlord*—Negotiations with Publishers - - - - - - 126

CHAPTER EIGHT. 1816-1818
Old Mortality to *The Monastery*—Meeting with Lockhart—Incessant Writing - - - - 150

CHAPTER NINE. 1819-1823
Ivanhoe to *St. Ronan's Well*—Family Life—Miss Edgeworth - - - - - - - 179

CONTENTS

CHAPTER TEN. 1823-1825
Marriage of young Walter—Growth of Abbotsford—*Redgauntlet* and *Tales of Crusaders*—*Napoleon* planned—Visit to Ireland - - - - 219

CHAPTER ELEVEN. 1825-1827
Advent of Disaster—The *Journal*—Death of Lady Scott—Work on *Napoleon*—*Woodstock* - - 247

CHAPTER TWELVE. 1828-1832
The Last Years—Lockhart to London—The *Magnum Opus*—*Count Robert of Paris*—Italy—Abbotsford—The End - - - - 278

EPILOGUE
Financial Aftermath—The Dualism in Scott's Life and Work - - - - - - - 301

CHAPTER I

"My Lord of Crèvecœur," said Quentin, "my family—"
"Nay, it is not utterly of family that I spoke," said the Count, "but of rank, fortune, high station, and so forth, which place a distance between various degrees and classes of persons. As for birth, all men are descended from Adam and Eve."

Quentin Durward, c. xxiv.

THE *Life of Sir Walter Scott* has been written by Lockhart in a manner that is not likely to be superseded or rivalled. But Lockhart's is a carefully composed picture in which some features of the original have been omitted, others skilfully softened; and the many letters which are now available show not only much inaccuracy in the details of Lockhart's narrative but a somewhat surprising element of what appears to be sheer invention of a picturesque and dramatic character, such as Lockhart had already practised in *Peter's Letters to His Kinsfolk*, *Noctes Ambrosianae*, and occasional contributions to *Blackwood's Magazine*. Moreover, in his design to at least minimise and to make explicable Scott's financial disaster, he allowed his mind to be clouded with prejudice and to be inoculated by Cadell with a false or partial view of the character and conduct of Constable and the Ballantynes. The aim of the present biography is, therefore, not to rival Lockhart's or other of the many Lives based on that work, but rather to supplement. Nor shall I essay to write a biography "in the modern manner". I will leave to Scott himself, or to the reader's own imagination, to supply pictures of the young Walter wending unwillingly to school, or pacing the floor of Parliament House, or entertaining guests at Abbotsford, or in his interviews, at the moment of crisis, with Cadell and James Ballantyne. I do not feel myself sufficiently superior to Scott to wish to take him down a peg, or to treat him with elegant banter. To me he is, if not a model of all the virtues, or the greatest of poets and novelists, " a very extraordinary man ", as Cadell calls him in a letter, a creative genius of the first order if we may judge by fertility and spontaneity, a man and writer in the study of whose motives and methods one comes closer to divining something of what one side of Shakespeare was like, the actor, the playwright, the purchaser of New Place and a coat of arms, if Shakespeare is a deeper searcher of the hearts of men, a poet of a far greater range of felicitous phrase and rhythm—and also apparently a more prudent man of business. It is not for the present writer to essay with others to follow in the footsteps of Mr. Strachey. Great brilliance is beyond his power. My model would rather be, and even with that I will not venture on rivalry, Mr. Dykes Campbell's *Life of Coleridge*. It is my hope not only to correct some errors of fact and date, but to suggest some aspects of Scott's character and life which too careful manipulation and idealisation have obscured, but which are of interest and importance to every serious student of literature and of human nature.

When G. R. Gleig, the biographer of the Duke of Wellington, reprinted in 1872 a sketch of the Life of Scott which he had contributed to *The Quarterly Review* in 1868, he found it necessary to prefix an apology for having apparently cast " the shadow of a doubt over the place which Sir Walter's family held in society. That his grandfather rented a farm under a distant relative is as certain as that his father lived and died a Writer to the Signet. But the farmer and the Writer were equally gentlemen by descent, by habits of life, by social relations, etc." It throws an interesting light on the spirit of Edinburgh society, suggests well the atmosphere in which Scott grew up—this concern to assert that your father was not a mere farmer, or a mere Writer to the Signet, but a gentleman by descent from old families and landed gentry. That sentiment helped to determine Walter to become an Advocate, not a mere Writer, and gave a very definite shape to his ambitions when he discovered that his pen was a potential source of wealth. Like Shakespeare a couple of centuries earlier, he would make for himself a place among those who, not by birth alone but by actual possession and status, were landed gentlemen, *armigeri*. This ambition in Scott was qualified by a sincere love of the country and country life. " It had been, though the gratification was long postponed, an early wish of mine to connect myself with my mother earth and prosecute those experiments by which a species of creative power is exercised over the face of nature." Moreover, with this as with all Scott's romantic sentiments, he could when called on to use his good sense discount it, and judge of things as they are. When his son Walter demurs to the connection with trade of the bride proposed to him, Miss Jobson of Lochore, Scott reminds him that they are themselves but cadets of cadets, and tells him that his sister Anne " makes herself a little ridiculous with her airs "— her Edinburgh airs. Nevertheless, the sentiment was deep and passionate, but unfortunately Scott lived two centuries after Shakespeare and was a contemporary of the French Revolution. The first shock had been given to the social fabric in which he hoped to gain for himself a secure and recognised position, and, like many around him, he felt in his bones that security was gone, that sooner or later the democratic movement would change everything he cared for in the social order. When a Whig First Lord of the Admiralty placed a frigate at his disposal for the last voyage to the Mediterranean, Scott's response was : " Things are still in the hands of gentlemen ; but woe is me. They have so undermined the state of society that it will hardly keep together when they cease to be at the head of it." So, from the outset, Scott was in politics a passionate partisan.[1] He can at times regret the bitterness of party politics and endeavour to prevent its affecting his attitude towards individuals. But perhaps a member of an established aristocracy can accept revolutionary changes with more equanimity than one who has just arrived, or believes himself on the way thither. Politics is the one subject in which Scott readily lost his balance, and I write as one who by no means regards Whigs and Radicals as indisputably in the right. The young peasant-born Sansculottist, Thomas Carlyle, came to have as great a contempt for Radicals and Democrats as ever Scott had, to feel and assert the need for a governing class; if he could not believe that the partridge-shooting, corn-law defending landed gentry represented any longer the class needed, that the dire necessity of his time was " a working aristocracy ".

This political bias was, I think, and that is why I have made it prominent, the chief effect of that pride in his ancestry—" Every Scotchman has a pedigree "—which the autobiography and letters reveal, qualified by a certain humorous recognition of the nature of these ancestors' achievements. For it is difficult nowadays to take much interest in Auld Watt of Harden and other Border

---

[1] " It is the same with me in politics. In general I care very little about the matter . . . but either actually important events, or such as seemed so by their close neighbourhood to me, have always hurried me off my feet, and made me, as I have sometimes afterwards regretted, more forward and more violent than those who had a regular jog-trot way of busying themselves in public matters. Good luck, for had I lived in troublesome times and chanced to be on the unhappy side I had been hanged to a certainty." *Journal*, Feb. 17, 1826. Lady Rosslyn rejected all friendly advances; and Lady Bessborough tells Lord Granville Leveson-Gower on August 27, 1808: " We dine again at the Rosslyns . . . Lady Rosslyn really would be very pleasant if it were not for her party violence, which exceeds everything I ever met with. She will not admit *any* of Walter Scott's Poetry into the house, and in shewing me his cottage said ' the Beast who us'd to live there and who I wish hanged ', and in passing Lord Melville's park she leant back lest she should be obliged to bow to Mr R. Dundas and said, ' I believe nothing will ever kill the old Devil; he ought to have been dead long ago ' —' and Damn'd,' added Mr. Brougham." *Lord Granville Leveson-Gower's private correspondence.* II, 323-4.

champions, whose life, when stripped of feudal glamour, does not really differ essentially from that of the gun-men of Chicago, plunder and murder their chief activities. " Beardie ", the poet's great-grandfather, was a devoted Jacobite, taken prisoner at Preston in 1715 and saved from death, Scott tells us, by the intercession of Ann, Duchess of Monmouth and Buccleuch. Walter Scott was a Jacobite too in sentiment, but that sentiment also was under the control of a directing realist and even rationalist outlook. Scott was of the Age of Hume as his treatment of the supernatural, alike in the romances and the *Demonology and Witchcraft* clearly evidences. Any such adjustment of the relations between reason and imagination as Wordsworth and Coleridge speculated about was not dreamed of in his philosophy.

Strangely different from these swashbucklers of the Borders and the Civil Wars are some of his ancestors in whom can be traced a deeper vein of feeling and reflection. His father's great-grandfather, Walter Scott of Raeburn, became a Quaker and suffered for his convictions; his mother's great-grandfather, John Swinton of Swinton, was also a convert, though perhaps for political reasons, " to avoid the fate of Waristoun and Argyle . . . it was a common phrase of the time that if Swinton had not *trembled* he would never have *quaked*. . . . I am glad I escaped the honours of the stiff-rumped Quakers which threatened to descend on me from two different channels." Scott had no love for saints. He warns James Ballantyne of all things not to marry a very religious woman, for nothing can be a greater cause of unhappiness in a family. But the Christian religion in which he had been brought up was for him an ultimate fact, the background to all our actions and experiences, not to be brought too much into the foreground. Religious duties were to be respected like other duties. In the hope of another life lay the only consolation for the sorrows and partings of this. Of what kind that life will be we do not and cannot know. " It is all speculation, and it is impossible even to guess what we shall do unless we could ascertain the equally difficult previous question, what we are to be. But there is a God and a just God—a judgement and a future life—and all who own so much let them act according to the faith that is in them." Of religious worship as practised in the Church in which he was brought up he had but doleful memories. He had groaned under many a sermon in the Tron Kirk. " The chief reason for entering a Scottish Kirk ", he reports a friend as saying, " is the pleasure of coming out again." It was probably the influence of his wife, a French Catholic rebaptised into the Anglican Church, which was responsible for his attendance at the Episcopal Chapel. But the Anglican ritual appealed to him, and one can see from the *Demonology and Witchcraft* (Letter VIII) that the *via media* achieved by that Church, the middle way between the Roman adherence to tradition (" vestigia nulla retrorsum ") and the Calvinist and Puritan rejection of every rag of papacy, between the Roman dependence on priestly authority and the too great dependence of the Calvinists on the populace, appealed to a mind whose natural bent was to compromise, to strike a balance between sentiment and sense, reason and imagination, if liable, especially in politics, to be more swayed by passion and prejudice than he would willingly have admitted, or could altogether approve when he looked back. He was far from sharing Southey's ultra-orthodoxy and fear of Rome.

Of more importance than these remote moss-troopers and Quaker offshoots are the poet's immediate kin. Walter Scott, or " Beardie ", to whom I have referred, was the second son of Walter Scott, the third son of the first Sir William Scott of Harden and his wife Ann Makdougall of Makerstoun—hence Scott's kinship with the Makdougalls. " Beardie's " eldest son, Walter, migrated to America. The second son, Robert, the poet's grandfather, became, after a brief experience of the sea, farmer at Sandyknowe " in the centre of which Smailholm or Sandy-knowe Tower is situated ", the home of the poet's early days. Robert Scott married Barbara, the daughter of Thomas Haliburton of Newmains, in whose property lay the part of Dryburgh, comprehending the ruins of the Abbey, which, for the want of male heirs, " would have devolved upon my father " (*Autobiography*). But alas ! a granduncle to whom it passed muddled it away in debts. The earliest extant letters of Robert Scott and his son, the W.S., father to the poet, are largely concerned with this Robert Haliburton's failure. The W.S. made an offer, through one Mr. William Elliot, keeping his own name out of the transaction, of £5,000 with permission to go to £50 more, but the estate passed for £5,500 to a Colonel Clarke Todd. Scott bitterly regretted this loss, and it was probably at his instance that his uncle Robert Scott of Rosebank, near Kelso, acquired from Lord Buchan in 1791 the right of burial in the Abbey grounds where the poet now sleeps (*Letters*, I, p. 15 note).

The poet's father, eldest son of Sandyknowe, became a W.S. in Edinburgh and prospered in his business, becoming head of the firm in which he had served his apprenticeship. The picture of him in *Redgauntlet* suggests the dry, canny Scots lawyer, but there were traits in his character which reappear in the son. He kept no books, so that the agent to the Trust after his death had to wade through a mass of correspondence to settle the exact history of this or that outstanding debt. There were so many of these due to him that it took from 1799, when he died, to 1814 to wind up the estate, and in more than one instance the losses had to be cut. Shortreed's notes, too, suggest that he was capable of enjoying a jest. In 1758 the W.S. married the eldest daughter of John Rutherford, Professor of Medicine in the University of Edinburgh, and his first wife, Ann, daughter of Sir John Swinton of Swinton, one of the oldest families of Scotland. The young couple settled first in Anchor Close, " a dirty narrow alley ", so Robert Chambers describes it in *Traditions of Edinburgh*, running down the hill towards the north—now a clean and uninteresting lane bordered on the west by the recent extension of the City Chambers. In this insanitary quarter poor Mrs. Scott settled down to a life of childbearing. " You have no time to write for bearing bairns," writes a Mrs. Smith, who had migrated to America. Here, Scott tells Henry Mackenzie in 1825, " my father and mother, healthy people, lost six children successively. They went to the south side of the town . . . and behold six children grew up to be men and women."[1] That, nevertheless, Mrs. Scott had vivid interests, social and literary, is suggested by other of these early letters. " How my heart would jump ", writes in 1765 the friend exiled at Charleston, " were I to find myself set down at the Anchor Close, or supposing I were to come slyly some evening and catch you reading a paper by Mr Spectator by yourself in the Drawing room." Another friend complains of having been interrupted in some reading " by a train of fine ladies who bounced in upon us—I am persuaded were I constantly living in your house I should be ready to cry out :

Shut, shut the door, good John, fatigu'd I said,
Tye up the knocker, say I'm sick or dead

---

[1] Like many of Scott's, this is a somewhat sweeping statement. Not all the children who died were born, or died, in Anchor Close. The firstborn Anne, born in 1759, lived to be eight years old, dying in 1767. Robert, born in August 1760, died in February 1761, and John, born in November 1761, died in November of the following year. The fourth child, and second Robert, whose name appears in Mrs. Scott's list of those who had been born before 1767 and was, therefore, reckoned by Lockhart among those who died in childhood, became the sailor who, after serving in the Navy, entered the East India Company's service, died and was buried at sea from the *Rodney* on the 8th June, 1787. Jean, born in March 1765, lived till July 1770, when she died of " chincough ". The first Walter, born in August 1766, died in October. A Barbara, of whose birth no mention occurs, was buried on 30th January, 1772. The John and the Walter who lived, were born, the former about 1768, and the latter on 15th August, 1771. Anne (1772), Thomas (1774), and Daniel followed. The latest letter which I have found addressed to Anchor Close is dated 1767.

for there is no resting a moment—but you Madam have been formed for society." Later letters show her growing serious and consulting the minister at Sandyknowe on points of doctrine. As a Swinton she formed Scott's closest connection with the upper class of Scottish and Edinburgh society. Otherwise, as Gleig justly says, the position given him by birth " was neither among the very high nor the very low, but in that middle class which constitutes the backbone of society both in England and Scotland ". And Scott never really forgets this fact, though from an early stage he sets himself to make his way up to a higher level—from his father's apprentices to the young advocates, sons of the landed gentry, and thence to the friendship of the young Lord Dalkeith and the Dundases and the Hamiltons and others, his attitude towards whom was always one of deference. He made no attempt to assert equality or familiarity, to be, as Byron boasted that he and Moore were, " the one by circumstances, the other by birth . . . free of the corporation." But that deference implied no servility. He was quite prepared to quarrel with a lord, even with the second Lord Melville, if need be, for Scott's feudal regard for rank was combined with a robust Scottish equalitarianism, the recognition that " a man's a man for a' that ", which made him equally at home with Lord Montagu, the Ballantynes, and Tom Purdie on a basis of mutual courtesy. He did not need, like poor Burns, to assert that equality by bluster or rudeness.

From both the paternal and the maternal side Scott and his brothers and sisters derived an unhealthy, even decadent, strain. Rheumatism he speaks of as an inheritance from his father, and the paralysis which overtook him at the end of his life had been his father's lot also. But it was from his mother that he inherited (and transmitted to Sophia) the tendency to gall-stones and its consequent, cramp in the stomach, from which he suffered so acutely in 1817 and again in 1819. Of the twelve children born to the W.S., six, as has been said, died in infancy. The air of Anchor Close and College Wynd [1] was in part to blame, and in 1773-4 their father built himself a house in George Square. In College Wynd or George Square five more children were born who survived infancy,[2] but of whom Walter alone " barely attained to the nearest limits of old age ". And he himself narrowly escaped an early death, for in his second year he was attacked by infantile paralysis, which left him permanently lame.[3] His life was saved by what proved also an inestimable boon for his imaginative development. He was sent to his grandfather's farm at Sandyknowe, where he lived in the open air, and for the first eight years of his life enjoyed the benefit of being surrounded by care and affection, at Smailholm with his grandparents, at Bath with his aunt, at Kelso and Prestonpans, enjoying that kind of spoiling which never injured anyone who was not perverse from the womb, if it made it a little harder to return to George Square, pious parental discipline, the bullying of rough older brothers, and the careless impatience of servants. " I had sense enough to

---

[1] " The old buildings of the College of Edinburgh . . . had for their main access, in former times, only that dismal alley called the College Wynd, leading up from the Cowgate. Facing down this humble lane was the gateway of the College, displaying a richly ornamented architrave. The wynd itself . . . was the abode of many of the professors. The illustrious Joseph Black lived at one time in a house adjacent to the College gate on the east side. Another floor of the same building was occupied by Mr. Keith, father of the late Sir Alexander Keith of Ravelston, Bart., and there did the late Lord Keith reside in his student-days. . . . The one peculiar glory of the humble place remains to be mentioned—its being the birth-place of Sir Walter Scott. In the third story of the house just described, accessible by an entry leading to a common stair, did this distinguished person first see the light, August 15, 1771." Chambers' *Traditions of Edinburgh*. The closing of the College Gate on that side and the running of Chambers Street along the north side of the College has left Guthrie Street as the only remnant of College Wynd. The University wall covers the site of the house where Scott was born.

[2] See page 8. But Barbara died, and Robert was born in Anchor Close.

[3] He also nearly suffered Dr. Johnson's fate of being infected by a wet nurse, not with scrofula but tuberculosis.

bend my temper to my new circumstances ; but such was the agony which I internally experienced that I have guarded against nothing more in the education of my family than against their acquiring habits of self-willed caprice and domination." To counter-balance these sufferings, he had " the partiality of my mother " and, at least on week days, the joys of reading.

All the details of Scott's childhood, whether gathered from his own autobiography and letters, from Lockhart, or from other sources such as the early *Life* by Weir and Allan, combine to give a vivid impression : the impression of a child of acute sensibility, but with the courage and good sense to fight against that sensibility, tempted, perhaps, to discipline and emphasise that courage as a less sensitive child might have felt no need to do ; a child of precocious intelligence and vivid imagination, averse from the arid paths of scholastic instruction in which a pupil is driven from behind rather than beckoned onwards by a vision of something to be obtained. " My little boy ", he writes in 1809, " is just entered at the High School and my imagination like that of Leontes in *The Winter's Tale* is running back thirty years and recollecting when I first crept through George Square with Robert Dundas to learn tasks to which I could annex neither idea nor utility." But if no lover of prescribed lessons, he is a reader almost from his infant years, absorbing fairy tales, ballads, Shakespeare, fiction, legend, and history. At six he is reading Falconer's *Shipwreck* and astounding Mrs. Cockburn by his dramatic declamation, his curiosity, and at the same time his ready acquiescence in solutions of orthodoxy, and his ambition to be a " virtuoso " and know everything. His memory for ballads can be traced back to his sixth year, if he was fourteen before Percy's *Reliques* awakened a consciously antiquarian interest in them and their recovery. Confined to bed in 1784-5, he consumes novels and fights his way through Vertot's *Knights of Malta* and Orme's " interesting and beautiful history of

Indostan ". At the end of his life, when on the last hopeless journey to the Mediterranean, he busies himself with a novel, which he feels is to be one of his best, *The Siege of Malta*. All that is coherent in that work proves to be an almost verbatim reproduction of Vertot's book. As the creative, controlling element in his mind failed him, the wonderful memory was still active, and he wrote as though it were his own what he had read and absorbed when a boy of fourteen. Romance, poetry, and history—with, later, law—were the chief elements in Scott's education. In more exact studies, philosophical and scientific, his training was of the slightest. His five years at the High School (1778 to 1784) gave him apparently an adequate grounding in Latin to which his own later reading added. But his English spelling was always uncertain, and his composition was not formed by rules and models. Lockhart, he writes in 1826, " kindly points out some solecisms in my style as ' amid ' for ' amidst ', ' scarce ' for ' scarcely '. ' Whose ', he says, is the proper genitive of ' which ' only at such times as ' which ' retains its quality of impersonification. Well ! I will try to remember all this, but after all I write grammar as I speak, to make my meaning known, and a solecism in point of composition, like a Scotch word in speaking, is indifferent to me. I never learned grammar ; and not only Sir Hugh Evans but even Mrs. Quickly might puzzle me about Giney's case and horum harum horum." (*Journal*). His own experience, however, made him, when helping to shape the curriculum for the Edinburgh Academy, determined that English should be a constituent element in the training given. To Greene and Jonson, at an earlier period, Shakespeare's scholarship and style had the same defects as Sir Walter's had for Lockhart—if only one could recover some such picture of Shakespeare's early reading as we have in such fullness of Scott's !

An omnivorous reader, reading in bed, or " lying upon his back on the carpet with all his books around him, his lame leg resting upon his left thigh and the book he was reading laid upon the lame foot as on a reading desk ", the young Walter was yet no retiring bookworm but by nature active and enterprising.[1] Despite his delicacy and lameness, he took his part in childish combats at the High School and in the fights with poorer boys in the vicinity of his home. We see him as the chief organiser of fireworks in the Square till a misdirected rocket scatters his audience; or a bold climber on the Castle Rock as in later years on expeditions of the Blair Adam Club, or on his visit to Ireland so late as 1825, in all of which was perhaps a little of the determination of one whose early lameness and delicacy had given him a certain sense of inferiority. " There is still the stile at which I can recollect a cross child's maid upbraiding me with my infirmity, as she lifted me coarsely and carelessly over the flinty steps which my brothers traversed with shout and bound. I remember the suppressed bitterness of the moment and, conscious of my own inferiority, the feeling of envy with which I regarded the easy movements and elastic steps of my more happily formed brethren." (*Chronicles of the Canongate.*)

And lastly the impression one derives is of a child of extraordinary sweetness and charm who gained the heart of everyone who knew him by his openness, his eager enthusiasm and readiness to communicate his interest; the sweetness of his temper, capable of anger but readily placated; and his wonderful dutifulness, by which I do not mean a too narrow cultivation of the " restrictive virtues " which may tend, as in Milton's case, to intensify rather than to correct egotism, but a readiness to admit and give full value to the claims—the rights and the

---

[1] " Mrs Ballantyne, Mrs Scott's old maid, who lives in our garden house, says she recollects to have heard that his uncle Captain Scott when he saw him lying on the carpet reading at his father's in Edinburgh and the Edinburgh school-boys playing in George Square asked him if he would not rather like to be playing out with those boys, he replied, ' No, Uncle, you cannot think how ignorant those boys are—I am much happier reading my books '."—MRS. SCOTT OF HARDEN to LOCKHART.

wishes—of others. It is not a quality that easily and often goes with genius, for the self-centredness, call it selfishness if you like, is or may be a self-protective instinct. Like the prophet and the saint, the poet must at times sacrifice father and mother, brother and sister, and perhaps most often his wife, poor woman. If Goethe is to be blamed for not visiting his mother in the later years of her life, why should Saint Xavier be extolled for refusing to take farewell of his mother as he made his way across Spain to embark for India ? And Scott had to pay a price for his regard for the wishes of others. Some of these are obvious —the time he wasted on electioneering in the Buccleuch interest, in looking after the interests of Daniel and Tom, preparing the marriage settlements of Miss Clephane, writing articles for Gillies, and endless other distractions before and after his catastrophe. But I think there were other and more obscure effects. If one is sensitive to the feelings of others, sometimes the only escape is a little concealment or even deceit. Scott entered his father's office though he disliked the work and detested the confinement, but read many a romance and played many a game of chess in office hours—just as other young men have done. But I am disposed to think that his later concealment of his business connections with the Ballantynes, and again of his activity as a novelist, had at least their partial source in the same desire to secure his personal freedom from expostulation and criticism. Against the *tracasseries* of a literary life, adverse criticism, and the asperities of literary controversy, he could determine to oppose the shield of indifference, though it is clear enough that he felt criticism like other men. Jeffrey's censure of *Marmion* made its contribution towards the starting of *The Quarterly Review* as a rival to *The Edinburgh Review*, and Byron's lines in *English Bards and Scotch Reviewers* stung him to the quick. But this was criticism of published work. It would have been different with social criticism of his participation in trade, and the expostulation of relations and friends ; nor would it have been easy within a small society like that of Edinburgh to turn out a novel each year if, in addition to printed criticism, one had to meet everyday acquaintances who insisted on giving him their views as to relative merits, or identifying, as Robert Chambers was to do later, persons and incidents in the novels.[1] The Ballantyne connection especially would have raised questions of right and wrong, of wisdom and unwisdom, that would have been more difficult to evade than when left to the decision of his own sanguine and impulsive mind, which undoubtedly made it possible for Scott at times to deceive himself. Secrecy left him complete freedom to pursue the three lines of life, social, literary, commercial, in independence of one another, so far as comment by others was concerned. For his conduct in each he had to answer to his own conscience alone, and his conduct to the last shows how acutely he felt his duty to the Ballantynes and his publishers. " I have been far from suffering by James Ballantyne. I owe it to him to say that his difficulties as well as his advantages are owing to me." With his publishers he might drive a hard bargain, perhaps play them off at times against each other. He would never deceive, or take advantage of, them. In the novels he felt his only duty concerned their moral tone and possible effect on young readers.

From the High School Scott proceeded to the University; but though he enrolled in Latin, Greek and Logic classes his education was seriously interrupted by the breaking of a blood-vessel in 1784. In March 1786 he was apprenticed to his father for a period of five

[1] Writing of her novel *The Inheritance* in 1824 Miss Ferrier says : " *Everybody* knows who the characters are, but no two people agree about them. I have heard of five or six Lord Rossvilles and as many Miss Pratts and Lady John Camp signs herself Mrs Major Waddell on account of her care of her husband which she says is her to the very life. In short whenever characters are at all *natural* they are immediately set down for being *personal*, which is a grievance." *Memoir and Correspondence of Susan Ferrier*, etc., London, 1898. Scott demurred to many of Chambers's identifications but it did not matter so long as nobody could speak to him about it.

years and groaned but endured under the confinement. During the first two of these his companions, Lockhart tells us, were chiefly his fellow clerks in the office. But in 1788, when attending the class of Civil Law,[1] he formed the acquaintance of young men whose aim was the higher branch of the law, and discovered that none beneath the level of an Advocate—leaving soldiers and the aristocracy aside—could in Edinburgh be accounted a gentleman. In consequence, those ambitions were quickened which were to determine the direction of his life, to assert for himself his proper place in the social scale, whether law or literature should prove the appropriate lever. To begin with he would be an Advocate and share the tastes and the amusements of the *jeunesse dorée* of Edinburgh. It was as part of his professional course that, in 1789-90, he attended the lectures on Moral Philosophy of the eloquent—more eloquent than profound—Professor Dugald Stewart, whose monument now graces the Calton Hill, set over against that of David Hume as a counteractive to any malign influence which might emanate from the tomb of so notorious an iconoclast.

[1] Scott's attendance at the University thus fell into two parts—a broken attendance on classes in Arts 1783-6; classes in Law 1788-92.

CHAPTER II

O Life ! how pleasant in thy morning !
Young Fancy's rays the hills adorning.
BURNS.

WITH 1788 closes the first chapter of Scott's life, in which he has lived among those of the class to which his father's family belonged, differing from them only in the range of his intellectual interests and in his extraordinary but not yet fully revealed gifts. It was quite natural that at Kelso in 1783 he should form a friendship in the village school with James Ballantyne who was to play so active a part in the drama of his subsequent life. There was no great social barrier to be passed. Nor is it in any way surprising that during these years he seems to have made the first step in his *éducation sentimentale,* and had an innocent love affair with a young girl whom later he would regard as socially undesirable. The story of his early love for an unknown " Jessie ", afterwards the bride of a young doctor who had studied in Edinburgh and made a practice for himself in London, is told in an unpublished Life of Scott among the Forster MSS. in the South Kensington Museum. It is a very poor biography, concocted from Chambers and Hogg and padded with chapters on the history of various forms of literature. The story of the early love affair is given on the authority of the lady herself. The evidence for its truth lies, it seems to me, in the letters themselves which she allowed the compiler to copy.[1] Who but the young Scott would have entertained the daughter of a small tradesman in Kelso with old ballads and songs, as

[1] *Letters of Sir Walter Scott,* Vol. I, pp. 1-8, referred to hereafter as *Letters,* with volume and page.

the youthful Oldbuck might have done? Scott's humour, too, is evident in the manner in which he tells the story of Lammikin, and his wonderful memory in the accuracy with which he then recalls the words of a ballad heard from a servant girl at Bath in his fifth or sixth year. The end of this youthful affair, begun in Kelso but continued in Edinburgh when the maiden was summoned thither to keep house for an aunt, a termination which left in her mind " a resentment that never subsided ", coincides probably with the crisis which marked his move up from the society of his father's apprentices to that of young budding Advocates, fully conscious of their social superiority to lawyers of the inferior branches, tradespeople, medical students (many of them Irish, like Goldsmith), *et hoc genus omne*. Edinburgh was long the Mecca of social snobbishness, drawing its lines very sharp and clear, and always at the top stood the toga and the sword—advocates and officers at the Castle.[1] Scott no sooner found his way into these circles than he determined to make good, to choose his friends among those who shared his literary tastes and whose more refined dress and manners appealed to his aesthetic temperament. "Jessie" and his father's apprentices fell into the background. Scott, like most of his townsmen, was somewhat of a snob, but the word is loosely, and often enviously, applied to very different impulses, from the parasitism of the climber, the vulgar uppishness of the " new rich ", to the quite natural taste for a higher distinction and refinement of manners and a greater freedom of outlook than is possible for those whose

---

[1] At a much later date, in 1825, Lockhart's friend Wright, in urging him to come to London as editor of *The Representative*, tells him he had come to the conclusion that Edinburgh was not a sphere " which your talents were calculated to adorn ", and goes on : " For what Scotland affords in regard to preferment calculated to satisfy an ambitious and aspiring mind I thought the claimants with title and hopes far exceeded those in England, and that there preferment was not so independently bestowed, and that there was not with you that regard paid to powerful and useful talents which prevails here."

horizon is too narrowly bounded by economic considerations. But for Scott to make new friends was not to abandon old. When his friends the apprentices complained of his cutting them for " the sake of Clerk and some more of these dons that look down on the like of us ", he replied that he would never cut any man unless he detected him in scoundrelism, but that no one had the right to interfere with his choice of friends. If he gave more attention to his dress and manners so that Sydney Smith could say later : " Who in the ordinary intercourse of society is better bred ? ", that did not involve any loss of naturalness and simplicity. " I was particularly struck ", writes Maria Edgeworth, who had seen much of the best society in London and Paris, " with his unaffected, gracious, simple and dignified manner of receiving all the complimentary visits and speeches made to him " in Ireland. " Sir Walter ", Robert Chambers reports, " speaks to every man as if they were blood relations."

About 1788 begins the second chapter of Scott's life, which may be said to close with his marriage in the end of 1797. His health was fully established. Apart from his lameness, he was not only healthy, whatever inherited germs of trouble might lurk in his constitution, but robust and powerful, with the breadth and depth of chest which so impressed Eckermann in Goethe. In the freshness of the morning he could lift a smith's anvil by the horn. His amazing energy was coming into full play as he launched into the social—and convivial—life of young Edinburgh lawyers, applied himself seriously to his professional studies, traversed the country on business for his father, or on walking and fishing expeditions with his new friends, and all the while continued the omnivorous reading which had begun when he was a child in George Square and with his aunt and uncle at Kelso. And he was finding now a quicker sympathy with his interests among these new friends, male and female—William Clerk of Eldin, Charles Kerr of Abbotrule, George Cranstoun,

George Abercromby, John James Edmonstone of Newton, Patrick Murray of Simprim, and, among the most ardent and intimate, William and Mary Erskine and Jane Cranstoun (sister of George), afterwards Countess Purgstall—the chief confidante, with the Erskines, of his second and most serious love affair, herself (I find it difficult not to believe) somewhat in the position of Viola when made the confidante of the Duke's passion for Olivia. Over all his friends he exercised the charm of the sweetness and simplicity of his own character, and the influence of one who pursued his studies legal, literary, and antiquarian, with a passionate ardour given to few men or women.

These studies, other than professional, were taking a more and more definite direction, but not as yet mainly literary. He wrote poems, which, to judge by those to "Jessie" and by the opinion of his friends, were of little worth. But history and antiquity, Scottish history and antiquity, were his most serious pursuits, determining the direction of his reading and giving a motive to his wanderings. The Borders he knew and was to know more thoroughly when he undertook his "raids" into Liddesdale with his friend Shortreed after being called to the Bar. His father's business had already taken him to the Highlands and introduced him to Highland chiefs or lairds who, like Stewart of Invernahyle, could entertain him with stories of the forty-five and the fifteen; and the Highlands, at least Perthshire, with Edinburgh and the south of Scotland, the Border Country, were to be always the country and people of which he wrote with most intimate knowledge and understanding. Two things must be kept in view in a study of Scott's earliest work—first, his antiquarian interest and secondly, how it came about that he carried this antiquarian interest over into creative work, and what was the character of that work as determined by his antiquarian studies on the one hand and his shrewd perception of what was required to awaken and captivate the taste of his own day—for Scott had no intention of imitating either Chatterton or Strutt and writing what could interest only an antiquarian, no more than Shakespeare was disposed to take lessons from Ben Jonson in " correct " comedy and historical tragedy weighted with " dignity of persons, gravity and height of elocution, fulness and frequency of sentence ". Both Scott and Shakespeare wrote to please their audience.

As an antiquarian interested in older literature Scott, of course, was but one of many in the last half of the eighteenth century. Bishop Percy's *Reliques* (themselves prepared for by earlier work) had stimulated the production of a long series of works, covering a wide field, English and Scottish, Celtic and Scandinavian, and it is necessary to remember how wide the field was, for Scott's interest covered almost the whole, with the exception of the Celtic, and his own work was influenced by almost every " kind " revived. We are apt to think mainly of the traditional ballads, historical and romantic, which appealed to Scott more strongly than to Burns, whose chief interest was the popular song reflecting the feelings and life of the peasantry. The ballad was certainly the principal subject of interest to most of the collectors, who were all enthusiasts for the authentic voice of nature, heard in those unsophisticated—as they hoped and believed—products of rural minstrels, going back it might be even to, shall we say, a communal level. " Captain Car ", says Ritson, " is an entire and ancient copy [of the story told in Edom o' Gordon], the undoubted original of the Scotish [*sic*] ballad, and one of the few specimens now extant of the genuine, proper old English ballad as composed—not by a Grub Street author for the stalls of London—but to be chanted up and down the kingdom by the wandering minstrels of the ' North Countree '." To recover the purely traditional, orally transmitted, ballad was the collector's dream; hence Ritson's indignation with Percy's dressing of the ballads to advantage, and hence Scott's and Leyden's eager raids in Liddesdale. There were two temptations to which the questers for these " authentic " ballads were exposed,—first, to " dress them to advantage ", make them better poetry than in the orally transmitted version they actually were ; the other was, to concoct ancient ballads, to follow in the wake of Macpherson and Chatterton. Both Percy and Scott yielded to the former temptation, though their dressing was not quite of the same kind. Pinkerton, Surtees, Cunningham, and perhaps Buchan later, succumbed to the latter, Surtees securing the inclusion in *The Minstrelsy of the Scottish Border* of a ballad of his own composition. The result is, that a sceptical editor like Mr. T. F. Henderson is suspicious of anything that claims to be a purely traditional ballad (*e.g.* " Tamlane " or " The Twa Corbies ") ; the better the ballad the more suspicious he is of the hand of the collector, especially if the collector be himself a poet.

But if the ballad was the most fascinating of older forms of literature for the believer in a " return to nature " and a lover of romance, it was by no means the only form being revived during these years that Scott was interested in, and was to be influenced by ; for all his best, which is his lyrical poetry, takes the form of a revived old mood of feeling and mode of composition. Older Scottish poetry, both popular and the courtly poetry of " the Makars " of the fifteenth century, was reprinted by Watson and Ramsay, David Herd, Lord Hailes, John Pinkerton, John Callander, William Tytler, Joseph Ritson, and others. English songs and ballads, *e.g.* the Robin Hood ballads, were reprinted by Ritson and George Ellis, and the latter was soon to be busy with the metrical romances of the fourteenth and fifteenth centuries. Both the earlier and the Elizabethan drama were finding students and editors. The interest in Anglo-Saxon and in Scandinavian poetry, quickened by Mallet and Gray, was increasing, and Scott acquired some knowledge of the Sagas through Bartholine's Latin versions and, later, from Jamieson, and had perhaps a limited acquaintance with the original language.[1] Beyond an early interest (and perhaps faith which he soon totally discarded) in Macpherson's *Ossian*, he seems to have taken no serious interest in Celtic poetry. His Border blood and love of his own Scottish tongue inclined him even for a time to accept Pinkerton's thesis of a Gothic, Germanic origin for the Pictish people and, without English intervention, of the Scottish tongue.

These were the fields of antiquarian study in one or other of which Scott was busy during those years of his apprenticeship, adding to his earlier reading in romance and history. It is of himself he is thinking when he says of Edward Waverley: " He had perused the numerous romantic poems, which, from the days of Pulci, have been a favourite exercise of the wits of Italy, and had sought gratification in the numerous collections of *novelle*, which were brought forth by the genius of that elegant though luxurious nation in emulation of the Decameron, . . . and the French had afforded him an almost exhaustless collection of memoirs, scarcely more faithful than romances, and of romances so well written as hardly to be distinguished from memoirs. The splendid pages of Froissart, with his heart-stirring and eye-dazzling descriptions of war and of tournaments, were among his chief favourites; and from those of Brantome and De la Noue he learned to compare the wild and loose yet superstitious character of the nobles of the League, with the stern, rigid, and sometimes turbulent disposition of the Huguenot party. The Spanish had contributed to his stock of chivalrous and romantic lore." This strain of historic romance and romantic history from Italian, French, and Spanish sources had preceded, it is well to remember, his introduction to German and Northern literature and antiquities. The study of these came apparently contemporary with his study of law as is indicated by the essay he wrote for Dugald Stewart in 1791 " On the Manners and Customs of the

[1] See Edith Batho's " Scott as a Mediaevalist " in *Sir Walter Scott To-day*, Constable, London, 1932.

Northern Nations" and the titles of various papers read before The Speculative Society, which he joined on the 4th of January of that year: "On the Origin of the Feudal System," "On the Authenticity of Ossian's Poems," "On the Origin of the Scandinavian Mythology." It is well to remember this because had it been otherwise, had German and Scandinavian literature been an earlier study, he might, like William Morris later, have been tempted to essay a closer, more pedantic, imitation of the prose of the Sagas instead of choosing as his models, in all that is most picturesque, dramatic, or humorous in his work, those great Latin masters, Froissart and Ariosto and Cervantes.

But though German and Scandinavian literature had no influence on his style, affected only his not very successful attempts in supernatural thrills, it was from German literature that the impulse came, which made of the young antiquary and omnivorous reader a creative writer, supplied the spark which fused the love of history and antiquities with the love of poetry and romance. Scott was, towards the end of his life, to be made President of the Royal Society of Edinburgh, and to listen from the Chair to many a lecture of which he confesses he understood not a word. His chief debt to that Society was an older one. In April 1788, he tells us, "the literary persons of Edinburgh... were then first made aware of the existence of works of genius in a language cognate with the English, and possessed of the same manly force of expression.... Those who were from their youth accustomed to admire Milton and Shakespeare, became acquainted, I may say for the first time, with the existence of a race of poets, who had the same lofty ambition to spurn the flaming boundaries of the universe, and investigate the realms of Chaos and Old Night; and of dramatists, who, disclaiming the pedantries of the Unities, sought, at the expense of occasional improbabilities and extravagance, to present life on the stage in its scenes of wildest contrast, and in all its boundless variety of character, etc., etc." (*Essay on the Imitations of the Ancient Ballad*.) All this was the effect of a lecture by that Man of Feeling and lover of cock-fighting, Henry Mackenzie (1745-1831), whose knowledge of German literature was derived entirely from French translations. And so was formed among the young budding advocates of Scott's circle a class of which he was at once the mainspring and the fly-wheel. Their German teacher would, in Teutonic fashion, have initiated them into the grammar of the language and read the simple banalities in which teachers delight, in this case Gesner's " Death of Abel ". Scott, impatient alike of grammar and piety, was soon at work on Schiller and Goethe ; and the young man who had written so much bad poetry was at last, by way of translation, to find his proper bent, his own individual style.

But that final step was aided by other than purely literary interests, connects itself with other activities in the life of boundless energy that Scott was leading during these happy years of recovered strength and rapid development. On the 10th of July, 1792 " Mr Walter Scott, son of Mr Walter Scott writer to the signet, was publicly examined ... and found sufficiently qualified " to be admitted to the Bar, just before the Session rose and five weeks before he had attained the legal age for admission. He appeared at the Jedburgh Assizes in September but declined the work offered him by Lord Braxfield : " I might have had employment, but durst not venture. Nine of the Dunse rioters were condemned to banishment, but the ferment continues violent in the Merse." The riots were the consequence of the enforcement of the Militia Act, and Scott was to be employed in more than one such case later. He attended other circuits, but it was not the custom to keep a record of the counsel employed in these provincial cases, and it was not till July 1795 that he made his first appearance in a case in Edinburgh. Indeed, the years following his admission were employed as much as ever, or more widely, in excursions prompted by antiquarian, historic, and poetic interest. In 1791 he had ridden over Flodden Edge and writes to Clerk his views upon the battle. (*Letters*, I, 18-9.) In 1792 he is at his uncle's cottage, Rosebank near Kelso, shooting duck with two " lobsters ", that is, young officers, and making a raid into Northumberland to view the Roman Wall and " the field of battle where the forces of Queen Margaret were defeated by those of the House of York ". (*Letters*, I, 24.)

Shortly thereafter he is introduced by his early friend Charles Kerr of Abbotrule (to whom in his years of trouble and separation from his family Scott had proved a friend in need) to Robert Shortreed, Sheriff-Substitute of Roxburghshire, and begins the more systematic quest for Border ballads which was continued for some seven years. Most of the letters to Shortreed were unfortunately burned on the occasion of a " flitting ". One letter that survived, and his letters to Murray of Simprim at Meigle, to and from Charles Kerr at Abbotrule, to George Chalmers, the antiquarian, and to James Walker the minister of Dunnottar in Kincardineshire, bear witness to his eager interest in ballads, in the sites of battles, in the excavation of castles, and the collection of antiquities of all kinds. In 1793 he seems to have chosen the Highlands instead of the Borders, and with Adam Ferguson visited various places in Stirlingshire and Perthshire. He heard from the father of Lord Abercromby of Rob Roy and his methods ; he visited for the first time an intimate friend of later years, " Buchanan the young laird of Cambusmore ", and the Rattrays of Craighall, relations of his friend and correspondent, William Clerk. He made his longest stay at Meigle with Murray, and from thence visited Dunnottar Castle and met in the graveyard Robert Paterson or Old Mortality. On the same excursion he slept at Glamis Castle and passed a night of such agitated reaction to the workings of his imagination as Lovell passed in Mr. Oldbuck's haunted chamber, and like, and yet how different from, Wordsworth's experience a year earlier in the " high and lonely " room in Paris,

> near the roof
> Of a large Mansion or Hotel.

Scott, too, felt the political agitations of the time as keenly as Wordsworth, but in a very different way. The chief theme, besides the antiquarian, of the letters of 1794, is the political riots and the swearing-in of special constables, the trial of Watt and Downie, and the " exit " of the former, " a very solemn scene, but the pusillanimity of the unfortunate victim was astonishing considering the boldness of his nefarious plans. It is matter of general regret that his Associate Downie should have received a reprieve which I understand is now prolonged for a second month—I suppose to wait the issue of the London Trials," that is, the trials of the Hardies, Thelwalls, Holcrofts, etc. The English prisoners were acquitted. " Downie and Watt ", Lockhart remarks grimly, " were not so fortunate." But they were definitely guilty of treason, Watt of collecting arms. They were tried by a Commission of Oyer and Terminer and not " by the violent and intemperate gentleman who sits in the Justiciary," *i.e.* Lord Braxfield (*Robert to Henry Dundas*, June 21, 1794), and " the prisoners had a fair trial ". (Meikle, *Scotland and the French Revolution*, Glasgow, 1912, pp. 150 f.) Their conviction served, of course, to confirm the prevalent view that all reformers were revolutionaries. But it is needless to go back to these old quarrels. We have lived through similar crises and know how hysterical feeling can become, and the illogical fashion in which we are prone to condemn outrages committed by our opponents and condone those of our own side. In the same letter of 1794 Scott refers to another effect of the disturbed times, the formation of volunteer corps. " Our volunteers are now compleatly embodied & notwithstanding the heaviness of their dress have a martial & striking appearance—their accuracy in firing & manœuvering excites the surprise of military Gentlemen.... Tom is very proud of the Grenadier company to which he belongs." Walter's lameness kept him from joining Tom, his younger and favourite brother, and it was not till 1797 that a horse troop was raised and he was able to take his part in the joy of playing at soldiers with the patriotic intention of resisting invasion and the ultimate practical advantage of gaining exemption from the Militia Act and compulsory service. "As I observe", he writes in 1803 to the Clerk of the Lieutenancy of Edinburgh, " by the inclosed summons that I am drawn a soldier of the army of reserve I beg to inform you it is my intention to claim the exemption provided in favour of Volunteer Cavalry having been for several years a member of the Edinburgh Troop of the R.M. Lothian V. Cavalry" (*Letters*, I, 196). By 1803 Scott was a married man with increasing responsibilities. Had volunteers been called for in 1797 Scott would not have hung behind. Still one can understand the bitter feeling of the lower class when they saw these patriotic gentlemen, who had been raised largely to keep them in order, exempted from the bloodier service to which they might be condemned by the luck of the ballot.

Through these years of antiquarian and literary reading and expeditions, of preparation for early work at the Bar, of political riots, trials, and military service, there runs another thread of interest which was also to be woven into his creative work when Scott at last found his *metier*—his most serious love affair. The object of this, apparently his second, certainly his most passionate, love was a Miss Williamina Belsches, daughter of a Sir John Belsches (after 1798 Sir John Stuart), Advocate, and his wife Lady Jane, daughter of the Earl of Leven and Melville. Into the intricacies of the Belsches' genealogy it is unnecessary to go as nothing came of the wooing. It is sufficient to note that by birth and expectations the lady belonged to a higher level of society than that in which Scott's father's family moved—a level to which he himself was yet no more than an aspirant, though by his blood he was quite entitled to claim admission if he had the means to maintain his footing there. He was, indeed, through his mother a very distant cousin of the lady. They both had Swinton blood. The earliest reference to the affair in Lockhart's *Life* occurs in a letter which he does not date, a letter said to have been written by David Erskine of Cardross. " Your Quixotism, dear Walter, was highly characteristic. From the description of the blooming fair, as she appeared when she lowered her *manteau vert*, I am hopeful you have not dropped the acquaintance. At least I am certain some of our more rakish friends would have been glad enough of such an acquaintance." Whether this was the lady in question is, I think, doubtful. In 1792 Scott writes to his friend, Clerk : " I have no chance of seeing *ma chere adorable* till winter if then," and in 1794 Charles Kerr, speaking of some verses, says : " There are some delicate touches in them which to a man like you in love must prove acceptable." But the nearest to a clear account of the history of the affair is given by Clerk, speaking from memory, in a letter of 1835 to Sophia Lockhart. " Your father's penchant for the lady began I think in the year 1790 (her mother Lady Jane was an acquaintance of his mother which led to a visiting acquaintance) it was a prodigious secret at first which I discovered by observing that he wore a sort of medallion in the style of Tassie's heads about his neck which had been made for him by a Mons. Guildbert, a french tutor, and shortly afterwards he told me all about it, he certainly was very much attached to her." In March 1795 Scott wrote to his cousin, William Scott : " The lady you allude to has been in town all this winter and going a good deal into public which has not in the least altered the meekness of her manners. Matters, you see, stand just as they did." But in August of that year he seems to have put his fortune to the test and sent her a written proposal. His letter, and her reply, he sent to Clerk to see what he could make of the latter which was apparently ambiguous. Her letter has disappeared, and was probably returned by Clerk. His own was sent to Sophia Lockhart by Clerk with the covering letter from which I have quoted. "It gave me the highest satisfaction to find, by the receipt of your letter . . . that you have formed precisely the same opinion with me, both with regard to the interpretation of ——'s letter as highly flattering and favourable, and to the mode of conduct I ought to pursue—for, after all, what she has pointed out is the most prudent line of conduct for us both, at least till better days, which, I think myself now entitled to suppose, she, as well as I myself, will look forward to with pleasure. If you were surprised at reading the important billet, you may guess how agreeably I was so at receiving it; for I had, to anticipate disappointment, struggled to suppress every rising gleam of hope; and it would be very difficult to describe the mixed feelings her letter occasioned, which, *entre nous*, terminated in a very hearty fit of crying. I read over her epistle about ten times a-day, and always with new admiration of her generosity and candour—and as often take shame to myself for the mean suspicions which, after knowing her so long, I could listen to, while endeavouring to guess how she would conduct herself. To tell you the truth, I cannot but confess that my *amour propre*, which one would expect should have been exalted, has suffered not a little upon this occasion, through a sense of my own *unworthiness*." If this is not the language of a warm and generous love, it is difficult to think what is; but it clearly implies that the writer has received encouragement, and Clerk's letter, though naturally guarded as written to Charlotte Carpenter's daughter, shows that was the impression of his friends also. "There can be no doubt she admired his talents and you will see from your father's letter that I then thought their affection was reciprocal in all respects —and perhaps it was so after all, but neither was in a

condition to marry, your father just come to the bar and
the lady entirely dependent on her father—so that when she
listened to the addresses of William Forbes, a rich young
laird and banker, she acted perhaps less romantically than
wisely." Against this view that Scott's feeling was recip-
rocated Lord Sands set a letter from Lady Jane Belsches
to Sir William Forbes which gives him repeated assurance
that he was her daughter's first love. " I shall never forget
how much she was prepossessed in your favour the first
evening she met with you . . . the same thing has never
happened of any other, having never once heard her
speak in the same way of any one of all the young men we
have seen and met with." But, one is tempted to say, this
is the mother for whom it is naturally delightful to find her
daughter falling at once in love with the most eligible
partner ; and later we shall see that she spoke to Scott in
1827 in terms that seem to imply at least some regret if not
remorse as though she felt that he had been somewhat
hardly dealt with. But since I wrote on the subject in the
February number (1937) of *Blackwood's Magazine*, Lady
Clinton has permitted me to see a letter which shows
clearly that, whatever encouragement she had shown
Scott in 1795 (and it is possible he exaggerated the significance of her letter), by the autumn of 1796 her heart had
passed to young Forbes. I will cite it later for the evidence it affords, and because as a letter it presents an interesting contrast to the letters of the young Frenchwoman
who took her place in Walter's life. What were her real
feelings is for us of less importance than what Scott felt,
and that is that she had surrendered her will to her mother.
That is the implication of the *Violet* and of a newly discovered poem which I shall print later. When James
Ballantyne, probably in 1808, suffered a similar fate Scott
wrote to him : " What *can* I say to you except that I feel
for what I know by never to be forgotten experience is a
situation scarcely susceptible of comfort but from generous
disdain of the wanton cruelty by which you suffer. . . .

Remember my breaking the wine-glass upon a similar recollection."

Before the end came, the passion for Williamina made its contribution to the fusion of the antiquarian and the poet in Scott. In the same autumn as he made his proposal to Miss Belsches and wrote to Clerk, Mrs. Barbauld visited Edinburgh and read to an audience, already interested, the translation made by William Taylor of Norwich of Bürger's ballad, " Lenore," full of the supernatural thrill which is the chief note of the German ballads. Scott was not present on this occasion, but, returning shortly afterwards, he " found all his friends in rapture with the intelligence and good sense of their visitor, but in particular with the wonderful translation from the German by means of which she had delighted and astonished them " ; and he at once determined to see the original. This was procured for him by the German wife of his immediate chief among the Scotts, Hugh Scott of Harden, later Lord Polwarth. The result was the translation of " Lenore ", made in the course of one night and taken the next morning to his friend, Miss Jane Anne Cranstoun, who was also his chief confidante in his passion for Williamina Belsches. This was followed by a similar translation of " Der Wilde Jäger ", and then, apparently on the initiative of Miss Cranstoun, the ballads were printed and an advance copy was carried by Scott as a present to Miss Belsches on the last visit he made to her at the house of her parents, Fettercairn in Kincardineshire.[1]

---

[1] Such at least is the story told to Basil Hall by the Baroness Purgstall when he visited her in 1834. See *Schloss Hainfeld, or A Winter in Styria*, 1836. I can find no allusion to this early printed volume in her letter, or in Scott's correspondence of the year. The earliest reference to the translation I have seen is in a letter of Kerr of Abbotrule of date 12th April, 1796. He had joined the army and at Shrewsbury, whence he writes, had made the acquaintance of Mrs. Piozzi. He speaks of " two of your letters one of which contained your beautiful translation from the German. Indeed I must confess that it is one of the prettiest things I ever met with. It is wild and fearful and dips deeply into the beauties of

The account of that last visit is contained in a letter to Erskine, though the main details remain in obscurity (*Letters*, I, 44-8). The letter was written from Aberdeen on 24th April, 1796, but Scott, in a manner quite common in his correspondence, wrote " September " for " April". Both the letter and one which he received from Miss Cranstoun (addressed by her to Montrose but forwarded to Aberdeen) indicate clearly the anxious spirit in which the journey was made and was followed by his chief confidante. Scott left Edinburgh in March to attend the circuit court at Aberdeen on 15th April accompanied by two of his young advocate friends—" Mountain Boys ", that is, members of the group of young, unbriefed barristers who spent their time in the Outer House of the Court of Session " giggling and making giggle ". On the way he was met by other friends and visited the field of Bannockburn, Cambusmore, and the Trossachs. There he was left by his friends to make his solitary journey up Loch Lubnaig " and round by Lochearnhead to Crieff " and thence to Perth. At Perth he found another friend and confidante, Mary Erskine, herself on the eve of becoming engaged to a young laird and lawyer, Archibald Campbell of Clathick, though she did not confide her secret to Scott till later. Receiving no invitation to visit Fettercairn, which was the true Mecca of his pilgrimage, " I tore myself from that quarter of the country & sad & slowly trotted on to Aberdeen with many an anxious thought upon the shadows clouds and darkness

romantic fiction.... Mrs Piozzi has not yet seen it . . . I shall see her soon and if she is possessed of either Taste or penetration it cannot fail to please her—depend upon one thing I shall write you her true sentiments." Possibly it was with some intention of presenting a copy to Miss Belsches that Scott was advised and resolved to print the ballad with one other at Miller's. By the time it was ready all was over with Scott's hopes.

Basil Hall's book referred to above seems to have provoked some resentment, I know not why. In a letter to Croker, Lockhart reports, on the authority of Lady Davy, that Basil Hall is to be cut in London because of his *Schloss Hainfeld*. But Lockhart, his father-in-law tells us, was a first-class gossip.

that involve my future prospects of happiness." At Aberdeen he doubtless attended the Court, where Lord Braxfield was one of the judges, but it was not the habit then to enter the names of counsel in the Minutes of the Court nor to extend the Minutes from the first scroll, so that we do not know in what cases, if any, he was employed. His father was the law agent for the city, and he tells us that he was " hospitably received by several freinds of my father "; and for his sake, though he does not mention this in the letter, made a burgess. " I am blithe to see your father's son on the causeway of our ancient town, Mr. Alan Fairford. Were you a twelve-month aulder we would mak' a burgess o' you, man ", writes Scott later in *Redgauntlet*, recalling his own experience. He visited the Leiths of Freefield and Glenkindie,[1] an old Aberdeenshire family, represented now by Lord Burgh. On his return thence he wrote the letter in question and next day, 25th April, set out on his return.

Meantime a letter had followed him from Edinburgh, addressed : " Walter Scott Esqr Advocate Montrose To be left at the Post Office till calld for ", which the postmaster had forwarded, striking out " Montrose " and writing " Aberdeen ". The postmark on the letter is " April 18 ", and the letter was lying beside Scott when he wrote and is worth reproducing in part as Lockhart has sorely mangled it. The writer was the enthusiastic Miss Cranstoun, who took apparently an even deeper interest in Scott's love affair than the shyer and more Victorian Mary Erskine. To Miss Cranstoun Scott had written, it would seem, from Perth a letter, now lost, which would explain some references in her letter. Her heart is full of the real concern of Scott's mind, not Aberdeen and a burgess ticket, but Fettercairn and Miss Belsches :

" I bless the Gods for conducting your poor dear soul safely to Perth—when I consider the Wilds the Forests &

---

[1] The wife (second or third) of the Laird was a relative of Scott's mother.

the Lakes the mishapen rocks that were piled around you, & the spirits with which you wd whisper to their startling echoes, it amazeth me how you escaped from the spot—had you but dismissed the little Squire and Earwig & spent a few days as Orlando would have done all posterity might have profited by it, but to Trot quickly away without so much as one Stanza to despair—never talk to me of Love again never never never—I verily believe you were getting the Galic Catechism all the time, such tremendous words can signify nothing but the names of the ten deadly sins. As for Rob Roy Macgregor if he be a more comical genius than our friend the Dn— one would ride twice as far to have the pleasure of his acquaintance. I am dying for your Collection of exploits and curiosities—Or as the Psalmist would say ' I have opend my mouth wide.' ' O fill it abundantly.' When will you return ? In the meantime Heaven speed you—' Be sober *and hope* to the end.' I have got a vile sheet of paper—it is impossible to make a mark upon it—

" Be it known unto thee that Will Taylors translation of yr. Ballad is publishd & so infinitely inferior is it in every respect I wonder how we could tolerate it.—Dugald Stewart [1] read yours to Greenfield the other day when he came to the fetter dance he look'd up & poor G. was sitting with his hands nail'd to his knees & the big tears rolling down his innocent nose in so piteous a manner that Mrs S. burst out laughing, an angry man Greenfield at such a cruel interruption, I have Stanley's addition to it but it is below contempt. . . . so that every day adds to your renown— This here place is damnd dull Clerk is in the Country getting strong Erskine in London, my dear Thomson at Dayly, Macfarlane hatching Kant & George Fountainhall, Monroe is making hot love to J. Dalrymple and upon my sincerity I have nothing else to tell you but

[1] Dugald Stewart's wife was Jane Cranstoun's sister.

that I am most affectionately Yours—many an anxious thought I have about you
       Farewell

WALTER SCOTT—ADVOCATE
 ABERDEEN
To be left at the
 Post Office till call'd for." [1]

Before Scott left Aberdeen the glass of his hopes had apparently risen. He was invited to Fettercairn, and, after a day or two at Dunottar Manse where he set Mr. Walker at work excavating in the Castle well and searching for ballads among servant girls and parish school teachers, he went on to Fettercairn. Miss Belsches had been unwell, which may have served as an excuse for his not having been received sooner. Some of the short time was spent in excavating the remains of Fenella's Castle, but his heart was still full of love and Miss Belsches gave him at least no definite indication that her heart was elsewhere, for on 5th May, when he was to depart, he climbed the neighbouring hill of Caterthun, and poured forth his feelings in a very characteristic blend of love and antiquarian interest.

1

Cold the wild blast that chills thy brow
And bleak thy summit C——r T——n
Yet lonely on thy cliffs of snow
I lingering watch the setting sun.

2

Long have the bards been low in death
That bade thy rocky crown arise
And frowning o'er thy brow of heath
Crest its gray circle to the skies

[1] For the correct dating of Scott's letter note : (1) that Miss Cranstoun's obviously refers to the same journey which he describes to Erskine ; (2) she reports the publication of William Taylor's translation, which appeared in *The Monthly Magazine* for March 1796 ; (3) the news about the Mountain, which Scott reports to Erskine, is derived from her letter.

3
Perhaps stern freedom on thy head
Reard the rude Granites flinty pile
What time her indignant votaries fled
The veteran legions lengthened file.

4
Perhaps in Denmarks conquering day
Here Odins ruthless altar rose
And thro the rough scarrd Runic lay
Streamd the red gore of captive foes

5
Or if we trust the Village tale
A wayward maid in witching hour
When stars were red and moon was pale
Reard thy dread mound by magic power

6
Yet not to trace whose deeds of yore
Have markd thy summit C——r T——n
On thy rude rampart bleak and hoar
I lonely watch the setting sun

7
Loth to resume my vagrant lot
While brightening in the distance far
Thy beams yet gild one sacred spot
And fondly seem to linger there

8
And linger still thou setting sun
And gild her walks and cheer her flowers
And chase each care, and chase each pain
That cloud my gentle Favourites hours

9
Mine be the blast on mountain brow
If evening's sunbeams round her play
And mine the storm and mine the snow
If hers the sheltered vale of May

10

And ever thro' lifes checquerd years
Thus *ever* may our fortunes roll
Tho' *mine* be storm or *mine* be tears
Be *hers* the sunshine of the soul—

5th May, 1796.

CA—T—R T—N.

On the 6th Scott was at Kinross, whence he wrote to Mr. Walker of Dunottar, and then, after a short visit to his old tutor at Montrose, proceeded to Edinburgh, arriving there a day or two before the opening of the summer session of the Court on 12th May. He had set out in a dispondent mood, but had returned apparently in better spirits. He had not been definitely forbidden to hope.

Work, or expectation of work, would keep Scott in Edinburgh till about 12th July, when he probably returned to Kelso, but by 26th August he was again at Cambusmore in Kilmadock parish, Perthshire, whence he returned to Kelso before 9th September,[1] for on that day (though he misdates the letter, writing " April " for what the postmark shows should be " September ") he wrote to Erskine, acknowledging a letter (*Letters*, I, 51-4) announcing the engagement of Erskine's sister, Mary, to Campbell of Clathick, a letter which Erskine forwarded to Campbell on 10th September : " the inclosed letter of my feal friend, to whom of necessity I communicated the event. . . . Scott was right in conjecturing that the news communicated to Thomson would go near to draw the breath out of him with joy ", and Erskine goes on to give a paraphrase of a letter similar to Scott's from Thomas Thomson, their common friend. Moreover, Mary Erskine herself was so touched by Scott's letter that she wrote—what seems to have been considered a daring thing for a young

---

[1] In September 1796 Miss Cranstoun writes to Thomas Thomson : " Erskine is reading the Knights of the Swan ; my dear Scott at Kelso, his Ballads in the press."—Cosmo Innes, *Memoir of Thomas Thomson* (1854).

lady—a personal letter of thanks to him of which a shortened and " manipulated " version is printed by Lockhart in his *Life*.

In both Mary Erskine's letter and Scott's there are references to his own love affair and its still uncertain issue. " Well do I remember ", she writes, " the dark conference we held together lately, the intention of unfolding my future fate to you was often at my lips when the gloom of the chamber would have prevented your seeing them, and had you not been to stay supper I certainly would have asked your approbation, for by the example of the Lords of the Creation are their helpmates guided to wave the privilege of asking advice." In the dark conference Scott had been the principal speaker and poured forth the doubts and hopes and agitations which are expressed in his letter to her brother referred to, and are still agitating him in his letter of 26th September in which he reports " the campaign of the formal Chevalier and his son and heir Don Guglielmo". By 12th October his fate was sealed. " William Forbes marries Miss Belsches," one of Scott's friends wrote to another, " this is not good news. I always dreaded there was some self-deception on the part of our romantic friend and I shudder at the violence of his irritable and most ungovernable mind."

" His irritable and most ungovernable mind "—that is a trait of Scott's which Lockhart's carefully arranged picture and also Scott's fundamental sweetness and placability have a little obscured, but it is more than once revealed in his letters. Crossed or wounded, he could speak harshly and unfairly to, and of, friends—Dugald Stewart, the Ballantynes, Constable—but, unless the quarrel was taken up obstinately on the other side, his angry mood soon melted. His tendency to a sanguine self-deception was to have, in time, more disastrous consequences. Scott deceived himself in many respects—as to his own prudence and economy, as to his indifference to worldly concerns, even, perhaps, as to his indifference to criticism and slight regard for his own work. He was but human, and if he had his faults, few men have had as many compensating qualities.

"His irritable and most ungovernable mind" expressed itself in some songs which show clearly that he thought of himself as deceived and abandoned for a wealthier wooer. "The Violet" is the only one which has so far found its way into print, but the following lines are contained in the same album as his last thoughts of love and tenderness, composed on Caterthun. They must have been written in the October which followed that agitating spring and summer :

> By a thousand fond dreams my weak bosom betrayd
> Believd thee for love and for constancy made,
> Believd that Indifference never could be
> When gentle Compassion had pleaded for me.

> The phantom swift flew, the Delusion is plain,
> Delusion too lovely alas ! and too plain,
> Too late 'Twas revealed and with anguish I see
> No comfort from love, no pity from thee.

> Ah fool, to exult, as wild fancy has done,
> While she dream'd such a conquest by thee could be won,
> Ah fool, to imagine such graces could be
> By Nature formd only for Love and for thee !

> For grandeur, for wealth your poor friend you resign,
> If Bliss they can give you *O may it be thine.*
> Farewell to the raptures of lowly degree
> You might have enjoyd with Love and with me.

> Unfriended by Fortune, untutor'd by Art
> I gave you my all when I gave you my heart,
> But many a gallant of higher degree
> Has none, W[illiamina], for love and for thee.

> Too proud to solicit, too weak to contend,
> That heart can but break, for it never shall bend,
> Nor bear the cold glance of *Acquaintance* to see
> In the eye which once softend with friendship for me.

SCOTT'S FEELINGS AND WILLIAMINA'S 41

Ah ne'er will that heart the last agony bear
When Envy must add to the pangs of despair,
When forgot each fond tie that once bound thee to me,
Thy charms the dear price of vain splendour may be.

O then ere the turf o'er these limbs has grown green,
Will my favourite forget that I ever have been,
No gentle remembrance will whisper in thee
" He fell a sad victim to Love and to me."

So ended in October 1796 the romance as far as Scott was concerned. But Williamina had apparently some troubled water to cross before she was married to Forbes in January of the following year. For her father seems for some reason to have demurred to the engagement. I have not seen any letters in which he makes plain his grounds, but Williamina's letter printed below is explicit so far as it goes. Who Mr S—— is I do not know. It is hardly possible that Scott or his father should have pleaded a precontract, for all that I have printed shows that Scott was quite uncertain as to how he stood in Williamina's and her mother's favour. The letter was written at Fettercairn on the 16th December, 1796, and posted at Falkland on the 18th :

" Friday Morning

I wonder if our difficulties and anxieties will ever have an end—I was reading your letter of Friday for about the tenth time, perfectly pleased and happy when my father returned from Balgonie and his countenance instantly informd me that his sensations were very different from mine—I do not know with what he is dissatisfied I only know that it is in consequence of a letter from Mr S——. I am persuaded you know nothing of this, were it only from the style of your last letter—*and you must make no enquiry about it* as that can only do mischief— On Monday or Tuesday if nothing extraordinary occurs we shall be in town—my father does not mean to answer Mr S——'s letter till he sees him, difficulties are much sooner removed in conversation than on paper—for many reasons I beg you may take no notice of this unless you hear of it from some other quarter—in truth I know not why I should mention it but I do confess I am teazed with this endless hesitation and I feel my spirits cannot much longer support this continual anxiety—If I am happy and comfortable for one day, the next never fails to bring with it new cause of uneasiness—In what a state of agitation has my mind been for nearly four months—I think it will require almost as many years of peace to restore its former tranquility—nothing on earth could induce me to pass such another period except for your sake—You have suffered as much as myself but you have not complain'd—I am far very far short of you in everything and in nothing more than in patience and strength of mind—however I am conscious of my inferiority and I will try to do better. In the meantime it appears to me that we are as far from certainty as we were two months ago, if you are acquainted with the meaning of all this I wish you would tell me for it puzzles and perplexes me in the extreme—they may retreat but I never can—at the same time I am perfectly conscious of what is due from me to my father—and to his will I must submit my conduct tho my affections are no longer in my power—from what a dream of happiness has this awakened me—from remembrance of the painful past I did but more enjoy the present and I now find myself (if possible) more anxious, more distress'd than ever—even the meeting which I have look'd forward to with so much pleasure will now be accompanied with doubt and anxiety —yet I trust we shall meet on tuesday I shall not write again unless we are detained and if it should be by a storm remember it will prevent my letter from reaching you—what a sad return is this for the dear kind letter I yesterday received—of one thing however be assured, it is not in the power of chance or change to deprive you of my regard—should I even never again repeat this assurance believe that it can end but with the life of your W. B. Of my father's future plans I know little—they are all I believe far from determined—all that I do know I shall tell you but I cannot write—do not let all this vex you too much I feel your uneasiness even more than my own—I trust all will yet be well."

There is more of Dorothy Osborne in that than in the somewhat arch epistles of the young Frenchwoman which we shall quote later. But it is all we know of Williamina, who remains the shadow of a shade. We have no letters of an earlier date from which we might form some estimate of what she had felt for Scott. But Clerk's letter to Sophia Lockhart, enclosing the letter given in *Letters*, I, 40-2, and that letter of Scott to Clerk, certainly imply that he had felt himself encouraged by the young lady. A lady does not point out to a young man, for whom she has no regard, what " is the most prudent line of conduct for us both, at least till better days which, I think myself now entitled to suppose, she as well as I myself will look forward to with pleasure." Scott's personal experiences are again and again woven into his work, but always with a difference that serves to objectify the picture. One side of his own character is vividly drawn in Wilfrid Wycliffe in *Rokeby*, the side which had, one suspects, made of his attachment a great imaginative experience. If Miss Belsches is anywhere sketched, it is certainly not in such a spirited young woman as Di Vernon (or only in her devotion to her father), but in gentle, yielding, dutiful characters such as Matilda:

> " The mild expression spoke a mind
> In duty firm, composed, resigned,"

or the more tragically passive Lucy, the Bride of Lammermoor. The " meekness " of Miss Belsches's character he had noted in the letter quoted. Meekness is not a conspicuous quality of Lilias Redgauntlet, whose " green mantle " has been thought reminiscent of the " manteau vert " quoted on an earlier page. Of that early love and his reactions to the letter of Williamina which, rightly or wrongly, raised his hopes there is, however, one clear reminiscence in *Rob Roy*. It is when the hero believes he has parted with Miss Vernon for ever : " At length tears rushed to my eyes, glazed as they were by the exertion of straining after what was no longer seen. I wiped them mechanically, and almost without being aware that they were flowing—but they came thicker and thicker ;—I felt the tightening of the throat and breast—the *hysterica passio* of poor Lear ; and sitting down by the wayside, I shed a flood of the first and most bitter tears which had flowed from my eyes since childhood." It was not easy for Scott to shed tears : " I do not know what other folk feel, but with me the hysterical passion that impels tears is of terrible violence—a sort of throttling sensation—then succeeded by a state of dreaming stupidity." (*Journal*, May 30, 1826.)

CHAPTER III

"Men have died from time to time, and worms have eaten them, but not for love." *As You Like It*, IV. i. 98.

"Scarce one person out of twenty marries his first love, and scarce one out of twenty of the remainder has cause to rejoice at having done so. What we love in those early days is generally rather a fanciful creation of our own than a reality. We build statues of snow and weep when they melt."
Scott to G. H. Gordon, June 12, 1820.

SCOTT'S sanguine, ardent, active temperament was not crushed or profoundly altered by his disappointment. The betrothal of Miss Belsches coincided in date with the publication of his two ballads from the German, which, however, attracted little attention outside the circle of his friends. In February of the following year, 1797, he plunged into the exhilarating activities of volunteering and drilling, riding and messing, with the friends among whom, besides James Skene, the young Earl of Dalkeith, and Robert Dundas, son of the great Lord Melville (fountain-head of all Scottish patronage), was William Forbes, the young Don Guglielmo, who had just carried off his lady-love. In March he is overflowing with martial and patriotic ardour to Patrick Murray of Simprim: "In case of an invasion one & all will be the word, unless with some very *black hearted* or *lily livered* rascals indeed" (*Letters*, I, 65).

Volunteering did not interfere with his endless reading, as his Note-Book for the year shows—Apuleius, Anthony-a-Wood, Delrius, Lessing, Marlowe's *Dr. Faustus* are a few of those recorded; and there can be little doubt that he wrote as well as read. What form his literary activities took in these years will be a matter of consideration later. But in September a roving tour through Tweeddale and over the Border ended at the now little remembered watering-place, Gilsland, and there began the final crisis of the heart in Scott's life. All subsequent crises were to be either literary or financial, the two closely linked.

For to Gilsland had come, in charge of the Rev. John Bird, the perpetual curate of St. Mary's Church, Carlisle, a young French lady and her companion. The young lady's name was Margaret Charlotte Charpentier, more generally known to her friends as Charlotte Carpenter; her companion was a certain Jane Nicolson. About them both hangs somewhat of a mystery, though we know more about them than Scott himself ever knew, and more than Lockhart ever discovered or would admit. Jane Nicolson was the youngest of three sisters—Catherine, who married a certain Stephen Barber, whose descendants are as unable as I am to indicate the Nicolson descent; Sarah, whom we meet more than once in the life of Scott as housekeeper to a well-known and successful French dentist in London, Charles François Dumergue, a great friend of Matthew Boulton the partner in Birmingham of James Watt. Of Jane, before she emerges as companion to Charlotte Carpenter, we know only that she was the companion chosen for her daughters by Mrs. Thrale when that lady became Mrs. Piozzi and left England. Owing to some suspicions about her character, she either left, or was dismissed by the eldest daughter, afterwards Viscountess Keith. That is all we know about Jane, postponing conjecture.[1]

Of Charlotte Carpenter, before she met Scott, we know just as little. Scott, when he met her at Gilsland and was carried off his feet by a fresh wave of passion, made no inquiries. When he wrote, at the request of his parents, to procure information, Charlotte, after reminding him that when Miss Nicolson was willing to supply such information he would not listen, goes on to give him a somewhat vague, if not evasive, reply. Her father had a place

[1] She claimed to be the grand-daughter of Bishop Nicolson of Carlisle (1655-1727), but without discoverable justification. See *Letters*, I, lx, note.

under the Government, and lived at Lyons in good repute and in *very good style*. He died when she was too young to know the value of such a parent, and the children were left to the care of Lord Downshire. Her mother moved to Paris, and, as she wished to have them educated and christened in England, the children were sent to Lord Downshire, and the mother soon after died.[1]

From some source which he does not state, Robert Chambers in 1833 informed the readers of *Chambers's Journal* that, when a young man, Lord Downshire, then known by the courtesy title of Lord Fairford, had been given an introduction by the John Bird mentioned above to Charlotte's father, Monsieur Charpentier, " who held the lucrative post of provider of post-horses to the Royal Family ". The unhappy result was her elopement with the young nobleman, whereupon M. Charpentier transmitted his children, a boy and a girl, to his frail wife with a desire, signified or implied, that she would undertake the duty of bringing them up, and brought up they were " with their mother under the general protection of Lord Downshire till at length the lady died ". The girl was educated at a French convent, the boy secured a good place in India, subject to a payment of £200 a year to his sister.

Further inquiries have cleared up some details of this story while leaving others even more obscure. Of Monsieur and Madame Charpentier we have one authentic and illuminating glimpse, of which it is very strange that Lockhart made no use, in close correspondence, as he was, while composing the *Life*, with Maria Edgeworth, for it comes from the first part of the *Life* of Maria's father, written by himself.[2] In the closing months of 1771

---

[1] Lockhart omits this part of her letter which runs in quaint English with a Cockney's trouble about aspirates : " My Mother went after to reside in Paris, has she had always been very desirous that we should be Educated, and even christen to the Church of England, we were sent to our Guardian Ld D. under whose care we have been left entirely."

[2] This was pointed out to me by my friend and partner, Mr. W. M. Parker, while we were at work on the *Letters of Sir Walter Scott*.

Richard Edgeworth and his friend Thomas Day, author of *Sandford and Merton*, went to France, and, after a few weeks in Paris, passed on to Lyons, where they resolved to spend the winter. " Mr. Day put himself to every species of torture, ordinary and extraordinary, to compel his antigallican limbs, in spite of their natural rigidity, to dance and fence and manage the great horse. In the meantime I lodged myself in excellent and cheerful apartments upon the ramparts. I boarded in the family of a gentleman who was at the head of the Military Academy at Lyons, where I soon learned to speak French so as to be intelligible. . . . Monsieur Charpentier, who was the master of the Academy at Lyons, had seen much of the world, and communicated agreeably what he had seen. He had been controller of the household to the embassy at Constantinople for upwards of twenty years, and had been no inattentive observer. . . . Madame Charpentier was young, beautiful, lively and accomplished, of an excellent disposition, and less fond of public amusements than most French women. During nearly two years that I was at Lyons I never had occasion to repent my having established myself in her family,[1] as I met with uniform kindness and confidence from every part of it."

So much for Edgeworth's account which makes of M. Charpentier a solid and real person, a man of some importance, not, as has been suggested by some of Scott's countrymen and biographers, the Keeper of a Mews. Of the young wife it suggests also an attractive picture. Now, if we add to this what is revealed by the baptismal registers of Lyons, we get some idea of the circumstances of, and the possibilities latent in, the marriage. A year before Edgeworth's visit a first child had been baptised, Margaret Charlotte, on 17th December, 1770. In June 1772, when Edgeworth was still at Lyons, or shortly after his departure, a son, John David (afterwards known as

---

[1] Edgeworth makes no mention of a child which was probably, in French fashion, sent out to a foster parent.

Charles) was baptised, and in 1775 a Noel, who seems to have died in infancy. But before any of these were born M. Charpentier had been in an important post in Constantinople for " upwards of twenty years ". It seems an inevitable inference that he must have been more than twenty years older than the Élie Charlotte Volère, whom he married presumably in 1769 or early in 1770. It is not entirely surprising, therefore, if the young wife and mother was betrayed into an affair that ended in an elopement with a younger lover.

But postponing conjecture again, the next fact that we learn about Madame Charpentier, after the birth of Noel in 1775, comes from the Chancery Court in England and is of a very mysterious character. In 1778 a spendthrift young Welsh landowner, Wyrriot Owen, being on the verge of bankruptcy, granted a mortgage on his estate in favour of a certain George Morgan, a lawyer. But endorsed on the deed is a declaration of trust, dated 2nd May, by George Morgan, to the effect that the money was not his property but held by him in trust for Madame Élie Charpentier, " wife of the Sieur Charpentier Écuyer du Roi de l'Académie de Lyons." In July of the same year Owen seems to have granted a Bill of Exchange on Paris, endorsed to her, for £250 in English money. In the same month he granted a trust conveyance of his estate for behoof of his creditors. A year later he died unmarried.

It is a strange story, and the more so that apparently no money ever passed to Madame Élie Charpentier and there is no evidence that she knew anything of the transaction. In subsequent decisions of the Court of Chancery the debt was allowed, but ranked after all the other debts on the estate, as it had been granted voluntarily, *i.e.* without value received. It remained, however, accumulating interest at five per cent, as stipulated in the mortgage, and in circumstances that may be detailed later the sum of £6,300 was paid in 1833 by Mrs. Barlow (widow of

Hugh Owen or Barlow, who had succeeded to the estate of Wyrriot Owen) to Mrs. Charles Carpenter as Executrix for the deceased Élie Charlotte Charpentier. Was Wyrriot Owen endeavouring to repay a loan, or loans, of money? Or was he the seducer of the young wife and endeavouring to secure her an annuity in view of his approaching bankruptcy? We cannot tell. Nothing was brought to light in the suit in Chancery except that Élie Charlotte Charpentier was formerly of the parish of St. George's, Hanover Square, in the County of Middlesex, but later of Paris in the Kingdom of France. In Paris she died some time in 1788.

In connection with this date two further facts are to be noted. In 1786 Lord Fairford married. In May 1787 were baptised at St. George's Church, Hanover Square, " Margaret Dr. of John Francis and Margaret Charlotte Charpentier December 1770, and John David s. of John etc. June 1772, 16, and with them Antionette Adelaide D. of Charles Francis and Ann Dumergue Aug. 1768, 13." In 1789 Charles Carpenter received an appointment in the East India Company's service. Putting all these facts together and keeping conjecture within as narrow limits as possible, I suggest that the breaking up of M. Charpentier's family was due to Wyrriot Owen, at some time between 1775 and 1778. Deserted by Owen, or herself severing the connection (he seems to have been an extravagant, rather worthless, person), she lived between London and Paris under the general protection of Lord Fairford until his marriage in 1786, when she went finally to Paris. Whether the words " under his protection " are to be taken in the more sinister sense conveyed by Chambers, or in a sense more compatible with the admiration and affection expressed for him by her daughter, I leave to the reader's own decision. That the daughter was, as Chambers says, brought up in a convent in France is supported by her somewhat imperfect English and foreign accent. The son was probably educated in England with a view to such an appointment as he later obtained. In 1787, I conjecture, Charlotte was brought to England and lived mainly with the Dumergues, whose housekeeper was Sarah, the sister of Jane Nicolson. The Boulton correspondence, preserved at the Assay Office, Birmingham, contains references to her as a member of the Dumergue household in 1789. As we have seen, the two children, with Dumergue's daughter, were baptised members of the Church of England. Of poor Madame Charpentier our last glimpse comes from the letter of a French Abbé to Lord Fairford in 1792. It suggests the woman, earlier portrayed by Edgeworth, charming and friendly but grown extravagant and capricious :

[*Translation*] [1]

" PARIS, 29 March, 1792.
5 Rue Favart, by the Théâtre italien.

I have the honour, My Lord, to apply to you with much sorrow for the amount of the advances which I have been so happy as to make to your friend, the unfortunate Mme. Charpentier. When the report spread that Mme. Volayre intended to have her daughter's effects sold, I meant to establish my claim *legally* by lodging an interdict ; but once the sale was announced as by your order I accepted no other court than yours.

" Miss Nicolson has been witness of all that I have done for Mme. Charpentier, and, indeed, shortly before the return of that lady [demoiselle—*i.e.* Miss Nicolson] to England, she [Mme. C.] sent tradesmen to me, whom she requested me to pay, asking me for an account of my advances, as is proved by one of her notes which I have the honour to send you. I took this account to her four or five times at least, but finding her often ill or without money, she put me off to the quarterly allowance which

---

[1] The French original, and the letters of Charlotte to Lord Downshire from which I quote, were lent me by the late Mr. James Glen, W.S.

she expected from your benefactions. What is more, she had this friendly habit with me even at the time of her last journey to go to you, since, far from repaying the advances which I had made to her, of almost 700 frs, as she had promised me on her departure, that is to say, three weeks after her arrival in London, my surprise was unequalled when out of the remittance which you were good enough to make me of a letter of exchange on Messrs. Aller, bankers, to pay M. Maillard, linen-draper, and the Marquis de Lamberte for a consignment of wine, there was left to me only a sum of 80 odd pounds (which you still reserved for some purchases to be made for Madame), and if I had not had bills which she had entrusted to me for her other creditors, I should not have been able to pay for two articles which she caused me to take from her upholsterer Muray at the price of 432 frs.

"It was the same with a watch-chain which she asked me to let her have to meet her financial expenses : she asked me the price, which was 7 Louis, having been sold to me a month before by a dealer of her acquaintance ; she answered me, '*I beg you to let me have it for 150 frs.*' She immediately put it on a watch which her son wore on his last visit to his grandmother—and all this with the intention of sending me the money from London.

"The embarrasment of giving you all these details costs me infinitely more than you could believe, and I have often groaned at my obligingness in accepting delays and excuses regarding her final settlement with me. Not to send you too voluminous a letter I simply state the amount which I set down as due to me on the 21 June, 1786, which shows that she owed me at first 32 fr., which, added to the first accounts, makes a total of 182 fr. 10 sous, in addition to the cost of the watch-chain (150 fr). Final account, 332 fr. 10 sous.

"I shall send you at the same time as this letter the further documents with which I shall justify the items about which My Lord may require more detailed explanations.

"I hope that he will permit Miss Nicolson, her sister,[1] the friends and children of the unfortunate Mme Charpentier, to find here the assurance of the sentiments which I have vowed to them for life.

"May you enjoy a health and happiness as complete as is respectfully wished,

> My Lord,
> by your very humble and most obedient servant, the Abbé de Chazelle, who keenly regrets that he has been unable to write to you with his own hand."

Such is the story, so far as I have been able to trace it, of Charlotte Carpenter's mother. One understands why Lockhart in part suppressed it, in part disguised it by a few attractive but misleading references to the French Revolution and aristocratic *émigrés*. In fact the unfortunate Madame Charpentier's life was over before the Revolution had, properly speaking, begun. It is an incident in the life of the France that was passing away. "The society at Lyons was at this time", says Edgeworth, "emulating the polish of Parisian manners, and approaching fast to the dissipation and relaxation of morals which prevailed in Paris," and he tells a story of a lady to whom the Mayor had spoken " in a sarcastic tone, with a quotation from the syllables of the Primer :—' Comment vous portez-vous, Madame Ba-Be-Bi-Bo-Bu ? ' She answered, ' Tres bien, Monsieur Ca-Ce-Ci-*Co-Cu* '—a sarcasm which was not applied at hazard."

What brought Charlotte Carpenter to Gilsland in 1797 was apparently a flirtation with some one regarded by Lord Downshire as undesirable, to put an end to which he packed her off with her companion, Jane Nicolson, to pay a visit to his old friends, the Rev. John Bird, mentioned already, and his family. They arrived in Carlisle just as the Birds were setting out for a holiday at Gilsland, and

---

[1] *I.e.* Sarah, Dumergue's housekeeper.

they took the young lady and her companion with them. To Gilsland, "the then peaceful and sequestered watering-place", so Lockhart calls it, came Scott, his brother John, and Adam Ferguson, making a tour on horseback from Tweedside through Carlisle, Penrith, the Vale of Eamont, Ullswater, and Windermere. Quiet and sequestered Gilsland may have been, but it was not without visitors and gaieties such as, on a larger scale doubtless, Jane Austen has described in *Northanger Abbey*, riding and driving excursions by day and dances in the evenings with cards for older people. The interludes to *The Bridal of Triermain* describe something of the life at such a place and the kind of persons who frequented it, " Fashion's train." Here, at any rate, Scott, on a morning ride with Ferguson, saw " a young lady taking the air on horseback " and traced her to Gilsland. " The same evening there was a ball, at which Captain Scott produced himself in his regimentals along with Ferguson similarly attired ; and Scott had the good fortune not only to dance with her "—if his lameness did not make it rather a sitting-out such as he had enjoyed with Mary Erskine a year earlier— " but also took her in to supper ". The result is seen in a letter which Charlotte addressed to Lord Downshire, whose consent, though she was already twenty-seven, a little older than Scott, she still thought it necessary to obtain for her marriage :

" CARLISLE Sept. 29 1797

MY LORD,

We have latterly been such ramblers, & so uncertain as to our plans, & place of residence, that I postponed the honor of inquiring after your health until we were settled. We went with Mr & Mrs Bird to Gilsland, we stayed there three Weeks, which time we passed very agreeably, they returned with us to Carlisle to introduce us to all their friends, who are the first people of this County but our stay here is only temporary, has neither the place, or expences can suit us, we are making

every possible inquiries, I fear that the situation we want will be very difficult to meet with it, we have not yet found any single thing cheaper than in the West of England. I am always troubling you with my little concerns, I intrude perhaps too much on your great Indulgence, to whom can I apply, but to you, who has protected me, & is my best & dearest of friends, will you allow me then my Lord, to appeal again to your friendship, & for your advice, as I shall be guided by it in every actions of my life. I shall then begin my Lord with informing you that during my stay at Guilsland I got acquainted with Mr Scott, a Gentleman of Edinburgh, he paid his addresses to me, which I have accepted only as far as it should be by your consent, & full approbation, he is of very good family, his profession is that of Advocate, & with his connections, & abilities he must rise, his fortune at present is moderate, but he has some great expectations, if you will permit my Lord, Mr Scott to address himself to you he could more fully explain his Situation, & refer you to some person, who could give you every information concerning his family & connections. I fear you will think me very hasty in declaring that with a man of Mr Scott's good principles, & qualities that he appears to possess, I think I can be more really happy with him, than with the most splendid fortune—may I hope my Lord, for the happiness of hearing from you soon, & if [*MS. torn*] me to take the liberty of addressing Mr Scott to you [*MS. torn*] me also to renew every sentiment of gratitude & with every wish for health and happiness to attend
    I remain My Lord
      Your much obliged
        C. CARPENTER.

Miss Nicholson present[s] her best Compliments.

PALMERS LODGINGS
 CASTLE STREET
  CARLISLE."

In this manner she announces her meeting with Scott, whose first letter to her (*Letters*, I, 65) was written presumably about the same time. Lord Downshire's reply to Charlotte's announcement arrived on 7th (?) October and was forwarded immediately to Scott with the warning to write soon, as Lord Downshire is to be called away to Ireland. Scott wrote at once, and Lord Downshire seems to have replied on the 19th, asking for more information regarding ways and means.[1] To this Scott doubtless replied at once, for in a letter of the 29th he is awaiting impatiently Lord Downshire's " final answer ", while he spends his time in galloping on the Musselburgh sands in the morning and translating little tales from the German in the evening. Meantime he has written from Rosebank, Kelso, on his way to Edinburgh, putting certain questions about her parentage, her brother in India, the necessity of which had apparently dawned upon him when he came to announce what was forthcoming in a letter to his mother and by word of mouth to his friends at Mertoun. No answer being received, he writes again on the 18th in some concern. " Do you really think that your Birth were it the most splendid in Britain would raise you in my opinion or would sink you were it otherwise—my esteem & affection are founded upon very different qualities and are unalterably your own, while you continue to value them—I would soothe national or family fancies where I could do so without going out of my own road, but otherways I know very well how to despise both " (*Letters*, XII, 54). Charlotte replied on the 22nd a little coldly. She will answer these questions when she hears from Lord Downshire, as advised by Miss Nicolson. The latter has been ill and she herself so busy nursing that " only once and that quite by accident I thought of you ". On the 25th she sends the somewhat evasive account of her parentage, which I have discussed above, and adds a

[1] Only the cover of this letter is preserved, but its contents are given by Lockhart, who dates it the 15th. The cover itself bears the date of the 19th.

little petulantly : " Before I conclude this famous Epistle I will give you a little hint that is not to put quite so many *Must* in your letter, it is beginning *rather too soon*, and another thing is that I take the liberty not to mind them much," but she is not to be taken too seriously for, after all, " you *must* take care of yourself, you *must* think of me." On the 26th she acknowledges the receipt of a miniature in a friendlier tone. Scott was considerably disturbed and just a little nettled by her tone, if one may say so of a man so much in love, and he replies on 29th October : " I have to thank my beloved freind for her two letters—the second was a relief *beyond what I can express* for the first surely left me under the impression that I had been unfortunate enough to offend you, an addition which was very unnecessary to my depression of Mind. When you were angry at me for insisting upon an inquiry which you certainly have satisfied with so much ease & credit to yourself, you surely my dear Charlotte did not recollect that I have other people besides myself to satisfy & that to do so in this country it is really necessary that I should say something of your family and parents—without doing this I could not promise that even your beauty & accomplishments would attone. . . . And let me add that nothing but such an explanation's being *immediatly necessary* could have led me to urge you to write or do any thing else that was disagreeable to you " (*Letters*, XII, 57). As to the hint about using the word " must " too often, " were I to be *trop recherché* in my expressions in our present situation that would be but a poor security for my continuing so hereafter—as it is, I think, you must be content with seeing the worst of me before hand—only unless you mean to hurt me more than I can describe never again suppose that I can intend any thing harsh or peremptory however careless my expressions may be—I love you my dear Charlotte as I do my own eyes, as I do my own soul but the warmth of that very attachment may sometimes hurry me into vehemence of expression which I do not intend especially as I never read my letters a second time" (*Letters*, XII, 58).

Scott had written to his mother on, or about, the same day as he wrote his first letter to Charlotte; and it is clear that the announcement was received with considerable dubiety by his family and definite opposition from his now ailing father. If that opposition is continued, he tells Charlotte in the letter of 29th October, " I am firmly determined to resign my prospects here and seek my fate in the West Indies and my freinds well know that if my resolution is taken, heaven & earth cannot divert me from carrying it into execution. But my sweet freind I wish I had as little real ground of apprehension from Ld. D as I have from my father & freinds but with him lies the rub" (*Letters*, XII, 59).

However she may have huffed at Scott's questions and " musts ", Charlotte had no desire to quarrel or to go to the West Indies, and on the 31st she writes to express her vexation that he could have thought she was angry because of his questions, and taken her quizzing so seriously. " Apprehension from Lord D." was also soon put an end to by the receipt of a letter from him on 29th October, and forwarded by Charlotte on 4th November, accepting Scott's proposals in the most flattering terms : " Sir, I received the favour of your letter. It was so manly, honourable, candid, and so full of good sense, that I think Miss Carpenter's friends cannot in any way object to the union you propose."

On the same day, 4th November, that she forwarded the letter, Charlotte wrote to Lord Downshire. " Last Nights Post brought me your letter for which no words can express the thanks and gratefulness of my heart, for the interest you have taken in my welfare. Your approbation insures me happiness, and also the satisfaction of knowing that having your sanction I am sure of acting to my Brother's wish. I have sent your Lordships letter to Mr. Scott, I believe it will bring him here very soon, I will then try to persuade him to differ our marriage until I have heard from my Brother, as such an occasion is always attended with some little expences, and has he is not *rich* we had better wait for the Pagodas, I should not like to go into his family without having a little of the needful. Pardon me my Lord for applying again to your great generosity, it grieves me to have to inform you that our little stock of money is nearly exausted, and if you will have the goodness to let me know if we are to apply to Mr Dumergue for the next Quarter, and now my Lord will you allow me to make another request, and hope your indulgence will excuse the too great liberty I fear I am taking in asking you to have the goodness of advancing me a triffling [*sic*] sum of money, as I find it is very uncertain when the affairs of the India House will be settled, and as I shall be obliged to purchase a few things, which I mean to do with the greatest economy." The allowance is doubtless Miss Nicolson's (in a letter of 1798 to Sophia Dumergue she mentions " Lord Downshire's having forgot to send Miss Nicolson's quarter ") ; the loan is an advance on money expected from her brother.

Scott received Lord Downshire's letter, forwarded by Charlotte, on the morning of either the 5th or 6th November, and set off the same day for Carlisle, getting as far as Selkirk that day, whence he wrote both to the Marquis of Downshire and to his friend, Robert Shortreed (*Letters*, I, 77-8). Both these letters, written on 5th or 6th November, are misdated : that to the Marquis by Scott himself (the original is extant) ; that to Shortreed either by Scott again or by Lockhart, misled by Scott's dating of the other.[1] " Scott ", says Shortreed, " was sair beside him-

---

[1] In that to Shortreed he says : " I shall be home in about eight days." The late Mr. James Glen pointed out to me that " the Courts usually met for the winter session on the 12th November, but in that year the 12th was a Sunday, and Monday was, I presume, then, as now, a blank day, so that the Court would meet on Tuesday, 14th November"—which agrees with the date of 5th or 6th for the two letters referred to. At the same time Scott must have been back in Edinburgh, for he writes from there to Charlotte on the 12th.

self about Miss Carpenter ;—we toasted her twenty times over—and sat together, he raving about her, until it was one in the morning."

Lord Downshire evidently responded generously to Charlotte's appeal for a " triffling sum of money ", for on 21st November she writes : " My Lord my heart overflows with gratitude, you are too good and generous to me, how I must be favoured for such a blessing in having you my friend and protector. I wrote to Mr Scott immediately to inform him of your wish to have the agreement drawn up ; he is at present in Edinburgh, he has taken a ready furnished house, in the new Town for six months, in the Spring we can have a great choice of Houses, and he thinks I can then please myself as to the situation and furniture, he is to return here about Christmas to fetch me. O my Lord tho' I have a prospect of happiness I cannot reflect on so great a change in my state of life but with fear, it is very awful to think it will be for life, how I will make it my study to remember and act by the good advices you have given me. Mr Scott's Mother and Sister have written to me very kindly, his family is very numerous, and with an Uncle and Aunt of his a Dr and Mrs Rutherford, they have sent me a very polite message by Mr Scott to say they would be happy to do every thing in their power to render Edinburgh agreeable to their new Neice.

" In a former letter of your Lordships you gave me to hope that on your return from Ireland you would perhaps see me, will you my Lord permit me to make it my most earnest request to have the honor of a visit from you, may I flatter myself for so great a happiness, and how happy I should be to present you to Mr Scott, and if on an acquaintance he should gain your good opinion I shall love him the more, be proud of my choice, and think myself one of the happiest of beings. I have heard from my good friends of Bond Street, they will have the goodness to execute my Commissions, for which you have so handsomely provided, and has I am going to send them a present I shall take that occasion of returning Mr Scott's letters. I hope it will not be long before we hear from dear Charles, he has been very ill, therefore I cant be angry with him, but only a little impatient for those promised letters. Miss Nicolson is very much obliged to you for your good wishes, there is not anything she would not do to oblige your Lordship, but when you advise her to marry she fears you forget that she is neither young, handsome, nor rich. I forgot to mention in my last letter that Mr & Mrs Bird were acquainted with Mr Scott, and that Mr B. was to perform the ceremony, etc. I remain My Lord Your much obliged and grateful C. Carpenter."

On the 26th she wrote again from Carlisle, expressing her anxiety about his journey to Ireland and her gratitude for a shawl : " I have written to Mr Scott to mention that circumstance of the Name which had not occurred to me,[1] he will send the paper for your Lordships inspection and approbation, and when it is returned for his signature and mine, if there is no obstacle, our marriage will take place soon after, which will be about Christmas . . . whatever success and good fortune and comfort I may enjoy in future I shall never forget a moment that it all origins from the blessing of having your Lordship for my friend and protector." She goes on to mention her brother's connection with a Mr. Haliburton, a relation of Scott's father (*Letters*, I, 83). On 10th December she writes to Charles Dumergue to thank him for the present of a teapot—" it is indeed the handsomest I have ever seen, you have always been too good and kind. . . . I shall never forget the attentions and favours I have received in your family. If I should ever be so fortunate as to persuade you to visit Edinburgh I believe it is not necessary to

---

[1] Writing to Scott on 23rd November, she says : " I have intirely forgot to mention to you that I have three names, Margaret and C C, it may perhaps be of consequence in the agreement you was to draw up, being never call'd but by the name of Charlotte it never once occur'd to me."

assure you that you would make me *very* happy, Mr Scott and me would take so much pleasure and delight in receiving such dear friends. . . . We cannot for the present fix exactly the time that we shall leave this place, as it depends entirely on Lord Downshire's returning a paper that Mr Scott has sent to him, I am most anxious to know if you have heard anything of his Lordship, I am always so very unhappy while he stays in Ireland." That was written on the 10th, and on the same day she wrote to Scott : " If I could but really believe that my letter gave you my dearest Scott only half the pleasure you express, I should almost think that I should get very fond of writing merely for the pleasure to indulge you—that is saying a great deal. I hope you are sensible of the compliment I pay you and dont expect I shall always be so *pretty* behaved. . . . It is very unlucky you are such a bad housekeeper—as I am no better. I shall try. I hope to have very soon the pleasure of seeing you, and to tell you how much I love you ; but I wish the first fortnight was over. . . . P.S. Étudiez votre françois, I have a french Grammar for you, remember you are to teach me Italian in return and call forth for all your patience. I shall be a stupid scholar. Aimez Charlotte." She wrote again on the 14th, " fixing *already* next Wednesday for your coming here, and on Thursday the 21st, O my dear Scott, on that day I shall be yours *for ever.* . . . P.S. Arrange it so that we shall see none of your family the night of our arrival. I shall be so tired, and such a fright, I shall not be seen to advantage." It was not till the 22nd that Scott reached Carlisle and they were married on the 24th. Scott's letters in the interval between his visit to Carlisle and return are full of his preparations and the new abode he has taken from a Mrs. Macleod which he enters finally on 21st November. " Look at *the date* my dear Charlotte, pray look at *the date* and tell me where I am got to now " (*Letters*, XII, 72-3), and he goes on to describe the appearance of his bachelor home and varied interests, literary, legal, military, in the manner of a scene from one of his novels. On 4th December he wishes to get into touch with Mr. Slade, the lawyer, as Lord Downshire is in Ireland. He wishes the contract to be drawn up exactly as her friends would approve. If that can be settled he will leave Edinburgh on the 16th : " If we have such a fine sunshine day as this for our journey *my own* Scotland will not appear quite so savage as perhaps Charlotte expects . . . we have some tolerably Bleak country to pass thro' " (*Letters*, XII, 81). The marriage was concluded " before the arrival of the deeds from Mr Slade ", but no difficulty ensued.

Lockhart has described, somewhat guardedly one suspects, the welcome accorded to Scott's wife by his parents ; the warm friendship felt for her by his only sister Anne, " that interesting creature, who seems to have had much of her brother's imaginative and romantic temperament, without his power of controlling it," and the enthusiasm with which she was received by the brothers of *the Mountain*. Mary Erskine had just wedded Campbell of Clathick and the enthusiastic Jane Cranstoun had become the wife of " Godfrey Wenceslaus, Count of Purgstall, a nobleman of large possessions in Styria ", and in the Walpole Collection is contained her reply to Scott's letter, apparently announcing his marriage, of which Lockhart has printed an extract.[1] Charlotte can hardly have taken the place of these friends intellectually, but her natural gaiety of temper and love of the theatre were quite to the taste of Scott and his circle. Leyden writes of her from India with genuine affection.[2] She so far interested herself in her

[1] " O, how delightful to see the lady that is blessed with Earl Walter's love, and that had mind enough to discover the blessing. Some kind post, I hope, will soon tell me that your happiness is enlarged, in the only way it can be enlarged, for you have no chance now I think of taking Buonaparte prisoner."

[2] " It is impossible however not to beg to be remembered to my dear Mrs Scott and the fact is that the Laswade Cottage, the blazing ingle &c still recur as the happiest scenes of my youth. God bless you and your family My dearest Scott, etc."—JOHN LEYDEN, 1811.

husband's work as to make fair copies of his ballads and even, later, of the poems for his friends. Hutton, the mediaeval and ecclesiastical historian, in letters to Scott acknowledges with gratitude copies of charters and heraldic designs made for him by Mrs. Scott at her husband's request.

In 1798 the Scotts, who, after a short stay in George Street, had taken up house in Castle Street, acquired as a summer residence the cottage at Lasswade, from which many of Scott's earlier letters are dated. From there Charlotte wrote to Lord Downshire on 24th August, 1798. "I deferd the honour of inquiring after your health until the times were a little quieted as I fear that during the disturbance I should only have intruded on your Lordship whom I hope is well. . . . I had wished to inform you sooner of our plan of taking this cottage which would not have taken place had I not been well assur'd of your approbation as I can convince your Lordship that we have acted within bounds of prudence, the rent of the house stands as at thirty pounds a year which for it we have very excellent accomodation, the house was built for Sir James Clark whose whim was to have it quite in the cottage style, it is even thatched which in my opinion is a beauty for a House of such little pretention, there is also belonging to it two large Fields and a little Garden that supplies us with all sort of vegetables, we intend next year to be great farmers as we shall have plenty of grass we shall keep a cow and a couple of Horse, at present Scott keeps only one, which he is obliged to do as he belongs to the Cavalry, on our marriage he parted with one to diminish his expenses but as we have a Country House we find we can keep another at very little expense which will not be till next Spring when I intend to fetch up all my courage and take to riding which will be a great convenience to us as we have great many neighbours by whom we are much visited.

"I am very much obliged to your Lorship for sending

me Charles letters which are indeed all that my heart could wish and much more than I can express of gratitude for his great kindness & generosity—the order of the two hundred and fifty pounds has been accepted for which I will send the receipt of it . . . " She has not heard from Miss Nicolson for some time : " I wrote to her a week ago to remind her of her promise of visiting us this Winter and to request her to give us that pleasure as soon as possible and hope I shall see her the beginning of October. Miss Jane had no other reasons for leaving me but that she could not find any family were [sic] she might have been boarded, her wish was to have been settled near me could she have met with such a situation and I should have been most happy if I could have prevailed on her to have stay'd with me,[1] but her wish was to have a home then she would come to visit me very often—she says she has wander'd long enough and wishes now to have a place she might call her home and live quietly, nothing could make me so happy as to see her well settled and would do all in my power to make her comfortable. Scott desires me to present his most respectful Compliments to you. . . . Your much obliged and ever grateful M. Charlotte Scott." She wrote again from the " Cottage " on 13th September, forwarding a letter to her brother and " to express the more than happiness I had on learning there was some chance of your Lorship visiting Edinburgh." [2]

---

[1] In a letter, written by Charlotte to her brother in India on 8th October, 1817, she says : " Miss J. Nicolson I hear is gone abroad. I am sorry to say she has given up my acquaintance as with the rest of her old friends."—Letter in Dr. Rosenbach's possession. Seen by me 26th May, 1933.

[2] Some kind critics of Scott have surmised that he hoped by his marriage to establish connections with the Marquess of Downshire and that the Marquess took no notice of him after the marriage. As a fact Lord Downshire expressed his intention of paying a visit to the young couple in Edinburgh, but in Ireland, to which he had gone just about the time of the engagement, he fell into disgrace by his opposition to the Act of Union, was dismissed from his regiment, was deprived of the Lord Lieutenancy of the County of Down, and had his name struck off the Privy Council. See the *Cornwallis Correspondence*, ed. Charles Ross, Vol. III (1859), the *Memoirs and Corres-*

A month later, 14th October, the first child was born. Scott seems to have written the same day to Lord Downshire, who replies from Ireland, promising to act as Godfather when " the little heathen is made a Christian ". But the child died the next day, and to Lord Downshire's letter of condolence Charlotte replied in an undated letter : " Had I been permitted to write I should long before this time have made an offering of my warmest thanks for your most affectionate inquiries after me, so much kindness and that from your Lordship could not but promote my speedy recovery and that of softening the disappointment I felt at the death of the poor Child. I was very ill and after having suffered so much I thought it hard to lose it, but I must think myself fortunate it was taken before I could have for it that affection that all Mothers must feel—I have been most kindly taken care of by all Scott's family, his mother could not have had more tenderness for her own daughter than she had for me and I was also attended by Dr Rutherford with the utmost attention and kindness. I cannot say enough of their goodness and I believe it is not necessary for me to assure you how affectionate and anxious Scott has been for me and how sensible I am of it. I am so far recovered."

In March of the following year the Scotts visited London, for Scott the first visit since childhood when he passed through on his way to Bath. There he made the acquaintance of the Dumergues and at their house met Lord Downshire. While the Scotts were in London his father died in Edinburgh, and a joint letter of condolence was sent from London (*Letters*, I, 90-2). And so may

pondence of Castlereagh (1848). He died in September 1801 and in an article in the *Annual Register* for 1822 on Lord Londonderry, p. 625, it is stated that owing to the disgrace to which he had been exposed he died of a broken heart, and that the Marchioness spared no expense nor exertion to avenge the insult offered to him.

In 1826 the man of business of the family, Mr. Handley, appealed to Scott on behalf of the Marchioness for aid in a claim she was putting forward in connection with the vacant Earldom of Stirling. (*Letters*, IX, pp. 478-80.)

end what I may call the second chapter of Scott's life. Thereafter literature and the career that success in literature opens to him become the predominant interest.

The story of those early loves presents a problem of character and feeling that is not altogether easy to solve. Was Scott a passionate man, and does the subordinate interest of the love-story, on which Balzac, his ardent admirer in other respects, comments as one might expect a Frenchman to do, reflect want in his own nature and experience ? Scott's early friends speak of his passionate, ungovernable nature as well as of the sweetness of his heart ; and one gets occasional glimpses of the underlying fires as in the story of his quarrel with his older cousin Scott of Raeburn, who had wrung the neck of a young starling which Walter had tamed : " I flew at his throat like a wild cat, and was torn from him with no little difficulty." His letters about Miss Belsches, and his letters to Miss Carpenter, bespeak something of the same passionate, impatient temper. Wherein then does he differ from the more common type of lover among artists and poets—Burns, Byron, Shelley, Balzac, de Musset, who flit like bees from one lovely flower to another and alone are generally spoken of as passionate ? Scott is more akin to Wordsworth who, it will be remembered, said he had not written love poems for fear of putting too much ardour into them. The statement has often provoked a smile, but the facts now known about Wordsworth's life have given it a measure of justification. Had Scott found himself in like circumstances to those of Wordsworth in France, and met with a passion of ardour equal to his own, he too could have thrown prudence to the winds. But in both men passion was modified, and to some extent inhibited, by other feelings, the strength of their affections for one. Affection and passion do not always, perhaps often, go together in equal measure. What did Byron care for any of those he loved ? It was not perhaps very different with Shelley. Wordsworth's affection for his friend

Coleridge, his brother John, his sister, and his children was a passion ; and there is the same strain of passion in Scott's feeling towards his family and friends.[1] In both, too, passion was controlled by that sense of dutifulness to which I have referred above, that inability to take the purely egotistic view of persons and relations which passion demands, that sense of responsibility from which Scott, with all his rashness, could never escape. In Wordsworth one has to add to this the more transcendental passion of the poet who is also a prophet ; in Scott, the active, impatient temperament which kept him from ever being sufficiently analytical of his own mind and motives. If he did not enter very deeply into the souls of the characters whom he drew, it was because he never entered very deeply into his own motives. Even in the later interesting *Journal*, though he speaks at times of his own character and feelings, his love of solitude, his proneness to dream and build castles in the air, he seldom or never analyses his motives. When the vision of ruin dawns upon him, he admits that Abbotsford has been his Delilah, and even that " I had a lesson in 1814 which should have done good to me, but success and abundance erased it from my mind". But he never recurs to this, or states fully to himself the measure of his own responsibility, considers the question of his long disguise of his financial activities, the manner in which, as Lockhart sees, he had misled his family and friends. He turns away from it to blame Constable, so far as in justice he can, and to plan for redress by his own unaided efforts. Only in this practical way does he admit his error. It is this dislike of analysing feeling that makes his heroes of so little interest, for it is in the mind and heart and soul of the hero, man or woman, that the conflict of a novel or drama must be worked out.

[1] " Walter and Jane appear cordial and happy in each other ; the greatest blessing Heaven can bestow on them or me who witness it. If we had Lockhart and Sophia, there would be a meeting of the beings dearest to me in life." *Journal*, August 16, 1826.

But, as we shall see, the novel for Scott is primarily a picture of life at a certain time rather than the soul's history of a Clarissa or even an Arthur Pendennis or Henry Esmond. He understands the passionate loyalty and affection of a Jeanie Deans. In the Master of Ravenswood he glances at a passion he could have understood but had never fully realised, and his treatment becomes a little melodramatic, but by no means as much so as has been maintained.

CHAPTER IV

> " The Minstrelsy has never yet found its way to the common reader. It is in my opinion the most amusing part of all Sir Walter's works—contains the germ of everything he ever did and only wants a little puffing to have an enormous run now.—The criticism of the time was all contemptible—I could not use a bit of it. What a progress in this sort of thing since 1802 and all owing to Sir W. himself."
>
> *Lockhart to Cadell*, Jan. 1, 1833.

WITH his marriage closes the first long period of Scott's life, what I have here called the first chapters: childhood and early education; adolescence, love, marriage. What remains is the history of his literary and social career, beginning slowly but gathering speed and force as he is driven onward by the impetus of creative genius and the passion of increasing wealth and success, the ever mounting strain of what he himself calls " a very exciting and feverish style of composition ", and the equal and more agitating excitement of " mercantile speculation . . . this mixture of necessary attention and inevitable hazard—the frequent and awful uncertainty whether prudence shall overcome fortune or fortune baffle the schemes of prudence."

For it was not, I think, as a novelist that Scott thought of himself as entering on a literary career. Even in the year of his marriage he had not determined on any such career. To Charlotte, when engaged, he speaks of the law as still his profession and his reliance for the future : " none of those who were calld to the Bar with myself can boast of having very far outstripd me in the Career of Life or of Business. I have every reason to expect that the Sheriffdom of a particular County . . . may soon fall to my lot, etc." (*Letters*, I, 66). But by the time, two years later, when he did obtain the Sheriffdom of Selkirkshire, adding £300 per annum to his rather scanty earnings at the Bar, he was already launching out in a bolder manner than is represented by the slender volume of translations in 1797. It was the arrival in Edinburgh of Matthew Gregory Lewis in the winter of 1798-9, which opened the channel through which so much was to flow.

Lewis's immediate interest was Scott's translations from the German ballads and plays, for these German products of " Sturm und Drang ", tales of Terror and of Wonder, were what Lewis was interested in as collector and author. He secured a publisher for Scott's very faulty translation of *Goetz von Berlichingen*, which is only one of the plays Scott had translated. Some of them are still in manuscript. *The House of Aspen*, produced at the same time, is an adaptation rather than a translation, a play " in the wretched German manner ", he called it later, but it was much admired by Richard Heber, who was surprised that Kemble declined to produce it. For Lewis's prospective *Tales of Wonder* Scott supplied, in addition to his translation of " Der Wilde Jäger ", already printed in the small volume of 1796, three original ballads in the same spirit, " The Fire King ", a very Lewisian piece of supernatural nonsense, the rather better " Glenfinlas, or Lord Ronald's Coronach ", one of his few ventures into the Celtic supernatural, and " The Eve of St. John ", a queer transferring of the " Lenore " theme to Smailholm and " Tweed's fair strand ". The verse is irregular, and Scott's management of anapaests, as later in *The Lay of the Last Minstrel*, is clumsy to a degree :

" O fear not the priest, who sleepeth to the east !
" For to Dryburgh the way he has ta'en ;
" And there to say mass, till three days do pass,
" For the soul of a knight that is slayne."

> He turned him around, and grimly he frowned ;
> Then he laughed right scornfully—
> "He who says the mass-rite for the soul of that knight,
> "May as well say mass for me."

To Scott's version of Bürger's "Lenore" Lewis preferred and printed Taylor's version from *The Monthly Magazine*, a banal performance in a somewhat Chattertonian English :

> She bet her breste, and wrung her hands
>   And rollde her tearless eye,
> From rise of morne, till the pole stars
>   Again did freeke the skye.

Scott's version is rather better though the faulty rhyme probably offended Lewis :

> She beat her breast, she wrung her hands,
>   Till sun and day were o'er,
> And through the glimmering lattice shone
>   The twinkling of the star.

But the fact is, that from German literature of the "Sturm und Drang" period—which was all he ever had any acquaintance with—Scott derived nothing directly, except it be some of the weakest elements in his work, from these early ballads and *The Lay of the Last Minstrel* to *Anne of Geierstein*. Indirectly, by way of example, they may have strengthened his interest in the ballad and mediaeval studies to which Percy and other of his countrymen had already directed him, and "Goetz von Berlichingen" may, as my old teacher Professor William Minto (*Encyc. Brit.*) argued, have suggested his attempting such a picture of Scottish life and warfare on the Borders as Goethe had of the German barons on the Rhine. The translation and imitation of German ballad and drama was but a slight bridge across which he travelled towards his own native and appropriate country. The real beginning, the taproot of Scott's later work as poet and novelist, is *The Minstrelsy of the Scottish Border*.

If we assume the authenticity of the letters to Jessie, Scott's memory of ballads goes back to his sixth year : " I remember in my childhood when staying at Bath for my health with a kind aunt of mine there was an Irish servant in the house where we lodged, and she sung me once two ballads which made a great impression on me at the time. One filled me with horror"—and he goes on in a later letter to quote *The Outlandish Knight* and *Lammikin*, citing the latter with a running comment in humorous style (*Letters*, I, 4-6). Percy's *Reliques* he read in his uncle's garden at Kelso when " the summer day sped onward so fast that, notwithstanding the sharp appetite of thirteen [1784], I forgot the dinner hour, was sought for with anxiety, and was found still entranced in my intellectual banquet. To read and to remember was in this instance the same thing." " The very grass seat ", he tells Bishop Percy later, " to which (when a boy of twelve) I retired from my playfellows to devour the works of the ancient minstrels is still fresh and clear to my memory." In 1792 he began his yearly raids with Shortreed into the Borders where he gathered what he calls " raiding ballads ", and in 1793 he writes to Patrick Murray : " As the facetious Linton " [Adam Ferguson] " will no doubt make one of the party I have got by heart for his amusement a reasonable number of Border ballads, most of them a little longer than Chevy Chase, which I intend to throw in at intervals just by way of securing my share in the conversation." His taste for collecting ballads was soon so well known that George Chalmers in February 1796 writes to him, from the Board of Trade, to ask him for a loan of them for his own *Caledonia* (1807-24). In replying Scott tells him " these ballads with a few others which I have picked up from tradition and which lie scattered thro other MS. of a more private nature I have sometimes thought of forming into a small collection, adding to them such of acknowledged merit as have already seen the light, but I am discouraged by the multitude of similar publications." What was meditated in 1796 began to take definite shape after the intercourse with Lewis. Scott found an enthusiastic, if somewhat fitful, collaborator in John Leyden, whose acquaintance he made through Richard Heber in the winter of 1799-1800. Moreover, while awaiting the long expected issue of Lewis's *Tales of Wonder*, he grew interested in the work as a printer at Kelso of his old friend James Ballantyne, and got him to print, under the title *An Apology for Tales of Terror* (1799), an eighty page quarto, containing ballads by himself, Lewis and Southey. This led at once to the further design of getting Ballantyne to print his long meditated collection of ballads. " I am still resolved ", he writes to James in April 1800, " to have re course to your press for the ballads of the Border, which are in some forwardness." But in the summer of 1800 another collector of ballads, Robert Jamieson,[1] a classical master in a school at Macclesfield, appeared in Edinburgh. He had acquired, through friends among the professoriate of Aberdeen University, a number of ballads from a Mrs. Brown, the wife of the minister of Falkland, from whom Scott had also got ballads through Fraser Tytler, later Lord Woodhouselee. The result was that when Jamieson called on Scott he " found you beforehand with him in the provincial poetry he had collected " (*Heber to Scott*, October 9th, 1800). The chief, or most novel, feature of Scott's collection was to be the " raiding ballads ", and Jamieson seems to have thought that Scott was to confine himself to these and leave to him the more romantic ballads (Jamieson, *Popular Ballads*, 1806, Introduction). But as early as June of 1800, Scott, in promising Heber to be a subscriber to Jamieson's ballads when published, writes " take care however that the Gay Goshawk or Brown Adam " (both of them romantic ballads) " do not

[1] He was a friend of William Smyth, tutor to Sheridan's son, Fellow of Peterhouse, and later Professor of Modern History, Cambridge.

slip into his collection for I have laid my clutches on both for the Minstrelsy of the Border," and on the 6th of October he informs Bishop Percy that the division he proposes to make is into " Raiding Ballads (as they are called) relating to the forays and predatory incursions made upon the Borders and the Romantic or popular Ballads founded upon circumstances entirely imaginary." When the first edition of the *Minstrelsy* appeared it contained in the first volume twenty-one historical (as he now called them) ballads and in the second volume some twenty-four romantic ballads with *Thomas the Rhymer* in three parts, of which the last two are of Scott's own composition. Two songs were included, " O gin my luve were yon Red Rose " and " O tell me how to woo thee " and, under the heading " Imitations of the Ancient Ballads," Scott's *The Eve of St. John* and *Glenfinlas* and Leyden's *The Cout of Keeldar* and *Lord Soulis*. Whether Scott poached upon Jamieson or not is not quite clear. Jamieson never resented it, and Scott later got him a post in the Register House under his friend Thomas Thomson. In any case he enriched what he took from any source by his delightful introductions and notes.

The publication of the two volumes in 1802[1] brought Scott communications from other enthusiasts, among them William Laidlaw and the poet James Hogg, who supplied more ballads, and were to be friends and clients throughout Scott's life, Hogg of a rather wayward kind. A second edition appeared in 1803 with a third volume, and with many additions and alterations in the first two. Joseph Ritson also was delighted with the first volume and wrote of Scott and Leyden to a friend : " I have two prodigious geniuses who are ready to give me

[1] In the second edition of *The Minstrelsy* which appeared in 1803 the additions are not confined, as is sometimes stated or implied, to a third volume. There were additions and alterations made in the first two volumes. This edition contained the bulk of the material in subsequent editions though a few things were added later. Scott had at first contemplated a single volume.

every satisfaction." He visited Scott at Lasswade and conceived a warm attachment to Leyden. With George Ellis, the editor at an earlier period of the *Anti-Jacobin*, Scott entered into correspondence over another scheme, the editing of *Sir Tristrem*, a middle English poem, a manuscript of which Ritson had found in the Advocates' Library, and he rendered aid, in return, to Ellis in the preparation of his *Specimens of the Early English Romances*, a work which was not without effect on his own later poems.

With the publication of *The Minstrelsy of the Scottish Border* (1802-3) and of *Sir Tristrem* (1804), which he not only edited but completed with a " Fytte ", or book, of his own composition, Scott, slipping his German moorings, was launched on the voyage that was to carry him from ballads to lays, from lays to historical novels. To appreciate what Scott did in the *Minstrelsy* and its relation in style, spirit, and use of historical knowledge to his later work as poet and novelist, one must study the ballads with Scott's Introduction and Notes carefully in Mr. T. F. Henderson's valuable and interesting edition (1902). Scott was no purist in the choice of his texts. He censured Ritson's savage attacks on Bishop Percy, and himself worked in the spirit of Percy though with a somewhat different conception of a poetic and ballad diction. The charm of his personality vanquished for the time being the irritable and eccentric Ritson when that scholar, vegetarian, and professed atheist visited the cottage at Lasswade ; but had Ritson lived to scrutinise the Border ballads as edited by Scott as closely as he examined those of the Bishop they could hardly have escaped his ultimate anathema. Scott composed his texts by a process of combining different versions, correcting and improving the phraseology, the rhythm and the rhyme, heightening by occasional words the archaic flavour, rewriting and supplying whole stanzas, lending to an often prosaic version the animation and colour of his own eager and buoyant temperament. Take a single instance, for I am not writing a treatise on the ballad. The older version of "Jamie Telfer in the Fair Dodhead" is in the matter-of-fact style of the traditional ballad; Scott's additions betray the hand that was to compose *Marmion* and *The Lady of the Lake*:

> My hounds may a' rin masterless,
> My hawks may fly frae tree to tree,
> My lord may grip my vassal lands,
> For there again maun I never be.

or

> Warn Wat o' Harden, and his sons,
> Wi' them will Borthwick Water ride;
> Warn Gaudilands and Allanhaugh,
> And Gilmanscleugh and Commonside. (etc.)

But most distinctive of all are Scott's alterations in the verses describing the fight. The old ballad is plain and matter-of-fact:

> Fa on them, lads! can Simmy say;
>   Fy, fa on them cruelly!
> For or they win the Ritter ford
>   Mony toom saddle there shall be.
>
> But Simmy was striken o'er the head,
>   And thro the napskape it is gane,
> And Moscrop made a dolefull rage,
>   When Simmy on the ground lay slain.
>
> Fy, lay on them! co Martin Elliot;
>   Fy, lay on them cruelly!
> For ere they win to the Kershop ford,
>   Mony toom saddle there shall be.

Scott makes his own family the heroes of the exploit, and his hand is unmistakable in the verses which take the place of these:

> Set on them, lads! quo Willie then
>   Fye, lads, set on them cruelly!
> For ere they win to Ritterford,
>   Many a toom saddle there shall be!

> Then till't they gae wi' heart and hand ;
>   The blows fell thick as bickering hail ;
> And mony a horse ran masterless,
>   And mony a comely cheek was pale !
>
> Then Willie was stricken o'er the head
>   And thro' the knapscape that sword is gaen ;
> And Harden grat for very rage
>   When Willie on the ground lay slain.
>
> But he's taen aff his gude steel cap,
>   And thrice he waved it in the air—
> The Dinlay snaw was ne'er mair white
>   Nor the lyart locks of Harden's hair.[1]

In the romantic ballads it is more difficult to detect Scott's hand and still more difficult to distinguish it from the possible contributions of Burns (to whom the finest touches in " Tamlane " are due), Hogg, and Sharpe. But in " Young Benjie ", for example, it is just where the MS. copy sent to Scott is silent that we get the most romantic touches :

> They've taen up the comely corpse,
>   And laid it on the ground—
> " O who has killed our ane sister,
>   And how can he be found ?
>
> " The night it is her low lykewake,
>   The morn her burial day,
> And we maun watch at mirk midnight,
>   And hear what she will say."
>
> Wi' doors ajar, and candle light,
>   And torches burning clear ;
> The streikit corpse, till still midnight
>   They waked, but naething hear.

It is difficult not to suspect that if the romantic ballads are, on the whole, more poetic than the historical, it is because

---

[1] Compare : And still, in age, he spurned at rest,
    And still his brows the helmet pressed,
    Albeit the blanched locks below
    Were white as Dinlay's spotless snow.
        The Lay of the Last Minstrel, iv, 9.

there is more in them of Hogg and Sharpe and Scott and others. If, as Mr. Henderson more than suspects, " The Twa Corbies ", as given in *The Minstrelsy*, is due in the main to Sharpe and Scott, it might in itself furnish a text by which to illustrate the difference between the traditional ballad as it was and as the Romantic Revival liked to see it :

    Mony a one for him makes mane,
    But nane sall ken whare he is gane :
    O'er his white banes, when they are bare,
    The wind sall blaw for evermair.

That is of the same spirit and mood as :

    O what can ail thee, Knight at Arms,
      Alone and palely loitering ;
    The sedge is withered from the lake,
      And no birds sing,

and Scott's own later " Proud Maisie ".

With the publication of *The Minstrelsy* Scott got into the full stride of his work as an editor and poet, and he was soon driving forward with all the impetuosity and tireless energy which had hitherto gone into reading and writing for his own amusement, studying hard and drilling as a cavalry officer, and persuading a young woman, whom he has met in September, to become his wife in December. While at work on the ballads, he had also been editing *Sir Tristrem* (1804), and corresponding with George Ellis on the date and authorship of that poem, while assisting Ellis in the collecting of romances.[1] He was making

[1] For the correspondence of Scott with Heber and Ellis see *Letters of Sir Walter Scott*, Vols. I, II, III and XII, where they are printed in full for the first time. A specially interesting letter is that of 1st July, 1807 (Vol. XII, pp. 290-5), where Scott tells Ellis how he has learned from a young German, Henry William Weber, of the existence of German romances on the subject of Sir Tristrem and the disturbing effect of this discovery on his theory of Thomas the Rhymer as an intermediary between the Celtic bards and the Norman minstrels. For Weber himself see the long note to this letter based on an appreciation written by Scott when Weber died. He is one of the men around Scott of whom Lockhart speaks with his usual rather brutal sarcasm.

friends on all sides and in all ranks—Lord Dalkeith, the Dundases, Lady Douglas, Lady Anne Hamilton, Lady Louisa Stuart, Richard Heber, James Hogg, Charles Kirkpatrick Sharpe, the Wordsworths, and a host of others. He visited London in 1803, staying with his wife's friends, the Dumergues; went on thence to the Ellises at Sunninghill; and was conducted over Oxford by Heber. Before *Sir Tristrem* was out, he was at work on the poem which was to confirm his popularity and to open before him the prospect of a literary career, which should more than make good any deficiencies in his earnings as an advocate. He has told us in a later Introduction how the thought of a ballad on the subject of a Goblin Page—suggested by Lady Dalkeith—grew into *The Lay of the Last Minstrel*. His own interest in the early English romances and lays, which Ellis was editing, must have counted for something, as well as Goethe's drama; but the immediate impulse came from hearing Coleridge's "Christabel" recited by John (later Sir John) Stoddart, who had come to Scotland, as his letters to Scott show, in quest of material for a *Monasticon*; and, indeed, Scott's debt to Coleridge goes beyond his not very happy use of what Professor Saintsbury called "freedom of substitution" —feet monosyllabic, iambic, and trisyllabic as determined by the fall of the accent. The most perfect part of Coleridge's wonderful fragment is the opening description of Christabel in the forest and that of her stealing back to her chamber with Lady Geraldine so silently as not to disturb her father:

> Outside her kennel, the mastiff old
> Lay fast asleep, in moonshine cold,

and

> They passed the hall, that echoes still,
> Pass as lightly as you will!

> " O softly tread," said Christabel,
> " My father seldom sleepeth well."

> Sweet Christabel her feet doth bare,
> And jealous of the listening air
> They steal their way from stair to stair,
> Now in glimmer, and now in gloom,
> And now they pass the Baron's room,
> As still as death, with stifled breath !
> And now have reached her chamber door ;
> And now doth Geraldine press down
> The rushes of the chamber floor.

The verse seems to have the quietness of the movements described. Scott is clearly imitating Coleridge closely in the similar account of Margaret stealing forth to meet her lover :

> Why does fair Margaret so early awake,
>   And don her kirtle so hastilie ;
> And the silken knots, which in hurry she would make,
>   Why tremble her slender fingers to tie ;
> Why does she stop, and look often around,
>   As she glides down the secret stair ;
> And why does she pat the shaggy blood-hound,
>   As he rouses him up from his lair ;
> And, though she passes the postern alone,
>   Why is not the watchman's bugle blown ?
>
> The ladye steps in doubt and dread,
> Lest her watchful mother hear her tread ;
> The ladye caresses the rough blood-hound,
> Lest his voice should waken the castle round, . . .

That is almost plagiarism and one understands Coleridge's resentment, exaggerated as it is ; but Scott's management of the irregular and accentual rhythms is both heartier and clumsier. Indeed, in the best of the ballads, say " Tamlane " and " The Twa Corbies ", there is more of imaginative poetry than in the whole of *The Lay*, the most perfect thing in which is another ballad, " Rosabelle ", as warmly coloured as the Chapel it celebrates is architecturally decorative. But the lovers of pure poetry are few ; the lovers of a good story told with the spirit and movement of Scott's cantering or galloping stanzas were many. Here was something new come out of all the antiquarian pother about ballads and the Gothic, something as new in its different way as *Clarissa* had been and *Waverley* was to be, and far more intelligible and interesting than Chatterton's and Strutt's archaism. Scott, as has been said, took the bread out of the mouths of the novelists.[1]

---

[1] "Walter Scott has no business to write novels, especially good ones. It is not fair. He has Fame and Profit enough as a Poet, and should not be taking the bread out of other peoples' mouths. I do not like him, and do not mean to like Waverley if I can help it, but fear I must."—JANE AUSTEN to ANNE AUSTEN, 28th September, 1814.

CHAPTER V

> "Ay, it was enough to tear me in pieces, but there was a wonderful exhileration about it all : my blood was kept at fever pitch—I felt as if I could have grappled with anything and everything ; then there was hardly any of my schemes that did not afford me the means of serving some poor devil of a brother author. There was always huge piles of material to be arranged, sifted and indexed—volumes of extracts to be transcribed—journeys to be made hither and thither for ascertaining little facts and dates—in short I could commonly keep half a dozen of the ragged regiment of Parnassus in tolerable case."
>
> SCOTT *to* LOCKHART, *Life*, c. xvii.

FOR Scott himself the success, relative of *The Minstrelsy*, complete of *The Lay*, was decisive. With the publication of that poem in 1805 the current of Scott's life began to flow in full force, and that, if I can manage the figure, in three channels which only at times are all of them visible to his friends and admirers—his literary work ; his social life of which the legal is part ; and his financial. The plan mooted in 1800 that James Ballantyne should remove his printing press to Edinburgh was realised in 1802 with the help of a loan from Scott. In 1805, after the publication of *The Lay*, Ballantyne approached Scott for a further loan, and Scott agreed to become a sleeping partner, investing in the business the legacy he had inherited from his uncle, Robert Scott of Kelso. Immediately he began to push the business with all the sanguine energy of his character, planning literary work of all kinds[1] and en-

---

[1] A letter in James Ballantyne's hand, now in the National Library of Scotland (MS. 910, f. 35) sketches plans mooted with John Murray. It is not dated but, I think, refers to negotiations going on when Constable stepped in with his offer of one thousand guineas for the unwritten *Marmion*. The schemes include (1) an edition of the novelists with biographies,

deavouring to make it a condition with publishers of what he wrote or edited that the printing should be done by James Ballantyne—British Poets, a *corpus historiarum* or full edition of the Chronicles of England, an edition of Dryden's Works, George Carleton's Memoirs, Sir Robert Carey's (Earl of Monmouth) Memoirs, Somers's Tracts, Sir Ralph Sadler's Life and Letters, and a new poem, *Marmion*, were all planned in the next few years and most of them executed. Lockhart has quoted Scott's own words, descriptive of the almost feverish exhilaration with which he plunged into all these varied undertakings, besides reviewing in long articles for *The Edinburgh Review*. As early as 1807 (two years before the publishing firm was instituted) Ballantyne writes to Robert Lundie, the parish minister of Kelso : " You will be happy to hear from me

(2) De Foe's works, (3) Swift's works. Murray thinks " Swift more uncertain than Dryden " *i.e.* as a commercial proposition, (4) Beaumont and Fletcher. Murray thinks this likely to be a " Respectable and valuable work ; but not extensive. Only 750 have been printed of Massinger, and 750 is now printing of Ben Jonson." The reference is to Gifford's editions, Massinger (1805), Jonson (1816). (5) An anonymous work—" perfectly approved " by Murray. What is referred to I do not know, unless it be that Scott was contemplating *Waverley*. It will be remembered that it was included in John Ballantyne and Co.'s printed list of " New Works and Publications for 1809-10 : " Waverley ; or 'tis Sixty Years Since ; a novel in three vols. 12mo." In September 1810 the early chapters were sent to James who commented on it in a letter of the 15th which is printed by Lockhart. Scott's own statement is that he sketched the first chapters in 1805 and, as Lockhart notes, the first of the MS. is on paper manufactured that year. (6) Minor Poets. " Barker is now printing such things—Wyatt, Surrey &c " is Murray's comment. (7) Daemonology—thus early in Scott's mind. We shall hear of it later. (8) Various Memoirs concerning Scottish and English history, " in the form of Cobbett's Historical Register." (9) Le Sage. But Murray would include only Gil Blas and The Devil, presumably Le Diable Boiteux. (10) Boyd's Works. " Has it been offered to usual publishers Cadell and Davies ? " Murray asks. This must refer to Hugh Boyd, claimed as the author of The Letters of Junius. Cadell and Davies had published his miscellaneous works edited by Lawrence Dundas Campbell in 1800. (11) A republication of Nash's pamphlets. (12) New Poem. " Only one opinion upon the subject. Most *certainly*." This must be *Marmion* and it was, as Lockhart hints, the knowledge that negotiations were in hand that induced Constable to step in and not only make his offer but to pay in advance. It was this payment in advance which was the bait

that our business is increasing with incalculable rapidity, and that we have every reason to flatter ourselves our reputation is not falling off. This is really providential, for my enterprizes were often so bold that nothing but the most decided success could have prevented the reproach of rashness from attaching to me."[1]

These were ominous words, especially as publishing was soon to be added to printing, and a third partner was to be taken in, viz. John Ballantyne, James's younger brother. He was twenty-eight when James moved to Edinburgh, and was carrying on his father's business in a manner all his own. " Could scarcely be happier. Hunted, shot, kept boisterous company, and neglected business the fruits whereof I soon found." By 1804 all was " wrong and changes in every way approaching ". In 1805 " all consummated . . . My furniture, goods, etc. all

that secured Scott for him, and that in the end was to make Scott as dependent on Constable as the latter on Scott. (13) Memoirs of the House of Somerville. (14) Popular Tales. " Mr Murray's father was the original proprietor. They never sold, and do not sell. Mr M. thinks they would do for the novels if they might not do alone." These are Scott's proposals. There follows a list of Murray's suggestions into which I need not go. The interest of the letter is the revelation of all that was in Scott's mind as early as 1806-8 including as they do many tasks which were not to be undertaken till a much later date.

If I am right then the letter must date from 1806, for on the 30th of January, 1807, Constable wrote to Scott: " We have much pleasure in accepting of the property of your new poem " Flodden Field " and not less in aggreeing to pay for the same the sum of one thousand guineas.

We propose offering Mr Miller and Mr Murray of London one half of the concern between them, the other we intend to reserve for ourselves—and we trust it will remain for ever in the hands of Edinburgh Booksellers for the honour and glory of Scotland—payment of the copy money shall be made to suit your convenience—and wishes—
                We remain with great regard
                Dear Sir
                Your obliged and obedient servant
                      ARCHD CONSTABLE AND COMPANY
WALTER SCOTT "

[1] Some Letters of James Ballantyne to Rev. Robert Lundie, Kelso, loaned to Nat. Lib. Scot. by Mrs. Eliza Maitland Bonar, granddaughter of Lundie. See *Scotsman*, 13th April, 1914.

sold at Kelso previous to my going to Edinburgh to become my brother's Clerk, whither I did go for which God be praised eternally on Friday 3rd January 1806."[1] John was installed as a clerk at a salary of £200 a year. But Scott's ambitions were mounting with the tide of his success. When Constable, that enterprising Edinburgh bookseller, *i.e.* publisher, heard in 1806 that Scott was engaged on a second poem, he was determined that Longmans should not have it and offered a thousand guineas " very shortly after it was begun, and without having seen one line of it " (*Lockhart*). But Constable's capital was not large, and he allowed one half of the copyright to be divided between Miller and Murray. By the summer of 1807 Scott was reciting or reading large portions of the poem to a friend, and in February 1808 it was issued with introductory epistles to each canto and long antiquarian notes. But in the course of that year Scott quarrelled with Constable, offended by his treatment at the hands of Constable's partner, Hunter; and, moved partly by political motives, the pacifist, defeatist doctrine which *The Edinburgh Review* was preaching to the Spaniards, but piqued also by Jeffrey's censorious review of *Marmion*, he was busy helping to found *The Quarterly Review*, published by Murray and under the editorship of William Gifford. The result of all this was, that John Ballantyne, who had arrived penniless in Edinburgh three years earlier, found himself in 1809 the apparent head of the publishing firm of John Ballantyne & Co., the Co. being his brother James and Walter Scott.

Scott, Constable, the Ballantynes—they were the characters in a drama which ended in a tragedy for the three principals, John having died before the final crash. It was an unwise step of Scott's to link his fortune so closely as he did with the Ballantynes; but it was a great mistake of Lockhart, trusting too implicitly to the prejudiced evidence of Cadell, to try to place on their shoulders the chief

[1] John Ballantyne's Diary, Pierpont Morgan Library, New York.

responsibility for the final disaster. Neither of the brothers was a sound man of business, John a little of a trickster and James somewhat of an epicure but with a strain of melancholy that prompted to fits of piety. They were both extravagant—John a scatterer, James an absorbent. But the sleeping partner was the active partner, and if he had to pay the piper, he always called the tune. They were absolutely at Scott's beck and call, could be summoned to Abbotsford at a moment's notice. When a dying man, John is scolded for wishing to settle at Kelso, too far from Edinburgh for him to act as Scott's agent in negotiations; and when James's wife dies, Scott is very sympathetic, but grows soon impatient of his absence from business for that and any other reason and is always a little contemptuous of his valetudinarianism, physical and spiritual.[1] But the root of the trouble which soon began to come is described with equal clearness by James and by Scott: " My brother John though an active and pushing was not a cautious publisher, and the large sums received [for *The Lady of the Lake*] never formed an addition to stock. In fact they were all expended by the partners who being young and sanguine men not unwillingly adopted my brother's hasty results," *i.e.*, I presume, his hasty calculations of loss and profit. So James wrote to Lockhart. Scott's account is almost identical: " You & your brother," he writes to James in 1816, " keeping the accompts we both drew according to our rated stocks with such indiscretion as it proved that the concern was run £4000 in debt which £4000 containing *your* draughts as well as *my own* I *alone* was under the

[1] " I am twenty leaves before the printers; but Ballantyne's wife is ill, and it is his nature to indulge apprehensions of the worst, which incapacitates him for labour."—*February 14* [1829], *Journal*.

" My dear James,—I am very sorry for the state of your health and should be still more so were I not certain that I can prescribe for you as well as any phisician in Edinburgh. You have naturally an athletic constitution and a hearty stomach and these agree very ill with a sedentary life."—*Letters*, II, 365.

necessity of replacing" (*Letters*, I, 511. The whole letter should be read). Profits spent which should have gone to increase capital and pay debts—that was one source of trouble. The other was, the difficulties inherent in a publisher's business. In 1815, when writing to the minister of Kelso, regarding a proposal by a young friend of Lundie's to set up a bookselling business there, James relates his experiences of literary men as advisers to a publisher. "The advice of *literary friends* I know from sad experience to be no adequate substitute for professional knowledge. I had them, God knows, not only of great talents, but of great coolness and judgement; and yet I cannot recall the single instance in which their advice was useful to me. One recommended the Culdees; another Singer's Dumfriesshire; a third, Beaumont & Fletcher; a fourth, Northern Antiquities, all of them speculations which, but for the printers Jas. B. & Co., would have ruined the booksellers, John B. & Co., and you are not to suppose that the mismanagement of John B. & Co. was to blame. No; it was the utter iniquity of the plans themselves, though recommended, examined in their details, and encouraged by voice and example by some of the most eminent men of the day. . . . My friend there is no conveying to you the gross ignorance which *we* exhibited throughout the whole experiment; rejecting what was good and choosing what was bad—and this, not that our taste, or knowledge of books was particularly defective; but that nothing is more different than knowledge of what ought to sell and knowledge of what will sell, in other words than knowledge of books and knowledge of bookselling. . . . Nothing in my opinion, in my conviction, can supply the place of long, creeping, cautious experience. Theory will as soon make a good general as a good bookseller." So ruefully speaks James, looking back on the years from 1809 to 1813. The firm started well, too well, with *The Lady of the Lake*; but *The Edinburgh Annual Register*, Jamieson's *Culdees*, Weber's *Beaumont and Fletcher*, the *Works of Anna*

Seward, etc., were not of a kind to make the fortunes of a publisher, and the business was soon in difficulties. *The Lady of the Lake* was the last long narrative poem which Scott wrote for the love of the thing as well as with a view to profit. Thereafter almost everything he wrote was with a view to meet engagements already incurred, to cancel or renew bills falling due at some approximating date.

Thus began to flow the strong undercurrent of financial activity, which was, more and more as time went on, to influence all the activities of Scott's life, literary and social. But meantime the current of his social life was broadening in the sunshine of recognition from every quarter and friendships in every class of life. The early years at the cottage in Lasswade, of whose purchase Charlotte had written to Lord Downshire, were among the happiest in Scott's life, while he corresponded about ballads and romances and *Sir Tristrem* with George Ellis, Heber, Joseph Ritson, Currie, Percy, and Anna Seward, years to which Leyden, Gillies, the Wordsworths and others looked back with delight. They came to an end when, in 1804, under pressure from Lord Napier, Lord-Lieutenant of Selkirkshire, Scott fixed his summer abode at Ashestiel on the Tweed, returning to Edinburgh to 39 Castle Street when the Law Sessions opened. *The Lay* had been written at Lasswade and in Edinburgh. At Ashestiel he composed *Marmion* and apparently the first chapters of what afterwards became *Waverley*. But while *Marmion* was composing, he had many other tasks on hand, and not alone such literary projects as have been referred to above. With the growth of his literary work it was becoming clear that his practice as an Advocate must dwindle, and Scott looked around for some other post with a fixed salary which he might hold along with his Sheriffdom. An elderly gentleman was persuaded to relinquish the duties of his office as one of the principal clerks of session while retaining the salary, a small addition to the private income of £12,000 a year which he, a bachelor, and his sister enjoyed between them. This arrangement required legal sanction, but with the help of the Marchioness of Abercorn and other influential friends this was secured. But 1806 was a critical year politically. Pitt died in January, and Grenville and Fox formed a Government. Lord Melville, that great fountainhead of patronage in Scotland, was impeached. Afraid that under the new Government his commission might not be passed, Scott hastened up to London and, through the aid of Lord Somerville, obtained from Lord Spencer the issuing of his commission. That was in February. In April came the trial, in June the acquittal, of Lord Melville. In a letter, written when a prosecution first was mooted (*Letters*, XII, 380-1), Scott shows himself a little uneasy as to possible errors or carelessness on Melville's part, but he quickly rallied to the hope and mainstay of Scottish Toryism, and, when a dinner of congratulation was held in Edinburgh, Scott " had the happiness to add something to the mirth, & I will say the enthusiasm of the Meeting, by the inclosed ditties, which I got Ballantyne the printer to hollow forth with the voice of a Stentor. I should be happy Lord Mellville saw them, as no man ought to feel or can feel more happy than I have done on this occasion " (*Letters*, I, 305). The ditties included the " Health to Lord Melville ", a robustious, bacchanalian ballad of the old political kind, in the closing verse of which Scott distinguishes between those members of the broad-bottomed administration who had treated him with courtesy and those who were principally interested in running down Melville—Whitbread and Fox :

> And since we must not set Auld Reekie in glory,[1]
>   And make her brown visage as light as her heart ;
> Till each man illumine his own upper story,
>   Nor law-book nor lawyer shall force us to part.
>   In *Grenville* and *Spencer*,
>   And some few good men, sir,

[1] *I.e.* no illumination of the town was permitted.

> High talents we honour, slight difference forgive ;
> But the Brewer we'll hoax,
> Tallyho to the Fox,
> And drink *Melville* for ever, as long as we live !

So Scott finally hoisted his flag on the Tory ship at what seemed a moment of bad fortune for the party. It meant a cleavage between him and some older friends such as Dugald Stewart and the Countess of Rosslyn, while it intensified hostilities with others such as Lord Lauderdale and James Gibson Craig. Indeed, Scott is at his worst in politics, not that the Whigs were a whit less bitter and unscrupulous if more complacently self-righteous. But in political matters Scott manifested a tendency to panic which contrasts strangely with his courage and stoicism in other matters.

But he reaped an immediate reward in the friendship of Canning ; and when, in 1807, the Tories returned to power, his next visit to London was a shining success. The letters which he wrote to his wife during this visit have only recently come to light, and they form an important supplement to Lockhart's narrative both as regards his stay in the South and by the glimpses they afford of his home-life in these early pre-Lockhart days. He had come up to defend the rights of the Clerks of Session in any changes to be made under the impending Judicature Act. " My dearest Love," he writes on or about 20th March, " I arrived here this morning after a very cold journey indeed—we were almost stopd by the snow at Morpeth & I have seldom felt colder weather than we had every night & morning.... On my arrival I found the surprizing but *most wellcome* intelligence that the Ministry were in the act of *going out* : & I have just met Lord Dalkeith who is in the secret & says every thing was settled yesterday. Castlereagh, Rose, Hawkesbury &c. come in & Lord Melville is to be at the head either of the Admiralty or of the Treasury. There's a turn for you—match it in your novels if you can. When I think what I witnessd last year in this very place it almost turns me dizzy. The Clerks &c all go—adieu a long adieu to all their greatness !—So the Law of Scotland will remain as it was or at least be touched with a respectful & lenient hand ... pray write & tell me all that you do & who takes notice of you & where you go & about the Laird & his sisters & brother not forgetting the Black Child. ... The Question about Catholic emancipation was that on which the King quarrelld with his Ministers ... I am invited to meet Canning & Frere at Roses's—they both come in, in high office" (*Letters*, XII, 94-6). Again, on the 24th : " I dine with a party of the *new men* today namely Canning, Frere, our friend R. Dundas & Sturges Brown.[1] They all express themselves highly delighted with my firm adherence to them in adversity & I hope to reap some good fruits from it. I think they should in some way or other relieve me of old George Home in whole or at least in part. My being on the spot is inconceivably fortunate—not a word of such a plan to anyone if you please Mrs. Mimi. ... Tomorrow I dine with Mr. Frere & some of the new Cabinet Ministers—theres for you. George Robison seems astonished at the attention shewn me here & hints as much. ... My health is perfectly good & my spirits would be abundantly so from the joyful change were it not [for] the melancholy state of Ellis & Mackenzie which counterbalances my happiness. Adieu my dearest love—assure the little people of my thanks & affection & comfort old Kiki" (*Letters*, XII, 97-8). " Old Kiki " is Camp, " the little people ", the Laird, etc., are, of course, Walter (born in 1801 and known as " the Laird of Gilnockie " or " Gilnockie " and by some other names later), Sophia (born in 1799), Anne (born in 1803), and Charles (born in 1805). " The Black Child " is probably Camp as the picture by Raeburn shows. Visiting the Abercorns in the recess, he finds himself among many distinguished people, including " Lord & Lady Aberdeen—the first a very

---

[1] William Sturges-Bourne (1769-1845), Lord of the Treasury, 1807-9.

accomplishd young man who promises to make a figure —our old freind Lord Brooke who desires to be rememberd to you Mrs. John Kemble & Lady Sutton (not our Lady Sutton but the wife of Baron Sutton) these with the family & some other *fashionables* as the phrase goes make a very pleasant society. . . . We expect the Duchess of Gordon & John Kemble today. I hope they will both come for the Duchess will be elbow-deep in politics & bring the very freshest news & I want to know Mr. Kemble : his wife is a very pleasant woman. . . . And now my dearest Lotty I am impatient to know what you are doing at home. I have always a little vision of you sitting with all the monkies teazing you and poor old Kiki sleeping upon the hearth rug. . . . I suppose by this time your gaieties are begun and that you have given a little fete in honour of the Change. I assure you my card-rack is quite coverd with invitations from Secretaries of State and Cabinet Ministers all of which is extremely droll. . . . Kiss my little girls & boys and pray tell me how the schooling goes on. The Laird I suppose is capering successfully.[1] I hope he does not neglect his head for his heels, but I know you will be angry with me for the suspicion & I am sure he will be the best boy in the world. Do kiss them all for me " (*Letters*, XII, 100-2). Besides the Abercorns, he visits Rose at Cuffnells and with him Portsmouth and the Isle of Wight. Returned to London, he is working hard to arrange something about old Home's retirement and a Sheriffdom for William Erskine. At Lord Abercorn's house in St. James's Square he is admitted to the Lady's boudoir—" there's for you. . . . I dined with Robt. Dundas, the Chief Baron &c were there all in brilliant spirits with the change. There is no doubt of its being lasting at least while the King lives ; unless they are obliged to take in Lord Sidmouth commonly called *the Doctor* who has contrived to physic every administration without exception of which he has been a part. The prince of Wales has

---

[1] Learning to dance.

renounced politics—he is terrified by the approach of death which by the best accounts is not far distant, etc." (*Letters*, XII, 108). He is dining out daily, he writes on 22nd April, and Tom, who has come to town, is to dine with him at Lord Abercorn's " & I fancy the Marquis designs to give him a lecture ". What this implies we shall see directly. " Only think how happy I will be to find myself at my own fireside again the bairns playing about & my dear Mimi presiding over the game " (*Letters*, XII, 110). But on the 27th he writes from Sunninghill, George Ellis's house, to tell of another visit :

> If yet higher the proud list should end
> Still let me say, no follower but a friend.

He has been to Blackheath to visit the Princess, the exiled Princess of Wales, who has received him with an almost embarrassing freedom : " ' Come my dear Walter Scott & see all my improvements ' & accordingly she whiskd me through her grotto & pavilion & conservatory & so forth asking me slily at the same time if I was not afraid to be alone with her." Scott is all on her side for the time being : " The Princess will emerge from all her distresses . . . & I think may soon look forward to a time when she will be enabled to gratify her freinds and make her enemies her footstool " (*Letters*, XII, 112). *Dis aliter visum*, and Scott also came to think otherwise. On 4th May he writes : " This day finishes my London carreer of dissipation. I think I hear you say *thank God for that* " (*Letters*, XII, 113). And so he returns home, travelling down to Loughborough with Wordsworth and in the highest spirits, visiting on the way the great Anna Seward, the Swan of Lichfield ; [1] and resumes his clerkly duties at

---

[1] " More immediately should I have noticed the kind contents of your letter had it arrived at a less interesting juncture. At two that day, Friday last, the poetically great Walter Scott came ' like a sunbeam to my dwelling '. I found him sturdily maintaining the necessity of limiting his inexpressibly welcome visit to the next day at noon. You will not wonder that I could spare no minutes from hours so precious and so few. . . . Not less astonishing than was Johnson's memory is that of Mr Scott ; like Johnson also his

Edinburgh and the editing of *Dryden* and the composing of *Marmion*. His experiences in London, his immersion in politics and politicians are reflected in the delightful introductions which he prefixed to each canto. They are addressed to the friends he had been meeting in London or who had been much in his mind while there—Rose, whom he had visited and accompanied to the Naval dockyard; poor John Marriott, of whose illness and its fatal blighting of his hopes he had written to Charlotte; William Erskine, the old friend for whom, while in London, he had been busy trying to secure a Sheriffdom; Skene, his fellow-volunteer; and George Ellis, whose failing health he had also bewailed in his letters. And into the flowing octosyllables he pours his quickened patriotism, memories of Nelson, Pitt, and Fox—this last an afterthought suggested by the Marquis of Abercorn—and the Duke of Brunswick, this a compliment to the Princess of Wales—and with these blends vivid descriptions of the country round Ashestiel in autumn, when he looks from his windows on scenes he at once regrets and is glad to leave:

> November's sky is chill and drear,
> November's leaf is red and sear,

so he begins, and the poem continues in like mood:

> That same November gale once more
> Whirls the dry leaves on Yarrow shore.
> Their vex'd boughs streaming to the sky,
> Once more our naked birches sigh, . . .
>
> And Blackhouse heights, and Ettrick Pen
> Have donn'd their wintry shrouds again:
> And mountain dark, and flooded mead,
> Bid us forsake the banks of Tweed.

recitation is too monotonous and violent to do justice to his own writings or that of others. You are almost the only poet I know whose reading is entirely just to his muse."—ANNA SEWARD to REV. H. F. CARY, May 10, 1807.

But the Border scenery brings back memories of early days :

> Then rise those crags, that mountain tower
> Which charm'd my fancy's wakening hour.
>
> . . . .
>
> It was a barren scene and wild,
> Where naked cliffs were rudely piled ;
> But ever and anon between
> Lay velvet tufts of loveliest green ;
> And well the lonely infant knew
> Recesses where the wall-flower grew ;
> And honey-suckle loved to crawl
> Up the low crag and ruin'd wall.
> I deem'd such nooks the sweetest shade
> The sun in all its round survey'd ;
> And still I thought that shatter'd tower
> The mightiest work of human power.

And this leads to the pleasures of sport, and so to the romances and Spenser and " mine own romantic town ". The cantos afford a more pleasing and a more revealing picture of Scott's mind than all the correspondence about publishers and printers, prices and bills. As with other poets, the best of Scott's life is in his creative work.

A more practical consequence of the visit to London and his quickened political interests was the already mentioned plan of a rival to *The Edinburgh Review* in *The Quarterly Review*, with plans for which he was busy throughout 1808 ; and on the heels of that came preparations for his own venture of the following year, the publishing house, one of whose chief glories was to be *The Edinburgh Annual Register*, a very costly business it was to prove. Nor was all this sufficient. As early as March 1808—*Marmion* published and *Dryden* drawing to a close —he has undertaken for Constable and Hunter an edition of the *Works of Swift*, and I have mentioned earlier the other undertakings which he was directing and superintending while contributing to *The Edinburgh Review* and beginning as an active adviser and contributor to *The Quarterly Review*.

These were the happiest years of Scott's life. He was happy in his family, as the letters I have cited show, happy in the country, happy in the friends he was making and the increase of influence he was acquiring, happy, above all, in the free flow of his boundless energies, his poems and the works he was carrying on personally or vicariously. The best picture of him at this stage is, Gillies tells us, the portrait prefixed to *The Lady of the Lake* in 1810, and his own description, Erskine says, of Redmond in *Rokeby* :

> A face more fair you well might find,
> For Redmond's knew the sun and wind,
> Nor boasted, from their tinge when free,
> The charm of regularity ;
> But every feature had the power
> To aid the expression of the hour.

Yet even in these years there were undercurrents of sadness and of a kind that added to the claims on Scott's energies. Like Napoleon's brothers and sisters, Scott's were a source of fairly constant anxiety. To judge from early letters, they were all attractive and even gifted children, if Walter's exceptional powers were early evident. In 1780 one aunt writes delighted with " your account of my young friends and their improvements. John I always was certain would do for a scholar, but what I hear from all quarters of little Walter's genius is astonishing and assures me I shall one day have some vanity in being his aunt. Do not let my dear and oldest acquaintance Bob think because I make mention of this I expect less of him than his brothers, on the contrary I shall be the more vain that they shine in different lines. Deliver my sweet niece a kiss. . . . I mean to bring her home two Indian cousins. . . . I shall have many a long evening's crack over a good fire in George's Square and Hyndford Close." Robert the oldest was sent, not to the High School, but to a rather superior boarding school, and among the Abbotsford papers is a petition in Latin for a school-holiday. He entered the navy in 1781, transferred afterwards to the East India Company's service, and dying on board the *Rodney* in 1787 was buried at sea. " My dear Bob has gone to heaven before you ", Mrs. Cockburn writes to his mother. Scott speaks of his haughty temper and capricious tyranny but adds " I loved him much for he had a strong turn for literature, read poetry with taste and judgement and composed verses himself". But a taste for literature is apt to make its possessor find the company of the average naval and military man tedious, and throw him back on undesirable distractions. For an Indian climate " his habits were ill adapted ". John entered the army and when quartered at Gibraltar (1795) sighs for books and more intelligent company. Tom's failure as a lawyer and estate manager for Lord Abercorn is traceable to his similar tastes and social habits, " an excellent heart and humour that used to put the table in a roar." He lost the agency for the city of Aberdeen. Even his father's trustees have to complain of his indolence in supplying documents and statements. But he had the same taste for reading. " He took no books with him except Rokeby," writes his wife in 1813, " and that only for your sake. . . . ' No, since I am to go into exile I will leave all behind me that helpt to lead me wrong.' " Walter hoped he might write for the *Quarterly*, or even a novel, but he replies : " I have to thank you for your good opinion of my poor abilities but alas ! whatever little humour I might once possess has now forsaken me I fear for ever. The life I am engaged in is so totally repulsive to my habits, the company of our officers so frivolous, the books I can get so few and uninteresting and the real cares of the world so many that Imagination has taken flight tired of such society." " I preferred observing the manners of the native Indians to the insipid conversation of our officers drawn principally from that never failing resource of Gentlemen of the Sword, the Army list the contents of which have more interest for them than the effusions of a *Southey* or a *Scott*." Anne the only sister, a dreamer like her brother but without his practical bent, died in 1801. Poor Daniel, the youngest, described by one correspondent as " a perfect child ", is described later by Scott to Ellis as a " soft ". He was sent early to America, probably to Charleston, but returned in 1799, was admitted a clerk at the Customs Office, got into trouble with some " designing woman " and was shipped off to Jamaica in 1804. Two years later he was home with broken nerves and health and reputation, and died at his mother's home in 1806. Scott superintended the education of his child.

Tom had inherited his father's business with the stewardship of the Marquess of Abercorn's estates at Duddingston, but by 1807 he is dining with the Marquess in London to receive a lecture, and by July of that year Walter writes to the Marchioness that Tom has outrun the bailiff. Walter, who was security for Tom, had to settle down with the help of a lawyer selected by the Marquess to do his best to wind up the business. By November he was able to write to the Marquis : " The debts have turned out heavier than my calculation and the funds have also turned out much better than I had expected." After giving such assistance as he could throughout the winter of 1807-8, Tom and his family removed to the Isle of Man, and, while Walter continues the troublesome winding up of details, he is busy also urging schemes of work for Tom, whether a history of the island or occasional articles of a light kind for *The Quarterly Review* which Walter will revise and touch up. All this time, be it remembered, he was Clerk to the Commission preparing for the new Judicature Act.

Some time before *Marmion* was finished, Scott is speaking in his letters to Ellis and Heber and others of a projected epic on a Highland theme. Whether in its earliest form this was *The Lady of the Lake* I am not quite sure. But in 1809 the publishing firm being formed, *The Lady of the Lake* was to be its first great achievement. Yet characteristically there is no mention of it in the letters of that year until December when he tells Lady Abercorn that he has made considerable progress in a new poem " which I intend to call the *Lady of the Lake* ". *Swift* and the *Quarterly* are the chief burden of the letters which he wrote from Ashestiel and from London whither the duties of the Commission took him, this time with his wife, during April, May, and a part of June. In June 1808 Scott had welcomed in Edinburgh, as friends of Lady Louisa Stuart, J. B. S. Morritt of Rokeby and his wife, and he entertained them later at Ashestiel on their return from Ross-shire. Morritt was a cultured man who had travelled in classical lands and was an ardent defender of the unity of Homer. On the visit to London in 1809 Scott met the Morritts again, and on his return journey in June he paid his first visit to Rokeby Park. Morritt became one of his most loyal and devoted friends, one of the very few to whom the secret of the Waverley Novels was entrusted. In London he had been, not so much this time as in 1807 the champion of the Tory party in Scotland, more the poet, the author of *Marmion*. He met Coleridge at a dinner and somewhat disconcerted him by reciting " Fire, Famine, and Slaughter " as anonymous lines and provoking much adverse criticism by Coleridge's friends before he admitted the authorship. Southey had visited him at Ashestiel in 1805, and Scott now endeavoured to use his acquired political influence to secure for the less popular author some remunerative post or sinecure. Byron he did not meet. That young man was just on the point of starting for the East, leaving behind him a satire which he had been printing and altering throughout the opening month of the year. It appeared anonymously in March, a second and enlarged edition following in October. Byron sailed from Falmouth about a week after Scott left London. The satire was well known to be his work. When Scott came across the poem is not quite clear, but it was certainly not when, on his Perthshire tour, he visited Hector Macdonald Buchanan. Lockhart has misdated that tour. On the rising of the Courts in July, Scott did not set out on a Highland tour but retired to Ashestiel, and there probably completed the first draft of *The Lady of the Lake*, for when he did go to Perthshire at the end of August he made the experiment of riding from Loch Vennachar to Stirling Castle to test the possibility of the ride described in the fifth canto of the poem. But already, in a letter to Southey of 10th August (*Letters*, II, 214), he had commented on Byron's references to himself. It is clear that they made him wince a little, the young aristocrat's scorn for turning poetry into money ; and perhaps he felt the charge the more acutely from the consciousness that this very year he was preparing to make literature more entirely a trade. Of *The Lady of the Lake* John Ballantyne & Co. were to reap the full share of the profits—author's, publishers', printers'. Unfortunately, as we have seen, these profits were not allowed to add to the much-needed capital of the business. But even poetry, *Swift*, the cares of publishing and printing, and legal duties, were not too much for Scott, for he was busy throughout 1808-9 securing a new patent and management for the Edinburgh Theatre and a performance of Joanna Baillie's *The Family Legend*.

The Lady of the Lake proved the most popular of Scott's narrative poems, and little wonder. To judge of Scott's poetry there is little use testing it by absolute standards which do not exist. All art for its effect depends to some extent on the circumstances amid which it appears. One must throw oneself back in imagination to the time, to the literature, verse and prose, when these poems appeared, to realise the freshness of the pleasure which they afforded ; and *The Lady of the Lake* is the most sunnily romantic of them all, with the novelty of the scenery which it described, the character of the people which it sketched, romantically certainly but just thereby delighting readers whom any more realistic treatment would have puzzled or repelled. Great poetry it may not be, but delightful poetry it was. That what he attempted Scott did well is proved by the way in which the poems have lived on when the innumerable imitations of them were still-born, when even Byron's continuation of the kind, poems which gained a glamour from their novel and equally romantic sentiment, and intensity from the larger infusion of the malevolent passions which, as Dr. Bain taught us in Aberdeen, are of so potent aesthetic effect, have lost their spell. Has any poetry since Shakespeare, allowing for all the difference in depth of insight and wealth of expression and rhythm, given so much the impression of a bubbling spring of original, creative power? Yet both wrote for money, with little or no thought of posterity, to which Wordsworth and Southey made such confident appeal.

CHAPTER VI

> "This mixture of necessary attention and inevitable hazard,—the frequent and awful uncertainty whether prudence shall overcome fortune, or fortune baffle the schemes of prudence, affords full occupation for the powers, as well as for the feelings of the mind, and trade has all the fascination of gambling without its moral guilt."
>
> *Rob Roy*, Chap. I.

THE publication of *The Lady of the Lake* in May 1810 marked, I think, the culmination of Scott's good fortune, untroubled as yet by financial anxieties. He was in the highest spirits, Lockhart writes, when, in July, he began to look round for some new theme, some new setting for a romantic poem. The Peninsula, where the British Army was engaged, was thought of, but eventually he made his first visit to the Hebrides along with his wife and eldest daughter, and probably got impressions for a later poem. Unfortunately, as we have seen, the profits on *The Lady of the Lake* were not used to accumulate capital for the business of the printing and the publishing firms. To unite the profits of printer and publisher is, doubtless, advantageous, but if it increases the gain it also adds to the possible losses, for a book that does not pay the *publisher* may, nevertheless, have been a good piece of business for the *printer*; but in the Ballantyne business the printer's profits were too often used to make good the publisher's losses. A success like this poem should have been used to provide a reserve against losses instead of being immediately spent by the partners. Before 1810 was out Scott is complaining of James Ballantyne's indolence, and a portion of the printing of *Swift* had to go to another firm; and Miss Seward's not very profitable *Life and Poems* was issued by John Ballantyne & Co. But in the following year Scott had two strokes of luck for which he worked hard. George Home was at last got rid of, so that the poet had a manger fitted to his stall, the salary (£1,300) as well as the duties of his office. Later in the same year Tom secured, by the influence of his brother and of a relative of his wife, the post of Paymaster to the 70th Regiment, and with the help of Walter's purse he and his family were enabled to discharge their debts and leave the Isle of Man. Scott and Robert McCulloch, brother of Tom's wife, had to become cautioners for Tom, which involved them in considerable anxiety later, but not, it would seem, in actual loss.

But if there was a fresh addition to his salary, there was soon also fresh expense. Scott's tenure of Ashestiel came to an end in 1811, and in the spring of the following year he removed to a cottage on the small estate of Abbotsford, near Melrose, and began the building and the purchasing of land which more than anything else was responsible for that anticipation of profits which proved so fatal to Constable and Scott. The only poem which 1811 produced was the quite negligible *Vision of Don Roderick*, the profits of which went to the relief of Portuguese sufferers from the invasion of the French.

With a steady income of £2,800 a year and the possibility of making another £1,000 by his pen, Scott should have been in the position to enjoy his life and write as he pleased. But the losses on almost every undertaking in publishing, except his poems; the sacrifice of such gains as were made from the printing house; the beginning of investment in land, were all tending to produce a serious position of affairs. Another poem must be finished and launched, but here again there were difficulties ahead. The vein from which he had drawn was not a very deep one, and a rival was in the field. Scott shared to the full in the quickening of the pulse which the appearance of *Childe Harold*, Cantos I and II, produced in 1812. To

Lord Byron he was introduced by letter through Murray, and a strong mutual interest and regard was formed and preserved.

But something had to be done and *Rokeby* was begun.[1] *The Bridal of Triermain*, in which, with Dame Una Pope-Hennessey, I suspect the presence of early work, was thrown off and issued anonymously in 1813. *Rokeby* is first mentioned to Morritt in December 1811. In March he reports that the first canto had been written and torn up. The vein would not flow quite so readily as was wont. Morritt helped to renew certain bills and invited him to check and enrich his descriptions by a visit to Rokeby, whither Scott went in September pursued by letters from the Ballantynes, urging the necessity of publication by Christmas and revealing the approaching crisis in their affairs. On 31st December he writes to James: "With kindest wishes on the return of the season, I send you the last of the copy of Rokeby. . . . There is something odd and melancholy in concluding a poem with the year, and I could be almost silly and sentimental about it. I hope you think I have done my best. I assure you of my wishes the work may succeed; and my exertions to get out in time were more inspired by your interest and John's, than my own. And so *vogue la galere*" (*Letters*, III, 209). The advent of trouble is foreshadowed in the division of the publication with Longman—Constable had been refused any share in *The Lady of the Lake* and Scott suspects him of trying to hold off Longman—and by the fact that John and James are each selling his share in the poem in advance and apparently to Constable. When the poem did appear in January 1813 it was variously judged, but it went through some five editions in the course of the year.

[1] In July 1812 he writes to John Ballantyne that it is advancing but slowly: "James & Erskine have alternately thrown cold water about my ears so that I have lost much of my confidence." By August he writes to John: "If there is any thing worse than your last statement I intreat you will let me know it—if not I think that the poem will extricate all, & I am now in full sail."—*Letters*, I, 417, 418.

Few but Scott could have written a poem of the kind under the circumstances of distraction, haste, and increasing anxiety in which *Rokeby* took shape, while he moved into a new house, planned further purchases and new building, corresponded with Morritt and Joanna Baillie and Lord Byron, while interchanging hurried notes with James and John Ballantyne. But the circumstances may have had something to do with the changed character of *Rokeby* compared with its predecessors, though one must also perhaps reckon with the influence of Byron. For in *Rokeby* Scott takes a long stride towards the novel of real life and character. The story is involved and needs, like the usual detective story, too much explanation as the end approaches ; but a little time, a little more care might have made it a poem of more serious interest than its romantic predecessors. Moreover, it has an adventitious interest. If, in the introductory parts of *The Bridal of Triermain* (1813), Scott went back in memory on the flirtation and courting at Gilsland, in *Rokeby* he revived an older and more poignant experience. In Matilda he drew, as he admitted, from his memory of the gentle and submissive Miss Stuart Belsches : [1]

> There was a soft and pensive grace,
> A cast of thought upon her face,
> That suited well the forehead high,
> The eyelash dark, and downcast eye ;
> The mild expression spoke a mind
> In duty firm, composed, resign'd ;
> 'Tis that which Roman art has given,
> To mark their maiden Queen of Heaven.
> In hours of sport, that mood gave way
> To Fancy's light and frolic play.

[1] " This much of Matilda I recollect, for that is not so easily forgotten, that she was attempted from the existing person and character of a lady who is now no more, so that I am particularly flattered with your distinguishing it from the others which are in general mere shadows."—To MARIA EDGEWORTH, 15th May, 1818.

In Wilfrid and Redmond Scott has drawn on his memories of his own youth. If in the former there is just a suggestion of his sensitive friend Erskine, the content is filled out from his own experiences of early reading and dreaming, his own delicate childhood and the affection of his mother :

> His sire, while yet a hardier race
> Of numerous sons were Wycliffe's grace,
> On Wilfrid set contemptuous brand,
> For feeble heart and forceless hand ;
> But a fond mother's care and joy
> Were centred in her sickly boy.
> No touch of childhood's frolic mood
> Show'd the elastic spring of blood ;
> Hour after hour he loved to pore
> On Shakespeare's rich and varied lore,
> But turn'd from martial scenes and light,
> From Falstaff's feast and Percy's fight,
> To ponder Jaques' moral strain,
> And muse with Hamlet, wise in vain ;
> And weep himself to soft repose
> O'er gentle Desdemona's woes.

If that is one side of Scott, isolated and embodied in an Erskine, the other, the counteracting strain, is portrayed in the daring and active Redmond, the young man that Scott made of himself as his health improved and as he realised the truth about life and human nature, and how the sensitive idealist fares :

> Woe to the youth whom fancy gains,
> Winning from Reason's hand the reins,
> Pity and woe ! for such a mind
> Is soft, contemplative, and kind ;
> And woe to those who train such youth,
> And spare to press the rights of truth,
> The mind to strengthen and anneal,
> While on the stithy glows the steel !

The year 1813 was the first crisis in Scott's heady career as poet, printer, and publisher, and has, as one consequence, the emergence of the novelist. *Rokeby* and *The Bridal of Triermain* did not provide the ready money needed at once to meet maturing bills. The banks were stiffening credit in view of a likely Government loan; booksellers were failing and leaving John Ballantyne with bad debts; *The Edinburgh Annual Register, Beaumont and Fletcher*, and other works were accumulating in stock. Already in October 1812 Scott is representing to James the dire humiliation of " striking sail to Constable in our own harbours . . . were it my sole concern I would rather submit to great deprivations than do so " (*Letters*, III, 166). By May 1813 it is clear that unless the accumulated stock can be sold for £6,000 or £7,000 " 50 per cent under its estimated value " then some £4,000 to £5,000 must be raised and kept floating. Constable is appealed to and takes stock to the value of £2,000. But a condition is that John Ballantyne & Co. must be wound up; Constable will not help a rival firm. " Adieu, my dear John. I have the most sincere regard for you, and you may depend on my considering your interest with quite as much attention as my own. . . . If to your real goodness of heart and integrity, and to the quickness and acuteness of your talents, you added habits of more universal circumspection, and, above all, the courage to tell disagreeable truths to those whom you hold in regard, I pronounce that the world never held such a man of business. These it must be your study to add to your other good qualities. Meantime, as some one says to Swift, I love you with all your failings. Pray make an effort and love me with all mine " (*Letters*, III, 272). It was on such statements that Lockhart based his attempt to make the Ballantynes the *fons et origo* of the first disaster; and, doubtless, it is worrying when one's agent forgets, or fears to warn you in time of maturing bills; but the deeper evil is the existence of the bills so far in excess or advance of incoming profits. Scott's closing words show that he is not making John the scapegoat.

But the difficulties were far from over. Throughout the summer Scott and John are running a desperate race with a Mickey Mouse pursuit of bills. By August Scott sees nothing for it but to sell his copyrights, and close the printing business. At Constable's suggestion, that someone outside the trade must be applied to for credit, Scott writes to the Duke of Buccleuch and begs him to grant him security for an overdraft of £4,000 ; and when the Duke's answer is delayed, Scott prepares for the end : " As to myself my dear James I must take my fate as I best can. Constable need not suppose that I will go mendicating from the booksellers a contract for a new poem. I would no more do so than you would sing ballads in the street for your relief. Scotland & I must part as old friends have done before, for I will not live where I must be necessarily lookd down upon by those who once lookd up to me. . . . I will see justice done to every one to the last penny & will neither withdraw my person nor screen my property untill all are satisfied " (*Letters*, III, 332). He contemplates the same fate as Tom. Even when the Duke, " my princely Chief ", came to the rescue, the trouble was hardly over, and ultimately it was only by the help of a redeemable annuity, involving heavy yearly payments, that smooth water was reached. Looking back on the episode later John recalls the breathless agitation of the months and the efforts of Scott. " The first partner stepped in at a crisis so tremendous it yet shakes my soul to think of it. By the most consummate wisdom and resolution and unheard of exertion he put things in train that finally (so early as 1817) paid even himself (who ultimately became the sole creditor of the house) *in full* ; with a balance of a thousand pounds."

It is a strange contrast that is afforded by the agitated letters to the Ballantynes on the one hand and the calm, sunny surface of Scott's family and social life presented in his letters to Lady Abercorn, George Crabbe, Miss Clephane, Joanna Baillie, and others. " I have been a vile lazy correspondent having been strolling about the country and indeed a little way into England for the greater part of July and August, in short ' aye skipping here and there ' like the Tanner of Tamworths horse." " The summer, an uncommon summer, has glided away from us at Abbotsford, amidst our usual petty cares & petty pleasures." Nor, it must be remembered, was the finance of John Ballantyne & Co. his sole worry that summer. Tom's regiment was ordered to Ireland and thence by way of Cork he sailed for Canada on 1st September, leaving his wife expecting a child ; and Walter had to supply financial help. He was still paying for Abbotsford ; he was contemplating the purchase of Kaeside ; and he was picking up old books, armour, and other knick-knacks.

One thing was clear, that a fresh poem must be got ready. In June of 1813, before the worst of the crisis is on, he is already negotiating with Constable for £5,000 between him and Longman, " the acceptances being made immediately discountable ", a suggestion which rouses Cadell's wrath. " I am perfectly astonished ", Cadell writes to Constable, " at Mr S. asking nay even hinting at such an idea as our paying say six or twelve months in advance for a Poem not written perhaps scarcely thought of—in what sort of situation would Longman and ourselves stand in if engaged to him for say £3,500 as in July and to be renewed till the Poem is published, then if Mr S. was to be summoned to the other world, and not a sheet at Press, how would we look ? what would the world say to it ? You will say I am a very gloomy fellow, but Mr Scott is not like his Poems immortal. . . . I think that £5,000 is too much for his proposed poem." Scott's naming so large a sum shows how great the profits of *The Lady of the Lake* had been.[1] In October, when the peak of the crisis was passed, he writes to James, fixing the price of the poem,

---

[1] By 1813 27,300 copies of *The Lay* had been sold, 17,000 odd of *The Lady of the Lake*. Even of *Rokeby* 3,050 quarto copies and 8,250 octavo copies had been printed and apparently sold before 1815.

which is as yet only in incubation, at £4,200 " but I have no objection that £1050 shall be made dependent on the success of the work ", for if Cadell & Davies take the work and they are the publishers, he suggests they must " accept for the whole sum in four bills at 12, 15, 18 & 24 months. . . . The last bill I shall relieve them from if the work proves unsuccessful. . . . You may shew Messrs. C. & D. that I have been always paid in advance." To most of us to-day it seems an astonishing phenomenon, a poet being paid at such a rate, in advance, for a poem which is still only in the poet's head. But it proves the unique popularity of Scott that publishers were willing and anxious to accept such terms. Constable (sharing with Longman, his London agent once more)[1] ultimately took the poem at fifteen hundred guineas for one half of the copyright, the other half remaining with Scott. *The Works of Swift*, too, which had been so long on the stocks, were got out in 19 volumes in 1814, and the *Memorie of the Somervilles*, to say nothing of an account of the Icelandic Eyrbiggia Saga in a work called *Illustrations of Northern Antiquities*, for which Henry Weber and Robert Jamieson were mainly responsible. On 17th September 1814 Scott is drawing in advance on all these works except the last, and driving on the printing and advertising of " The Lord of the Isles : a Poem by Walter Scott, Esq. . . . as it will put a different face upon our transactions. I have made up my mind to do my best upon it."

But before *The Lord of the Isles* was completed another venture was on the stocks, and a new road to success was opening. *Waverley* was in process of completion and duly appeared in July—the publisher Constable—on a half-profits arrangement—the printer James Ballantyne & Co. But before speaking of *Waverley* and such problems as it raises, I must say a word on Scott's life other than financial during these months and on the close of his work as a narrative poet. If *Rokeby* had run a race with John

[1] Constable had quarrelled with Longman about 1806-8.

Ballantyne's letters and bills and James's desire to have it out before Christmas, *Waverley* and *The Lord of the Isles* had an even more agitated course to sail, for, though bankruptcy in August 1813 had been averted, every month brought its crested wave of bills to retire or renew. Yet but little of all this appears in the aspect of his life which was open to the world and his friends. The latter, indeed, Morritt, Hartstongue—a faithful spaniel who, in Dublin, beat up game for Scott's *Swift*—, Charles Erskine, John Murray, all had to lend a hand in accepting bills and guaranteeing overdrafts, without ever clearly knowing why. In early November Morritt writes he has heard " that your poor friend Ballantyne had failed & with great grief that you were likely to be a sufferer to a very great extent by his failure, indeed to an amount which if true must be very distressing."[1] Scott is not to let his obligation to Morritt increase his embarrassment. " I will settle with Hoare when the time of payment comes." Two months earlier Southey has to complain to Scott of John's failure to pay certain debts promptly, for Southey contributed the historical part of *The Edinburgh Annual Register* and had held a share in that unfortunate project. But Scott is able to reassure them both while he corresponds with them on *Rokeby* and *The Bridal of Triermain* and the offer which has been made to him of the Poet Laureateship and his desire to secure the same for Southey; while he entertains Lady Abercorn with gossip and stories, writes to a brother poet in George Crabbe, receives from Joanna Baillie a lock of Charles I's hair, and tells her how he feels towards that monarch : " Tory as I am my heart only goes with King Charles in his struggles and distresses for the fore part of his reign was a series of misconduct. However if he sowd the wind God knows he reapd the whirlwind and so did those who first drew the sword against him few of whom had occasion to congratulate their country or themselves upon the issue of those disastrous wars."[2] Abbotsford and its grounds are

[1] *Letters*, III, 383 and note.   [2] *Letters*, III, 311.

growing and so are the children, and George Thomson, the original of Dominie Sampson, is engaged as their tutor. With Daniel Terry he corresponds about purchases of armour, etc., and concerning that actor's own plans. Moreover, he is in 1814 already raising money not alone with a view to the debts which he is clearing off, but with an eye on Kaeside as an addition to Abbotsford. Withal, his interest in public affairs is acute, and he rejoices with Southey and Morritt over the defeat of Napoleon and the first entrance of the Allies into Paris: "Joy—Joy in London now—and in Edinburgh moreover my dear Morritt for never did you or I see and never shall we see —according to all human prospects—a consummation so truly glorious as now bids fair to conclude this long and eventful war." That is in April. In May Morritt visits Paris and becomes convinced that Napoleon was an avatar or incarnation of Satan, so much evil has he worked in the French character; but he can find no enthusiasm for the Bourbons.

When *Waverley* is out, and *The Lord of the Isles* is taking shape in his mind, Scott accepts an invitation to visit the northern and western islands in the Lighthouse Commissioners' yacht. "I have been busy with this matter since I was here," he writes to Constable on 22nd July, "and I really think that, with the advantage of my proposed tour —where we are to visit everything curious from Fife-ness to Greenock, whether on continent or island, I may boldly set considerable value on the fruit of my labours.... The poem will go to press almost immediatly on my return, and be out, as I conceive, in January at latest." And so on the 29th he sets out on that tour, the diary of which bulks so largely in Lockhart's *Life*. The letters he wrote to his wife have recently come to light and supplement it interestingly. To the company on board—which included the minister of Tingwall parish, the original of Triptolemus Yellowley—he was the soul of the party, giving no evidence of the anxiety with which he awaited letters from the

Ballantynes, but obviously at times, in the evening when the others were below in the cabin, pacing the deck and muttering to himself, intent on the composition of his poem. " I remember ", writes Lord Kinnedder (Erskine), " that at Loch Corriskin, in particular, he seemed quite overwhelmed with his feelings ; and we all saw it and retiring unnoticed left him to roam and gaze about by himself, until it was time to muster the party and be gone." He seems at Kirkwall and Torloisk to have missed his letters, both home letters and Ballantyne's, and is growing anxious by the time he reached Campbeltown where he found not altogether reassuring letters from Constable and James. This was on their return from the Giant's Causeway, where he had heard, quite by chance, of the death of his early friend and patron, the Duchess of Buccleuch, to whom when Countess of Dalkeith he owed the suggestion of *The Lay of the Last Minstrel*. Anxiety for his own financial position and sorrow for his bereavement are blended in his letters to Ballantyne and Constable. " I wish I could as easily wash my deep sorrow out of my mind as I can dismiss the apprehensions of the loss of world's gear ; but I am most deeply distressed indeed on account of the generous and noble survivor, and the more than kind friend whom I have lost," and again : " I have made up my mind to do my best upon it [i.e. *The Lord of the Isles*], and I thank God that did I need (as who does not) a lesson of patience under the disappointments and struggles of life, I should find it in a friend at no great distance, who is bearing distress of a much deeper nature with the most manly fortitude." The letters which passed between Scott and the Duke are printed by Lockhart. It is strange that, with all his good sense and right feeling, he was incapable of learning one lesson of providing against the vicissitudes of fortune, that, as Carlyle says, if one cannot increase one's numerator one may always reduce one's denominator. If the financial outlook is so troubled, why, oh why, contemplate the purchase of Kaeside and expensive armour for the overdecoration of Abbotsford ? By October of this year he is contemplating a new novel, the advances on which will enable him to discharge his personal debt to Charles Erskine : " This is a new perplexity—for paid he must be forthwith, as his advance was friendly and confidential" (*Letters*, III, p. 505). The letters between Scott, the Ballantynes, and Constable, during the closing months of 1814 and the early months of 1815, reveal the same anxious endeavour to meet or to renew bills, and to provide mutual accommodation between the firms of John Ballantyne & Co. and Archibald Constable & Co. (*Letters*, I, Appendix, and II and III *passim*). For the fact is, though Scott was not fully aware of it, that Constable and Cadell were themselves in very deep water. With Robert Cathcart as partner, in 1812, just before his reconciliation with Scott, Constable had bought *The Encyclopaedia Britannica* and was preparing to enlarge it with a supplement for which he was paying generous sums to authors of reputation. Dugald Stewart got £1,700 for his forgotten dissertations. By October 1814 Constable is endeavouring to get Longman as a partner in *The Edinburgh Review*, and the death of Cathcart has made the burden of *The Encyclopaedia* almost too heavy. Like Scott he is contemplating the possibility of an end. " I have not acted dishonestly to any one in my dealings. If I have embarked largely in Bookselling have I not been encouraged to do so ? I have it is true been most unfortunate in following many plans more for the benefit of my connections than that of myself" (*To Cadell, 18th October,* 1814). It is little wonder that he was unwilling, in addition to granting bills in advance on each edition of *Waverley*, on *Swift*, etc., to take over any portion of John Ballantyne & Co.'s unsaleable stock. As a consequence of all this financial trouble and endless quest of credit, and despite the success of *Waverley*, of which four editions were issued in the year of its publication, *The Lord of the Isles* had to be pushed forward for issue in January 1815.

Lockhart's description of its being composed by Scott at Abbotsford in September and October while the children went and came about him can apply only to its final stages, for the poem had been planned and even to some extent drafted before *Rokeby* was published.

But before pursuing farther the account of Scott's life, so agitated below the surface, so prosperous and sunny in all that the world saw of it, I must turn back for a moment to *Waverley*. Scott himself made so much mystification about his work that one may not complain if his statements are sometimes suspect, and the same is true of Lockhart. *Waverley* is the first of the novels of which we hear a word. Had Scott already written novels which, after the success of *Waverley*, were taken from the recesses where they reposed and prepared for the press? If so, why at this tremendous juncture, when he is still struggling with a mountain of debt, was no other of these thought of except the fragment of *Waverley*? Submitted to James Ballantyne, it was justly enough criticised as long-winded and as not really contributing much to the understanding of the hero's character; though these early chapters are of great interest to the student of Scott's own development. Would James have been equally condemnatory of *The Monastery, Redgauntlet, St. Ronan's Well,* and *The Fair Maid of Perth*? These, always excepting *Redgauntlet*, seem to us now inferior novels, but that is by comparison with Scott's own work. The letters with which *Redgauntlet* opens would, doubtless, have scared James; but in 1809-10, when *Waverley* was first advertised in John Ballantyne & Co.'s printed list of " New Works and Publications for 1809-10 ", or in 1813-14, when anything and everything was to be done to save the business, would not even *The Monastery* have seemed at least worth trying compared with most of the novels which Mrs. Scott was ordering from the circulating library?[1] That Scott had written much of every kind, verse and prose, before he found his

[1] For a list see *Letters*, XII, 95, note 1.

way we know well. Of his attempts at prose romance he gives us two specimens, "Thomas the Rhymer" and "The Lord of Ennerdale" in the General Preface to the collected edition, and prints there also the already published conclusion he had written to Strutt's *Queenhoo Hall*. Of the early poems any that have come to light bear out the judgement of his friends given at the time that they were not of much value. Were the attempts in prose any better? His first ambitions, too, seem to have been for the stage. He translated at least five plays from the German and composed two original dramas, "The House of Aspen" and "Halidon Hill". Where is one to get in time for a series of works at this early period? If all that is meant be that Scott may have used in his novels earlier matter I am prepared to admit that this is quite possible —and only awaits proof. For, and this is essential to a right judgement on Scott's historical romances, the novels as composed (or recast, if you wish it) from 1813 onwards bear the clear mark of being the work of a man who had passed the early years of romance and has in view something of quite a different kind from the romantic tales he wove for Irving on Arthur's Seat or the German fiction of terror and romance which was in vogue in his early days. Already, when preparing to write *The Lady of the Lake*, he had spoken in a letter to Ellis or Heber of the want in all modern epics of the element of reality and everyday character and incident. They are all too heroic. But in the poems, unlike Milton, he had the use, as it were, only of his left hand. The characters, if not too heroic, are too thin and poetical, as the taste of the time required. His humour can find no adequate outlet, never rises above the facetiousness of "Peter and Powle", for there is a strain of facetiousness in Scott's humour even in the prose introductions written in character, for example by Jedediah Cleishbotham and others.

In turning to the prose novel Scott considered carefully what it was he wished to do. In Chapter I of *Waverley*,

"Introductory", he sketches with amusing clearness the types of novels most in vogue. "Had I ... announced in my frontispiece, 'Waverley, a Tale of other Days', must not every novel-reader have anticipated a castle scarce less than that of Udolpho, of which the eastern wing had long been uninhabited, and the keys either lost, or consigned to the care of some aged butler or housekeeper....? Would not the owl have shrieked and the cricket cried in my very title-page? . . . Again, had my title borne, 'Waverley, a Romance from the German', what head so obtuse as not to image forth a profligate abbot, an oppressive duke, a secret and mysterious association of Rosycrucians and Illuminati, with all their properties....? Or if I had rather chosen to call my work a 'Sentimental Tale', would it not have been a sufficient presage of a heroine with a profusion of auburn hair, and a harp, the soft solace of her solitary hours....? Or again, if my Waverley had been entitled 'A Tale of the Times', wouldst thou not, gentle reader, have demanded from me a dashing sketch of the fashionable world, ... a heroine from Grosvenor Square, and a hero from the Barouche Club or the Four-in-Hand, ...?" It is an informing picture of the background to the Waverley Novels, the background of the fiction of the day, and explains the sense of surprise and delight which they awakened. Scott is aiming neither at the antique for its own sake as Strutt had done in *Queenhoo Hall*, nor, on the other hand, at a picture of manners such as in a novel of contemporary life is a chief interest. "The object of my tale is more a description of men than manners. A tale of manners, to be interesting, must either refer to antiquity so great as to have become venerable, or it must bear a vivid reflection of those scenes which are passing daily before our eyes." His aim is to throw "the force of my narrative upon the characters and passions of the actors;—those passions common to men in all stages of society, and which have alike agitated the human heart, whether it throbbed under the steel corslet of the fifteenth century " or any later costume.

That is Scott's aim, and it is by this that his achievement must be judged. He will give a picture of life at different ages in which there must be a certain colouring from the description of the setting, the costumes, the manners, the language of the time, but not too much. Some reproduction, for example, of the language of our grandfathers will suffice, he declares, after his early experiment in *Queenhoo Hall*, to suggest the idiom of olden times. More will only cause obscurity. Many writers have in fact surpassed Scott in the accurate portrayal of the manners, including the sentiments, of a past age. Few have equalled him in giving the impression of real life and character in such a wide range of period, of locality, of rank, of idiosyncrasy, from the Crusades to his own day, from the Shetlands to Byzantium and Palestine, from Kings and Captains to peasants, beggars, and rogues; from a Cromwell or a Louis XI to half-wits like David Gellatly and Madge Wildfire. Wherein Scott fell short was not through carelessness in any of these details, which are matters of small importance if we get truth of character and passion. The chief limitation to his popularity to-day is in the field he has chosen for his own—the field of passion and character. Like Shakespeare in so many respects, the ebullient creativeness of his genius, the wide range of his sympathies, the charm of his genial humour, the wisdom of his criticism of life, the poetry that pervades his best prose and wells out in his lovely lyrics, he lacks almost entirely Shakespeare's command over the great passions of the heart; almost entirely but not altogether, for if he is no great hand at lovers or in portraying the passions, whether of ambition, revenge, or religion, in his great historical characters, he can express, as Shakespeare perhaps could have done but never has done, the simpler but no less strong passions of simple people—the grief of the Mucklebackits, the devotion of Jeanie Deans, the single-minded, passionate determination of the Porteous mob, the generous indignation of Meg Merrilees over Ellangowan's expulsion of the gypsies, the blind Alice's interview with young Ravenswood and Lucy Ashton : " Hearken, young man," she said, " your fathers were implacable, but they were honourable foes ; they sought not to ruin their enemies under the mask of hospitality. What have you to do with Lucy Ashton?—why should your steps move in the same footpath with hers?—why should your voice sound in the same chord and time with those of Sir William Ashton's daughter?—Young man, he who aims at revenge by dishonourable means "—

" Be silent, woman ! " said Ravenswood, sternly ; " is it the devil that prompts your voice?—Know that this young lady has not on earth a friend, who would venture farther to save her from injury or from insult."

" And is it even so? " said the old woman, in an altered but melancholy tone—" Then God help you both ! "

But the finest example of Scott's power to put into the mouth of simple people words expressing what they feel, if perhaps they could never have so expressed themselves, is Jeanie Deans's appeal for her sister's life to Queen Caroline. As an example of a poet's power to find words for a great occasion, an historic occasion of which no record is extant that can do more than give a general indication to the poet, it is comparable to Shakespeare's expansion of Plutarch's " Antonius making his funeral oration in praise of the dead, according to the ancient custom of Rome, and perceiving that his words moved the common people to compassion, he framed his eloquence to make their hearts yearn the more, and taking Caesar's gown all bloody in his hands, he laid it open to the sight of them all showing what a number of cuts and holes it had upon it." But Shakespeare's audience did not look for eloquent language or generous feeling in the mouth of a common person, one of the " mutable, rank-scented many ". Their day was not yet come. Many of his countrymen can never forgive Scott for being a Tory and opposing the Bill which gave power to the middle classes and the moneyed interests. But it was the Scott of the novels who taught not only novelists, but historians, to take some notice of the common people. Many things in the literature of the eighteenth century had prepared the way for a sympathetic, sentimental, or revolutionary consideration of their sufferings ; but Scott was the first to give them a place in the picturesque pageant of history.

Some such general note on the novels to come may be forgiven me here as my space will not permit any detailed criticism. All that can be said on them from the traditional point of view has been said by many writers from Adolphus and Senior to Bagehot, Lang, and others, and finally in Lord Tweedsmuir's delightful *Life*. I must consider them mainly as events in Scott's life, as shadows of his own experiences.

Waverley reveals at once what he was after, what he was to achieve, and wherein he was to fall short. The opening chapters were intended to prepare us for the romantic adventures of Edward Waverley, to show how he, like Don Quixote, had, by the irregular nature of his education and the over-indulgence in romance and poetry, overdeveloped the imaginative side of his mind and was thus likely the more easily to become affected by the exciting atmosphere of a rebellion, the motives of which were chivalry and loyalty. But Cervantes makes Don Quixote the centre of his story, and preserves him as such throughout. Scott fails to do so. Waverley has more of prudence and principle than of romantic imagination. That he had the imaginative poetic temperament we have to be reminded as in the description of his behaviour at Holyrood : " Waverley, as we have elsewhere observed, possessed at times a wonderful flow of rhetoric ; and, on the present occasion, he touched more than once the higher notes of feeling, and then again ran off in a wild voluntary of fanciful mirth. . . . Many ladies declined the dance, which still went forward, and, under various pretences, joined the party to which the ' handsome young Englishman ' seemed to have attached himself, etc., etc." It is not so that Scott describes a conversation in which Jeanie Deans, or Meg Merrilees, or Andrew Fairservice, or Bailie Nicol Jarvie takes part. He does not describe it at all, he renders it, which is what Cervantes does for his hero who is the centre of every episode and ready to discourse at length upon his own motives, his own fantastic reading of events. Edward Waverley has no such interest for us. In a novel by Balzac or Victor Hugo he would have been a devoted lover, sacrificing prudence and principle to his passion for Flora MacIvor ; and he would have shared the fate of Fergus at Carlisle. For Scott his lovers and their adventures provide merely the occasion for a vivid picture of scenes illustrating the historic episode as his imagination conjured it up from his knowledge of the period and his interest in life and human nature. From the novelists of his own day, as he has described their works in the passage I have quoted, he derived nothing but what is weakest in his work, the sentimental element and the necessity for a note of edification. The hero will always be a man of principle. Scott's direct line of descent, if that counts for anything, is from the picaresque romance, Defoe, Fielding, Smollett. He delighted his readers by giving them the same sense of real life but in a more romantic setting of place and time, with more varied and exciting characters and less of that lowest side of life which had been essential to the early picaresque novel in its reaction from the lofty heights of the Amadis romances.

But I must turn back to the picaresque of Scott's own life, for so it seems fair to describe that aspect of Scott's activities of which there was little or no evidence in the sunny surface of his increasingly prosperous social activities as a Sheriff, a Clerk of the Supreme Court, a landed gentleman, and a poet of repute. It is just at this time that Byron places him at the apex of an egregious poetical triangle with Rogers a little below, Moore and Campbell following, and Wordsworth with Coleridge in a lower chamber just above " The Many ".

Scott returned from his tour to the Islands to find, as has been said, that his early patron the Countess of Dalkeith had died, and that money troubles (the maturing of outstanding bills) were acute. He has not landed before he is in anxious communication with Constable and James Ballantyne. On 27th September he writes to John : " I find that by the end of Jany. if the *Register* sells the debt will be reduced to between £2000 & £3000 & if money can be got on the P.O. [the Printing Office] proportionally lower. As to the *Register* James is in despair but his heart has been in his breeches about every thing since I came home. Whereas matters though bad enough are certainly mending with us & I would have given £1000 this time last year to have seen them so far on. Debts reversions from Bankrupt estates, the resources of the P.O. & my own with such small sums as can be had from stock will gradually melt down the remainder " (*Letters*, I, 458). But in October James had a distraint for debt served upon him in Edinburgh while he was at Kelso on a visit. On the 21st of that month, however, Scott writes to John: " if you can pick up any cash by Novr. good & well —if James gets his loan still better—but let the worst come to the worst ' Coragio Bully monster '. October is over & I will make the best fight I can till you like the God Thor bring your hammer to my aid," *i.e.* his auctioneer's hammer. " And in December ", he continues, " the poem will be afloat—in January the regr.—in feby. the new Novel " (*Letters*, I, 470 and see notes on p. 471). If we must condemn Scott's recklessness, something human in one enjoys his sanguine gaiety. John, whose honesty was far from being above suspicion, suggested that in order to get other publishers than Constable to help with the unsaleable books, the next edition of *Waverley*, as well as the new novel, should be offered to Longman, Murray, or Blackwood. Scott turned this down (*Letters*, III, 506), but arranged to have the new novel printed first and then offered to the publishers mentioned, " first to Constable and Longman—second, to Murray and Blackwood—to take the whole at such a rate as will give them one-half of the fair profits; granting acceptances which, upon an edition of 3000, which we shall be quite authorized to print, will amount to an immediate command of £1500; and to this we may couple the condition, that they must take £500 or £600 of the old stock." All this before a word of the new novel had been written, that is if we can accept Lockhart's account of the phenomenal activities of this year—the greater part of *The Life and Works of Swift*, *Waverley*, *The Lord of the Isles*, two Essays for the *Encyclopaedia Britannica* Supplement, *Memorie of the Somervilles*, and *Guy Mannering*. The no-dating and misdating of Scott's letters, and the fact that Lockhart manipulates dates as well as texts of letters, make it difficult to be precise. But I think Lockhart exaggerates. The *Encyclopaedia* article on " Chivalry ", asked for in April 1814, was not written till 1817.[1] *The Lord of the Isles* was on a subject on which he had meditated a poem earlier. He was busy with it on, and immediately after, his return, and the note of 7th November to Joseph Train (*Letters*, III, 513), on which Lockhart relies for his being then at work on the poem, suggests to me that it was for the Notes he is seeking information regarding Turnberry Castle. That *Guy Mannering* was not begun until after the receipt of Train's communication, which Scott acknowledged on 7th November, is hardly compatible with the fact that not only is a new novel on offer in a letter of 14th October, but that in a letter, which Lockhart dates October 14 but which *may*

---

[1] " I will get to *Chivalry* next week. I will not have time to make the article long but will try to make it lively."—To ARCHIBALD CONSTABLE, 5th Sept., 1817 (*Letters*, IV, p. 506). " Chivalry " appeared in 1818; " Romance " in 1824; and " The Drama " in 1819.

be later, it is already called *Guy Mannering*.[1] That James Ballantyne, writing to Maria Edgeworth on 11th November, says the novel would depict manners *more ancient* than 1745 is explicable if Scott's first intention was to frame his tale " out of the incidents of the life of a doomed individual, whose efforts at good and virtuous conduct were to be for ever disappointed by the intervention, as it were, of some malevolent being, and who was at last to come off victorious from the fearful struggle ". Such a story would have found a more appropriate setting in the seventeenth century, given something of the atmosphere of Hogg's *Confessions of A Justified Sinner*. I suspect that the work of the closing six weeks of 1814[2] consisted in giving final form to a story over which he had been brooding for several months and probably composing in the intervals while he waited for the successive proofs of *The Lord of the Isles*. The poem appeared on 18th January ; the novel on 24th February.

For the story in its final form Scott drew again, but in a more indirect way, with more transfiguration, on his own experience—Colonel Mannering has, like Scott, experienced and suffered from an injury to his affections. Scott has not made much of the story of jealousy, the duel, and the death of Mannering's wife; but he was able to find in the character some traits he could admire and make his own, the man of honour and gentleman who has suffered but has grown, not cynical and embittered, but rather more chivalrous in his care of his daughter and the protection of Lucy Bertram and her awkward tutor. Julia herself has traits of the young Frenchwoman he had wooed at Gilsland ; and for the adventures of Brown he is able to draw on his own experiences of raids in the south of Scotland.

[1] *Letters*, III, 505, and I, 473. Lockhart omits the words "the name is Guy Mannering".

[2] " What I have often heard Scott say, that his second novel ' was the work of six weeks at a Christmas '."—*Lockhart*, chap. 34.

CHAPTER VII

> " But *sans phrase* I should be happy to do anything you might consider as useful, and that not in a Mercantile way, because I make it a rule to cheat nobody but Booksellers, a race on whom I have no mercy."
>
> SCOTT *to* THOMAS SHERIDAN, September 19, 1811.

Guy Mannering was published in February 1815. On the 31st of March [1] of that year Scott travelled up to London with his wife and eldest daughter : " Mrs Scott and Sophia are with me and we came up by sea very successfully and even pleasantly bating three circumstances—1st. That the wind was in constant and methodical opposition. 2nd. That a collier brig ran foul of us in the dark and nearly consigned us all to the bottom of the sea. 3rd. and last we struck on a rock and lay hammering for two hours untill we floated with the rising tide " (*Letters*, IV, 42). His chief task in London was to negotiate marriage settlements for his young friend Margaret Clephane—she and her sister had chosen him as their guardian—with Lord Compton, later Marquess of Northampton ; and he takes endless trouble over the matter. He dined twice with the Prince Regent, and delighted him with his conversation and stories. The Prince presented him with a " gold snuff-box set in brilliants ". But a more exciting tour followed his return, for on 28th July he set out again with three friends, John Scott of Gala, Alexander Pringle the younger of Whytbank, and Robert Bruce, the advocate, to visit the field of the recently fought battle of Waterloo,

---

[1] Lockhart misdates this visit with strangely minute inaccuracy. He states that Scott was in London " by the middle of March " and returned to Edinburgh on 22nd May. He did not leave Edinburgh till the 31st of March and sailed for Scotland again on the 11th of June.

from which he proceeded in the wake of the Allied Armies to Paris. Long letters to the Duke of Buccleuch and Joanna Baillie describe his survey of the field and incidents of the journey to Paris, where he met, as Lockhart tells, all the distinguished crowned heads and captains, and gained the regard and confidence of the great Duke himself. He left Paris on 9th September and returned to London, where he dined with Byron on the 14th.[1] He reached Abbotsford after visits to Warwick, Kenilworth, and Sheffield, and it was on this occasion that he wounded Mrs. Scott's feelings by failing to notice the " new chintz furniture " with which she had adorned the drawing room.

But Scott had business in view throughout this tour. Before leaving Edinburgh, he had concluded a profitable engagement with Constable, Longman, and Murray for *Paul's Letters to His Kinsfolk*, which was published in January 1816; and two not very happy poems, "The Field of Waterloo" and "The Dance of Death", "a hurly-burly sort of performance", were published, the first in October 1815[2] and the latter in *The Edinburgh Annual Register*, 1815-6. Nor was that all. *Harold the Dauntless*, " a sort of tale of errantry and magic which *entre nous* I am very fond of

[1] " A DINNER AT SIR JAMES BLAND BURGES'S IN LOWER BROOK STREET, AUTUMN, 1815.—I was once invited to dinner by Sir James Burges, father of my friend, Captain Burges of the Guards : it was towards the end of the season 1815. I there met, to my great delight, Lord Byron and Sir Walter Scott. . . . Walter Scott was quite delightful ; he appeared full of fire and animation, and told some interesting anecdotes connected with his early life in Scotland. I remember that he proved himself, what would have been called in the olden times he delighted to portray, ' a stout trencher-man ' ; nor were his attentions confined by any means to the eatables ; on the contrary, he showed himself worthy to have made a third in the famous carousal in *Ivanhoe*, between the Black Knight and the Holy Clerk of Copmanhurst. . . . Walter Scott gave one or two recitations, in a very animated manner, from the ballads that he had been collecting, which delighted his auditory ; and both Lord Byron and Croker added to the hilarity of the evening by quotations from, and criticisms on, the more prominent writers of the period."—*Reminiscences and Recollections of Captain Gronow 1810-1860* (1889), I, pp. 149-151.

[2] Separately, and also as a part of *The Vision of Don Roderick, The Field of Waterloo, and other Poems*.

though ashamed to avow my frailty " was out in January 1817. All these are more or less negligible now, though Sir Colin Campbell pronounced the description of the battle of Waterloo in *Paul's Letters* to be the best he had seen. In some respects the description in the *Paris Revisited in 1815 etc.* (1816) of poor John Scott, editor of *The Champion* —who died later a victim to one of Lockhart's many quarrels—if less military is more vivid in its human details.

But a new novel was also incubating (or on the stocks). For if *Guy Mannering* was issued in February 1815, Constable and Longman had in January contracted for *The Antiquary*, the name already given, " to be published 4 June 1815 " (Constable to Longman 23 Jan. 1816[1]: " It is now twelve months since it was contracted for "). In April Scott writes from London to James Ballantyne : " I shall begin the Anty. on my return which will be about the 1st week of June." In October he writes to John : " The Antiqy. goes on instantly after or rather before Paul is done at press." Lady Louisa Stuart has heard of it in the same month ; and on 22nd December (*Letters*, IV, 145) he tells Morritt of his various activities and goes on : " I shall then set myself seriously to the Antiquary of which I have only a very general sketch at present. But when once I get my pen to the paper it will walk fast enough. I am sometimes tempted to leave it alone and try whether it will not write as well without the assistance of my head as with it." Finally, to James on the 29th :

" Dear James—I'm done, thank God, with the long yarns
    Of the most prosy of Apostles—Paul ;
And now advance, sweet Heathen of Monkbarns !
    Step out, old quizz, as fast as I can scrawl."

[1] Indeed in a letter of 23rd Jan., 1816, to Longman & Co. Constable says : " We are sadly perturbed about the Antiquary and can say nothing to its progress—we wish you could without any allusion to this write us shortly as to the injury we are all sustaining by its delay. It is now twelve months since it was contracted for, to be published by 4 June 1815 " (*Constable's Letter-Book*). Scott must have had the story very clearly in his mind, if not on paper, to promise it so definitely in January 1815.

A long period of incubation, with the possible sketching of chapters in the intervals between the arrival of proofs of other undertakings, and then a final committal of the whole to paper as fast as his pen could go, that I think was the method of composition. It is borne out by such letters as we have—the Erskine letters, written with the novels as submitted for criticism, being lost—asking for books and information needed for the work in hand.¹ One rather suspects it was Shakespeare's method of working too. Flaubert's and Ben Jonson's was a very different one.

There were still, as recently published letters reveal, financial reasons for pushing on work that was likely to pay.² " For heavens sake ", he writes on 17th October, " press on Paul to avoid hobbles in November." " I think Harold will come within the month & with Paul will add £800 to your finances which will make them flourish as December has almost nothing." The fact is, the bills in connection with the unhappy experiment of John Ballantyne & Co. were not cleared off till 1817, if then ; and already Scott in anticipation of their discharge was purchasing more land. " Our matters seem now so nearly ended that I have thoughts of entering into a transaction

---

¹ And, as I shall show more fully later, by the water marks on the paper Scott used in such autographs as are still extant or accessible.

² How Scott thought of his financial position is very difficult to ascertain and understand. While all the Ballantyne letters are filled with devices for meeting bills and anticipating of profits—" Mr. Constable proposes 6000 of Waterloo to which I have no objection the price he proposes to be 5/. If so settled I presume I should have something handsome to draw for which will help out matters well. I pray you to push on Paul. Taking the edition at 6000—12/ & deducing £300 already received there will be £800 & upwards to draw which will do much to clear next month."—*Letters*, I, 486.— while he is pressing on work in this feverish way to surmount recurring crises, he can write to Lady Louisa Stuart, perhaps, with Morritt, his most trusted friend : " I have been tempted to write for fame, and there have been periods when I have been compelled to write for money. Neither of these motives now exist. . . . But the habit of throwing my ideas into rhyme is not easily conquered, and so, like Dogberry, I go on bestowing my tediousness upon the public."—*Letters*, IV, 114.

for a farm lying contiguous to Abbotsford ", *i.e.* Kaeside ; so he writes to John in the letter of 17th October ; and there were other drains upon his purse. " My brother has drawn on me for £200 at fifteen days sight. I can manage £100 but shall be pinchd for the rest unless you can help me about that time. He tells me he is writing a novel—if so I think it will prove a good one." Poor Tom's good intentions all went the same way, but *The Antiquary* was out in May 1816 (a year late) in which month John Scott —the Major—died leaving something to be divided among the brothers.

In *The Antiquary*, as in *Guy Mannering*, the sentimental interest traceable to Scott's own experience—which is what gives its warmest life to a novel—is again not to be sought in the young lovers, who are of the normal type—dutiful and honourable but insipid—nor in the tragic history of Lord Glenallan—but in Oldbuck, the Antiquary himself, whose character and humours form a warm and diffusive influence throughout the novel. Oldbuck is Scott himself—though in externals he may have borrowed traits from George Constable. He, too, has suffered a disappointment in love which has left an indelible scar upon his heart. But that is long over, except when, for a brief moment, the story told by the old domestic, Elspeth, brings it again to life ; and Scott is able to develop the humorous strain in his character as he could hardly do in Colonel Mannering. Oldbuck is Scott the antiquarian of the years of ballad-collecting and the editing of *Sir Tristrem* and the discussions with George Ellis regarding Thomas of Ercildoune and the Gothic or Celtic origin of the Picts—the same grown older, a little more pedantic and humoursome, and a little miserly in his expenditure—but all qualified by his essential kindness of heart and high principle. The main interest outside the character of the Antiquary is not really, as Mr. E. M. Forster asserts, the story of Lord Glenallan and his recovered son Lovell, but the scenes and characters that are woven into this loose framework : Edie Ochiltree and poor Oldbuck's praetorium, Edie and the escape of Sir Arthur and his daughter, one of the greatest scenes in all the novels, the suggestion for which Scott derived from a letter of Currie's, the first biographer and editor of Burns. There is less of history in the story, but as much or more of drawing straight from life, as the inimitable scene in the village post-office (chap. xv), or the burial of poor Steenie Mucklebackit (chap. xxxi). And then there is the last scene with the old nurse Elspeth (chap. xl) and the ballad she sings. There may be many greater novelists than Scott in the analysis of character and subtle shades of feeling, and in variety of intellectual and sophisticated types of society. Not many, apart from Shakespeare, could write scenes in which truth and poetry, realism and romance, are more wonderfully presented.

In these three novels then, it seems to me, Scott starts from a personal experience, a hidden memory of events and sufferings in his own life, but does not, either because he cannot, or does not wish to, make the principal theme the elaboration of this experience and its emotional consequences in any detail, but fills out the picture from his stores of antiquarian, historical, and literary reading reinforced by his own sympathetic knowledge of character —especially the simpler, more strongly marked traits and humours of the people.

For his next two novels Scott made a new venture in publishing. Lockhart, relying doubtless on Cadell, has attributed to John Ballantyne's guile the proposal to try another publisher besides Constable. This is not borne out by the correspondence between Scott and John. Constable, as a fact, was feeling the strain of advances on *Waterloo* and *Paul's Letters* and new editions of the earlier novels, and of accommodation bills. " I would deal with C.", Scott writes to John in October, " as little as possible untill his notes become more marketable," and again a little later : " I fear we shall have too much of Constables paper with *Antiqy.* so you must manage to get Longman's acceptances for as much as you can of Lady of [the] Lake." Feeling the strain, Constable was not too willing to take over more and more of John Ballantyne & Co.'s stock.[1] He seems to have thought also that printing might be done more cheaply than by James Ballantyne, or that James might be the better of a little threat of competition, such as Cadell tried in the years after the disaster. With a view, therefore, to securing a new source of credit, a new help to clearing off the old stock, while retaining the printing in James Ballantyne's hands, Scott threw out a bait to Blackwood and Murray. Blackwood, with Murray as his London agent, was eager to get an interest in Scott's poetry, and with that in view had been generous in work for the printing press : " Within these three years I have given him nearly £1400 for printing, and in return have only received empty professions made, to be sure, in the most dramatic manner." Indeed, as early as 1813 he had become retail publisher for John Ballantyne & Co. just before that firm was wound up. " This will be of very great use to me as it interests Walter Scott deeply in all my concerns" (*to Murray, 10th March,* 1813). Then had come *Waverley* and *Guy Mannering*, the latter completely eclipsing *The Lord of the Isles*, the Ballantynes acting as agents for the mysterious author, and Scott strongly suspected of being the person. " I regret the loss of *Guy Mannering* ", Blackwood writes to Murray, "much more than the splendid two guinea quarto [i.e. *The Lord of the Isles*]. If Walter Scott be the author of the novel he stands far higher in my opinion in this line than in his former walk. Ballantyne

---

[1] In April 1815, a third edition of *Guy Mannering* being got ready, Constable writes to Longman, who was manager for this novel, that it is the intention of Scott and the Ballantynes to ask that " we purchase Books of their stock to the extent of £500 " on this new edition. " We hope you will resist such a large purchase from their stock for so small a number of *Guy Mannering*—they only asked £500 on the first 4000 of this novel and £600 on 5000 now in progress, we therefore conceive they cannot look for a purchase of more than £250 on 2000 of Guy now at press—all this in confidence."

made great professions of his regret that we were not the publishers." But Blackwood was, like others, uncertain as to the author : " There is much greater invention, and far more feeling, than I have ever seen Walter Scott display in any of his works."

James clearly baited the water with half promises and expressions of discontent with Constable : " He assured me that Mr Scott would take an interest in me, and that matters would take that turn with you & me which I had so long been wishing to bring about. Constable, Ballantyne told me in confidence, had been doing everything he could to tease and torment Mr. Scott " (9th Feb., 1816—Smiles, *Memoir of John Murray*, I, 455). The ground well prepared, therefore, James on the 10th or 11th April approached Blackwood with a definite offer : " Till now he had only made professions : now he would act " (*Blackwood to Murray*, April 12—Mrs. Oliphant, *W. Blackwood and His Sons*, I, 57). " He said that he was empowered to offer me, along with you, a work of fiction in four volumes such as ' Waverley ', &c. ; that he had read a considerable part of it, and knowing the plan of the whole, he could answer for its being a production of the very first class ; but that he was not at liberty to mention the title, nor was he at liberty to give the author's name. I naturally asked him, was it by the author of ' Waverley ' ? He said it was to have no reference to any other work whatever. . . . He only requested that whatever we might suppose from anything that might occur afterwards we should keep strictly to ourselves : that we were to be the publishers." Blackwood is convinced that " they are anxious to get out of the clutches of Constable, and Ballantyne is sensible of the favour I have done and may still do him by giving so much employment, besides what he may expect from you. From Constable he can expect nothing."

So far from James and John being the directing agents in these negotiations, it is clear that James offered more favourable terms than Scott would agree to : " Having only authority from me to promise 6000 copies" [thereafter fresh bargains would have to be made] " he proposes they shall have the copy-right *for ever*. I will see their noses cheese first. He proposes I shall have 12 mos. bills —I have always got 6, however I would not stand on that. He talks of volumes being put into the publishers' hands to consider & decide on. No such thing—a bare perusal at St. John Street only. . . . It is *not* stipulated that we supply the print & paper of successive editions. . . . I will have London Bills as well as Blackwood's." Blackwood's bills would involve more transactions with Edinburgh banks, of which there were already enough. " If they agree to these conditions—good & well—if they demur Constable must be instantly tried—giving half to Longman—& *we* drawing on *them* for that money or Constable lodging their bill in our hands " (Scott to John Ballantyne, 30th April, 1816, *Letters*, I, 498). No sign there of Scott being led by the nose. Nor was Scott endeavouring to escape from the clutches of Constable, as Blackwood soon discovered. In a letter of 20th October 1814 Scott, in apologising to Murray for giving him no share in *The Lord of the Isles*, had written : " In casting about how I might show you some mark of my sense of former kindness a certain MS history of Scotland in letters to my children has occurd to me which I consider as a desideratum : it is upon the plan of Lord Littletons letters as they are calld. A small experimental edition might be hazarded in spring without a name not that I am anxious upon the score of secrecy but because I have been a great publisher of late," and on 10th June 1815 he writes again : " I intend to revise my letters on Scottish history for you but I will not get to press till November." [1] But now, in the summer of 1817, while he is awaiting impatiently the MS. of the promised novel,

---

[1] On 14th November 1816 he tells Lady Louisa Stuart : " My ostensible employment is a view of the history of Scotland long since written and on which I set so much value that I shall revise it with great care."—*Letters*, IV, 294.

Blackwood learns from Ballantyne, when " perhaps from the wine he had drunk [he] was very communicative ", that " about six weeks ago—at the very time our transaction was going on,—these worthies, Scott, Ballantyne & Co., concluded a transaction with Constable for 10,000 copies of this said History of Scotland in 4 vols. and actually received bills for the profits expected to be received from this large number." Yet when asked previously about this history, when it was to be ready, Ballantyne had denied all knowledge of such a work. " Now after this what confidence can we have in anything that this man will say and profess. I confess I am sadly mortified at my own credulousness. John I always considered as no better than a swindler, but James I put some trust and confidence in. You judged more accurately for you always said that ' he was a damned cunning fellow ' . . . Constable is the proper person for them ; set a thief to catch a thief. . . . One in business must submit to many things, and swallow many a bitter pill when such a man as Walter Scott is the object in view " (Smiles, *Memoirs of John Murray*, I, 462-3).

What James told Blackwood was this time the truth. On 3rd June 1816 Constable writes to Longman to inform them " that we have arranged some very important literary matters with Mr. Walter Scott, in particular the publication of a General History of Scotland in 3 vols octavo—to be published at Christmas. . . . On account of profits on this we have granted Mr. Scott bills viz. at 8 and 12 months p. £700." Constable has further arranged to bear all the expense of *The Edinburgh Annual Register* for the year 1814-15. " . . . In addition to this we have engaged for a £1000 of the E. A. R. in setts charged at 25 per cent from sale price . . . by bill at 12 mos." The history is to end with the rebellion of 1745. So Constable rides off with what had been promised to Murray, then in alliance with Blackwood, hence Blackwood's indignation. But by October Constable learns that he has not landed quite so big a fish as he had hoped. Scott will not give his name to the work and his suggestion " by the Author of Paul's Letters from the Continent " does not appeal to Constable, who writes dejectedly to Longman that with Scott's name attached a large number might have been printed, without it they had better not go beyond two thousand. However, printed it never was, unless it became later *Tales of a Grandfather* or the *History of Scotland* contributed to Lardner's Cyclopaedia. The bills remained a debt to Constable like those granted for the projected second visit to the Continent.[1] That he wrote some part of it at this time seems almost certain from references in his letters not only to publishers but to the Duke of Buccleuch.

The whole of the transactions makes strange reading. The transfer of the projected History is probably explicable. Scott had promised it to Murray as a compensation for keeping him out of *The Lord of the Isles*. As he then gave him two novels, he probably felt that the debt had been discharged, the History released, and it might now be used to keep Constable in hand. The aim and object of the whole affair was to get ready money for purchases of land and the finishing of Abbotsford, to get rid of John Ballantyne & Co.'s old stock, and to clear off the borrowings from friends including the Duke of Buccleuch. The first of these Scott, rightly or wrongly, regarded in the light of investment.

Blackwood's irritation about the History was partly due to his fear that it was delaying the appearance of the *Tales*, for James had promised a first sight of the MS. " in the course of six or eight weeks " after the 12th April, but month after month had passed and nothing was forthcoming. It was not till 23rd August that Blackwood was able to announce to Murray the arrival of the MS. and his intense enjoyment of the opening chapters of *The Black Dwarf*. That enjoyment was a little premature, as Scott

---

[1] See *Archibald Constable and His Correspondents*, III, p. 442, for the list of " claims brought against Sir Walter Scott's estate on account of contracts pending or unfulfilled " which include : " History of Scotland 1816, Travels on the Continent, 1818."

himself anticipated, for in acknowledging Ballantyne's report he writes : " I return the letter of Mr Blackwood and am glad he is pleased, but he will like the second volume better than the first and so will you."[1] Sure enough Mr. Blackwood did not at all like the conclusion of the first story when it reached him and, less polite than Constable or Cadell, frankly told James so, appealing to Gifford's opinion (which Murray had secured for him) for support, and even suggesting a better possible termination. The result was the explosive letter of 3rd October to James (*Letters*, IV, 276-7) to which Lockhart gave an even more explosive content. But *Old Mortality* more than made good Blackwood's disappointment, and *Tales of My Landlord : First Series* were out on the first of December 1816 with a result that entirely delighted Murray. " It is even, I think, superior to the other three novels. You may go on printing as many as you can, for we certainly need not stop until we come to the end of our unfortunately limited 6000 " (*To Blackwood*, 13th Dec.) ; and though his letter to Scott (14th December, *Letters*, IV, 318-9) failed to draw a confession of authorship, it secured for *The Quarterly* a review of his own novels by their author, a kind of mystification in which Scott took endless pleasure.

[1] " I return the letter of Mr Blackwood and am glad he is pleased ; but he will like the second volume better than the first and so will you, I think. But I want some Covenanting books sadly to ascertain and identify my facts and dates by before committing myself to the inevitable operations of the proofs. The following I especially want " (here Mr Cleishbotham enumerates Wodrow's History of the Sufferings of the Kirk and a number of others all of which I had it fortunately in my power to send to Ballantyne along with some others which I know he would like to see). [*Murray's parenthesis.*] "Without the means of the most accurate confirmation of what I have written with these volumes Jedidiah hath too much regard unto verity to print or publish. The sooner they can be supplied the sooner you will receive the copy. I have some thoughts of writing a Glossary in the name and style of said learned Jedediah. I am, if I may say so, confident of the success of the work ".—SCOTT to BALLANTYNE as reported by him to Blackwood and by Blackwood to Murray. Smiles, *John Murray*, I, 467.

Ballantyne adds : " This is no bad heartening although it must be confessed that authors are not the best judges of their own compositions. I do not hope to like the Covenanting tale better than the Black Dwarf."

But Blackwood, it is clear, got a little on Scott's nerves[1] and, with the expiry of the fourth edition, the *Tales* passed over to Constable and Longman & Co. with whom Scott was again in active collaboration. The History of Scotland hung fire, but on 7th May 1817 Constable was able to report to Longman " an agreement for a new work by the Author of Waverley, it is to be entitled Rob Roy in 3 vols. and published in September ",[2] and on the 16th he sends to John Ballantyne a list of the stock of Ballantyne & Co. " which we have selected agreeable to arrangements gone into upon the same principle as *Guy Mannering* and *The Antiquary*." The matter had been settled at a meeting between Scott, Constable, and John Ballantyne at Abbotsford on 5th May, when John was able to announce to his brother : " Wish me joy. I shall gain above £600—Constable taking my share of stock also—The title is Rob Roy —by *the Author of Waverley*." The arrangement as regards

---

[1] If Blackwood felt sore over the diversion of the History, Cadell was no less so over *The Tales*. On 3rd December he writes to Constable, reporting also the success of *The Tales* : " Some good judges say that the second, Old Mortality, is the best of the Author's productions—I am not inclined in any great degree or at any time to call names—but this I will say that there was a monstrous want of candour in the Author of these books going past us in the way he has done, when we undertook the History and Register he should have told us of the other and his reason of going elsewhere—We must just be quiet and wait till the current brings the thing again our way." " Blackwood has they say got off his first 2000 Tales of my Landlord—we wd have discussed 5000 in less time " (19th Dec., 1816).

[2] As early as April Scott, in writing to James Ballantyne on the request of Blackwood to postpone the printing of the fourth edition of the first series suggesting that Constable might buy over the remainder of this edition, the remainder of the 6000 which he had fixed as the limit to Blackwood's and Murray's right to issue, he writes : " Indeed were Constable to engage in the transaction I would probably give him four volumes more by next season on proper conditions and John might have such a share in the transaction as he could manage safely for himself. I would expect either a good lift of stock or something very handsome for 6000 of the new Jedediah." Possibly it was Scott's intention to make *Rob Roy* the first of two more *Tales*, but he changed his mind till the first series was into Constable's hands and delighted both Constable and John by returning to " By the Author of Waverley." The second series in the end contained only one story *The Heart of Midlothian*.

old stock was £600 for 6000 copies, Scott's price for the novel £1,700 payable in May. Paid by bills Scott doubtless was by that date, but the novel was not ready in September—not till three months later, 31st December 1817.

To the causes of this delay, and the novel itself, I shall recur later, but meantime I think it well to continue the history of the negotiations of these years, 1816-18, because they are the most complicated and agitated till we come to the great and final crisis, and they practically determined the financial history of Scott, Constable, and Cadell. Lockhart has told in his piquant way the story of the negotiations regarding the Second Series of *Tales of My Landlord*. As I do not entirely trust the accuracy of that account, I shall confine myself to what the letters of Scott, of Cadell, and of Constable suggest. Scott's main anxiety now, when money seemed to be flowing in and was yet always needed to meet immediate claims, was to clear off the bond for £4,000 into which the Duke of Buccleuch had entered in 1813. When negotiations began is not quite clear, but by 6th September 1817 Scott writes to John, who has been abroad and is then in London, that James " tells me nothing can be done in London respecting the money I want to pay off the Bond, owing to Rees's absence. I must therefore enter into treaty with Constable (so soon as R. R. is out) for the continuation *Tales of my L[andlor]d* 4 vols. which will make the £4000 forthcoming especially if I change the publishers of the first four volumes" (*i.e.* transfer *The Black Dwarf* and *Old Mortality* to Constable, which was done as soon as the fourth edition, the 6000 copies, was sold out). On the 9th Scott has heard from John of Longman's proposal and writes to James on the 10th to announce that " they are willing to clear our hands of the whole remaining stock on getting the next Tales ", and Constable must play up accordingly, he " will not I am sure wish or expect me to be a loser by my preference of him ". Both Longman and Constable are to be informed that " Murray has through an indirect channel offerd advantages equivalent or more than equivalent in a pecuniary point of view : but I cannot stomach some things which occurd formerly ". So James is told for Constable's information ; and on the same day Scott, in demurring to one part of Longman's proposal, viz. that John Ballantyne & Co.'s books are to be taken *at a valuation*, adds : " Murray has made advantageous offers so Longman & Co. must be sharp." If there was any playing off of publishers against one another, Scott's was the directing hand. John had been abroad and had involved himself and James in financial loss. In fact John, as James had done with Murray and Blackwood earlier, ran a little beyond his instructions with Longman, and Scott, taking the matter into his own hands, instructs James on 14th September to offer Constable the *Tales* " to be ready by Whitsunday ", Constable granting " acceptance for authors profit at six months ", and taking " the *whole* remaining stock of J. B. & Co. on the same terms of discount acceptance etc as formerly ". But Constable is to offer Longman " half the above bargain and there may be a reserve made of some small corner for the doughty John to cover his swindling losses at home and abroad ". In the end Longman, to Cadell's great disappointment, refused to accept any share in the *Tales*, boggling apparently at the arrangements made as to that Old Man of the Sea, the *Edinburgh Annual Register (Constable to Longman & Co.,* 18th May 1818, *Constable's Letter Book*).[1] Constable took " the

---

[1] When later, in June 1818, Cadell was in London, Longman & Co. complained that " they had accepted all the conditions we offered—and I have no doubt there has been a misunderstanding about which as I told them they can only blame themselves ". Longman himself was a little sarcastic about Constable's bargain : " You seem to give the author everything he asks " and " have you any better hold on the author by taking all the stock. I think not, by giving him so much you enable him to ask high terms in future and perhaps he may not stay with you " ; and as a fact, the manœuvring of John and James did give Cadell and Constable some anxiety later on in 1818, but I do not find they had any authority from Scott for such tactics.—*Archibald Constable and His Literary Correspondents,* III, pp. 110 ff.

whole of the transaction on ourselves as indeed the responsibility of it has been hitherto ". What that responsibility was, and how much it was felt by Cadell, is clear from his letters to Constable.

The stipulation which, Cadell felt, involved the greatest danger, was that " as many acceptances etc. must be granted in November as will take out of the way the £4000 bond ". But the novels were not written, were still in Scott's mind, *Rob Roy* was only finishing, and *Scott was ill*. What would be the position of Constable & Co. if they granted bills for £4000 in November, for work to be out at the earliest six months later, in the event of Scott's death before anything was completed ? " I say *to you* & to no one else that W. S. is not long for this world & I am acting in everything accordingly." Not only did Cadell fear the risk, but even to have it known that they had accepted such bills would affect Constable & Co.'s credit which was too much strained already. " But with all this there is a lamentable want of capital " : that is the constantly repeated cry of Cadell in his letters to Constable. Accordingly Cadell set himself to postpone the commitment till 18th May when, he hoped, the new tales would at least be in the press. The negotiations are a little difficult to follow but are not without interest. Longman did not definitely refuse till May 1818, and Cadell hopes they may grant bills in advance " for their one third of £4000 *now* and so much more for profit ". But John Ballantyne is to have one fourth share of the profits—*i.e.* in the final division of profits on the arrangement between author and publisher—in return for which he had undertaken to contribute £1,000 towards the November clearance of the Duke's bond. Now John had, or professed to have, £1,000 ready for this purpose, and Cadell adroitly managed to persuade Scott to be satisfied with this for the present, Constable & Co. undertaking to " take up the bond for £4,000 at Whitsunday with interest, etc., due from this term, this therefore stands for £4000 advanced on their part at this term. The bargain provides for £1,000 more in case I shall want it. I have only the prospect at present of needing £500 or so which you will please to provide. The remainder will be wanted at Candlemas as it is in payt. of some land" (*Scott to John*, 24*th Nov.*, 1817, *Letters*, V, 17), and on the next day: "My land-merchant having come to town a day I must settle a large sum with him tomorrow. You will therefore please pay £500 into the Bank of Scotland to be at my credit these [*sic*] being so much in proportion of the advance on a late bargain. I hold Messrs. Constable & Co. to have already advanced £4000 this will make £500 more all that I have occasion for at present" (*ditto*).

This was then the position as regards Constable: "We go on with all our operations as if the sum *was paid* it being held as *pro tanto* of the bargain concluded with John Ballantyne" (*Cadell to Constable*); but they have till Whitsuntide before issuing bills for the sum, John providing meantime. John clearly felt he had been caught out, probably not really having the £1,000 in cash, and several letters from Cadell to John show that he tried to push it off at once on to Constable. In the end Cadell was able to use his hold on John to purchase the fourth share which had been allotted to that worthy.

What Cadell procured as a safeguard requires a somewhat careful reading of Constable & Co. to Mr. Scott on 21st November 1817 which is printed in *Archibald Constable and His Literary Correspondents*, Vol. III, p. 105. They undertake "the obligation of making good this payment of £4000 sterling, at the next term of Whitsunday ... we engage also to pay the annuity on said bond for that period of six months, and to relieve you of all expenses and trouble attending it from this time; the legal steps being taken, we can insure the bond being put into your hands cancelled at May 1818." Then comes the clause of which Scott perhaps hardly realised the effect: "It being understood that this bond of £4000, when so paid or delivered up, goes in part of the sums to be made good by us in the transaction with Mr. John Ballantyne before alluded to." What this implies is, I take it, that if Scott did not write the novels arranged for in " the transaction with Mr. John Ballantyne ", then Constable was *not* liable for the bond. This explains Cadell's somewhat exultant letter to Constable three days later : " It gives me sincere satisfaction to assure you that I have got Mr. Scott's Bond arranged, the payment stands over till May, our taking upon us the extra charge of interest, the other parties to the Tales paying their proportion of this extra sum & the six months interest—it is needless for me to say that this is to us a most beneficial transaction, it lessens our risk in his life, and keeps our name out of operations, it was finally adjusted on Saturday. . . . It would take up too much time and space to explain how this was managed tho I have no hesitation in telling you candidly that you *could* not have done it for you *would* not have done it & when I shall explain all the circumstances you will be apt to say that I am something of a h[umbu]g—I did not think I had so much *face* left but so it is, what is more I got it so adjusted that the offer came from Mr. S. himself. I called on him & sorted it in ten minutes. . . . I expect to-morrow to get his life insured." Accordingly on the 25th he writes again : " It gives me pleasure to tell you but no one else *knows it*—that I have at last got Walter Scott managed—Mr. T. and I got it sorted this morning—I have signed the declaration required for the insurance and it is off. The man himself is looking remarkably well—what with this and the Bond altho I do not care about praise or commendation of myself—it being only bare duty to myself and those concerned, yet I feel much satisfaction in having got them both done so quickly —this I will say as to the Bond you would scarcely have let me do or say what I did in this respect." On the 28th he continues : " I think you are wrong in the construction you put on the mode of adjusting the Tales with Longman, I send you copies of my communications with Mr. Scott on the subject, by which you will see I have (at least I think so) not belied my character of a Writer in the perfect corner I have secured ourselves in this matter, my letter was to Mr. Scott and you will see by his letter (and I have nabbed two to John Doe to the same purport) goes clearly to show that we are held *as having at this time* advanced the £4000—and come what will we are covered from any claim that can be made upon us should Mr Scott die, for to you I mention this, but I am diffident of doing so *in writing* to any one. *My letter to W. S. is as good as his* in the eye of the law and as to the Bond, why, should he die we have nothing *to do with it*, the Duke pays the Piper and *our letter* stands *against his*. At least I think this is the present aspect of the matter. L. & Co. nor ourselves have any Bill to grant to W S on this score at all, they *grant to us*. We have virtually paid the Bond—W S says so & L & Co must grant only to us—the sum being already made good by our responsibility in the matter" (*Nat. Lib. Scot.*, 322). If I understand this at all, it must mean that while Scott's letter would imply that Constable & Co. had taken over and paid the Bond, Cadell's would imply that they had agreed to make themselves liable for £4,000 as part of a bargain which Scott's death, without having delivered the MS., would annul.

By these negotiations Constable finally secured Scott for themselves, for some manœuvring by John later in 1818, when Murray was to visit Edinburgh, was directed merely to securing " that both he and ' James, poor fellow ', as he observed, must have *slices* ", have their shares, in any book brought out, well in advance by bills. That autumn, *e.g.*, a bargain was concluded for a " New Travels on the Continent " of which John " is to have one-third, and *us* two-thirds, the number 10,000, and the division half-profits." But the prize was won at a great cost to Constable's firm and therefore ultimately to Scott himself. Before the crash came, Cadell has to tell, Constable again and again that they are more dependent on the Ballantynes' bills than Ballantyne & Co. are on them. " Their bills to us are sooner cashed than ours to them." Scott had no idea what an unstable foundation he was putting so great a strain upon : " Constable's business seems unintelligible. No man thought the house worth less than £150,000. Constable told me, when he was making his will, that he was worth £80,000 " (*Journal*, Jan. 29, 1826). Robert Cadell had no such illusions.

I have followed up these negotiations, passing over the other currents of Scott's life, because they were critical and definitive, so that I need not follow up the financial history further beyond what may be necessary to say of the state of affairs when the catastrophe arrived. There is no mystery about Scott's insolvency, though it is impossible to disentangle the accounts as between Scott and his partner. More important is it to form a fair judgement of Scott's conduct in all these affairs; and I will venture to state mine in a series of propositions.

(1) Scott early realised that he had in his gifts as romancer, first in verse and then in prose, a mine of wealth, and he was determined that he and not the publishers should be the chief gainer thereby. He knew or believed it was generally the other way. Publishers grew rich. He was determined to exact his full price, as a man does who is selling a house, or a painter for his picture, a musician for his performances, a public entertainer for his appearances. Why an author should not do the same is difficult to understand. Poet, artist, novelist, musician, tight-rope dancer—all are public entertainers, and have the right to be rewarded according to the willingness of the public to pay.

(2) Nevertheless the prices which Scott asked were in themselves fair, as Cadell admits : " Scott was throughout liberal to his publisher—he might have asked higher prices—if he had done so he would have got them—but when a price was once fixed he took the same money for

those that followed[1] without making any change: in Waverley for example the First edition was published on the principle of the Booksellers taking the risk of paper and printing and dividing the gain with the author [2]—the arrangement went on with all the after editions altho it is clear from the extraordinary popularity of the Author he might have exacted higher terms." For most of the novels after *Waverley* the method adopted was somewhat different. Scott sold to Constable and Co. the right to print two thirds of the first impression of 10,000 (in some cases 12,000) books for a fixed sum. Until 1822 or thereabouts the price of the two thirds was £3,000, but it seems to have been thereafter reduced to £2,500. The remaining one third was reserved for James Ballantyne, but in regard to one half of this third James acted as Trustee for Sir Walter. Constable & Co., on the book being published, bought the reserved third share of the books amounting to say 3,300 at trade prices, and granted bills therefor—bills for value received.

(3) The Ballantynes were his agents, John for negotiations (though James was also used) with publishers, James for the work of general criticism, criticism and correction of details of style and punctuation, the transcription of Scott's autograph, proof-reading, etc. " I am labouring ",

[1] That is the editions of the same novel, not each subsequent novel.

[2] What half-profits come to is indicated by Scott in a letter to James Skene on 7th January, 1816 (*Letters*, IV, pp. 163-4). " To understand this, however, you must be aware that first the publisher subtracts from the gross sum about £27 or £28 per cent. as the allowance to the retail booksellers, so that the calculation is made upon what they call sale price. From what remains there is deducted the expenses of print, paper, engravings, etc., and something in the way of incidents or advertising. All these speaking roughly, come to more than a third of the gross amount, the rest is considered free profit and divisible. Upon the best calculation I can make an author gains generally about one-sixth part of the whole, or half a guinea upon three guineas. I believe upon the whole it is the fairest mode of transacting business, and at present, when capital is ill to come at is perhaps the only eligible one." But Scott did not in the case of *Waverley* pay for the paper, etc. In some cases one finds him reserving the right to supply paper hoping, I suppose, to be able to get it at a lower price than the publisher would charge.

he writes to a friend in 1814, " to get the author to discard certain Scotticisms, in which he too much indulges ; amongst them the too frequent use of words peculiar to himself—' meet ' for ' becoming ', ' guerdon ' &c. They are good enough in themselves, and I should not object to them in Southey or Byron. But it is because they occur constantly in his pages that I hate them there. They tinge the whole composition more or less. His principle is give me beauties and I forgive faults. But silk and sackloth should not be united though I do not contend that all should be embroidery." John Ballantyne was a trickster and inclined to use his powers as negotiator to secure advantages for himself, as Cadell's correspondence shows. " I am quite clear ", Cadell writes to Constable, " that the way to manage Mr Scott is to attack him in person, apart from the Ballantynes, and speak to him in a plain, business-like manner. I am sure he likes that better than diffidence . . . he likes candour and openness." They were both extravagant, John in horse-racing and other gaieties, James in dinners and entertainments. John's cautioners at the Bank had ultimately to pay up. If James reduced his debts of 1822 by the date of the failure, it was apparently at the expense of the printing business. Scott treated them with absurd generosity, allowing for their usefulness. There was none of the meanness of Pope's dealing with Browne and Fenton, or of Dickens's allowance to his wife after he had compelled a separation and was able at the end of a lecture to roll amid cheques.[1]

(4) While the prices he asked were fair or moderate Scott put an undue strain on his publishers by his demands for payment in advance by bills, and on the

[1] At least his staff : " Dickens's fourth series of readings began in October 1868 . . . He was well received at Manchester, but even better at Liverpool, where he read on 25 October . . . Hundreds of persons were turned away. Dickens's staff ' rolled on the ground ' of his room ' knee deep in cheques and made a perfect pantomime of the whole thing '. Similar scenes followed. Everywhere he was greeted with furore—the money poured in in cataracts." Thomas Wright : *The Life of Charles Dickens*, 1935.

printing business by the loans which he raised from it for expenditure on land and Abbotsford. He seems never to have had ready money at command. Any sudden expense, a journey to the continent, the purchase of his son's commission, required bills to be discounted on some work yet to be done. Even Sophia's dowry was paid in bills so that she too ranked among the creditors.

(5) But the cause of the failure as it actually eventuated was that the firm of Constable and Co. was itself on the edge of bankruptcy throughout the years of Scott's later connection with it. If in 1813 Constable helped Ballantyne and Co. to escape disaster, it seems to me clear that it was their connection with Scott which kept the firm and its credit afloat from 1814 to 1826. The letters of Constable to his partner in 1814, while the former was in London trying to obtain necessary support for their large engagements, show him ready to throw up the sponge and "retire to some quiet corner if to live in little better than poverty—I hope in peace—out of the world's eye. I should be content with very small matters—and I desire nothing so much" (28*th October*). "If you apply to the directors of the Bank of S. and are refused our difficulties will get abroad and ruin will be the result" (7*th November*). That was their position before they had become deeply engaged for Scott and his works or loans. By 1823 they are finding Ballantyne and Co.'s counter-bills to them more easy to negotiate than are theirs to Ballantyne and Co. So Cadell tells Constable. Scott had apparently no inkling of the actual condition of affairs.

When all is said and done, Scott was a dreamer, a poet " whose temperament ", as Robert Chambers says, " was sanguine and ideal as ever poet manifested, though in his case usually veiled under the air of worldly seeming." Nor was the Edinburgh in which Scott grew up an environment likely to encourage unworldly ideals—a dissolute upper class, a conceited, prudential middle-class, a religion more concerned with the abstractions of theology than with " whatsoever things are true, whatsoever things are honest, whatsoever things are just, whatsoever things are pure, whatsoever things are lovely, whatsoever things are of good report ; if there be any virtue, and if there be any praise think on these things."

CHAPTER VIII

*One crowded hour of glorious life
Is worth an age without a name.*

I HAVE thought it well to follow up these negotiations, because they are at once critical and typical and will save me much discussion when the hour of destiny arrives in 1825-26. I must now turn back to Scott's doings other than literary, and to a word on the novels themselves. The expenditure of energy in these years seems incredible, and was bound to carry with it some consequence to his health, that robust health which had succeeded to a delicate, precocious youth. *Paul's Letters*, *The Antiquary*, the History of the Year 1814 for *The Edinburgh Annual Register*, *The Black Dwarf, Old Mortality, Harold the Dauntless*, the History of the Year 1815 for *The Edinburgh Annual Register*, the Introduction to *The Border Antiquities, Rob Roy*, all were issued in the course of two years and even if we conjecture that some of them, as *Harold the Dauntless*, were begun earlier, this does not materially reduce the work of composition, proof-reading, etc. And alongside this stream of publication went all the negotiations which I have described. Nor were the negotiations about the successive novels the only financial business of these years. In the autumn of 1815 James Ballantyne, who had been jilted by some unknown lady in 1808-9, became engaged to a Miss Hogarth. But her brother, George—the father later of Catherine Hogarth, who became the wife of Charles Dickens—demurred to the marriage until James should be entirely free of obligations for the firm of James Ballantyne & Co. Scott, accordingly, took over all the debts and all the profits—never so large as the principals were disposed to believe—of the firm, allowing

James a salary of £400 a year, but retaining his claim for £3,000 which he had formerly advanced to the printing business as a debt due to him by James personally.[1]

With all this in hand, Scott was acquiring more land. The purchase of Kaeside was completed in 1816 : " The author of a late popular novel understanding his second edition is getting fast on has requested me as his substitute to draw on our friends at the Cross for £350 to accompt of profits. As this venerable person has lately bought the Kaime of Kinprunes & has had to pay the purchase money thereof occasions his being thus importunate. I will draw the bill myself if you will send me a stamp " (*To John Ballantyne, May* 1816, *Letters*, IV, 235-6). " I believe I wrote to you that we now extend ourselves as far as Cauldshiels Loch " (*To M. W. Hartstongue*, 28*th Nov.*, 1816, *Letters*, IV, 306). In December 1815 he with James Hogg—who had apologised for a rude letter over the preliminaries to his *The Poetical Mirror*—was busy organising, of all things, a football match between the lads of Yarrow and the sutors of Selkirk. He was extending and furnishing Abbotsford with the help of Terry and George Bullock, of whose death later in 1818 he believed himself to have had ghostly indication by an inexplicable noise as of moving furniture in a room where nothing was found to have been disturbed. He had a fairly continuous succession of guests in 1816, including his wife's early friends, Miss Dumergue and Sarah Nicolson, elder sister of Jane. To Morritt, who himself—and there were others—came later, he writes on 21st August : " We accomplishd with some difficulty a visit to Loch Katrine and Loch Lomond and by dint of the hospitality of Cambusmore and Ross we defied bad weather wet roads and long walks. But the weather settled into actual tempest when we settled at Abbotsford and though the natives accustomd to bad

---

[1] James was readmitted to partnership in 1823, when provision was made for the liquidation of the £3,000 by his assigning to Scott his share of profits in five novels then contracted for. But see Mr. Glen's letter in *Letters of Sir Walter Scott*, I, pp. lxxxvii-ix.

weather ... contrived to brave the extremities of the season it only served to increase the dismay of our unlucky visitors who accustomd only to Paris and London expected *fiacres* at the milestane cross and a pair of oars at the Deadmans heugh [1]... I walkd them to death—I talkd them to death—I showd them landscapes which the driving rain hardly permitted them to see and told them of feuds about which they cared as little as I do about their next-door news in Piccadilly. Yea I even playd at cards. ... Yesterday they left us deeply impressd with the conviction which I can hardly blame that the sun never shone in Scotland" (*Letters*, IV, 268). A too vivid picture of many a summer holiday in Scotland, but also of Scott's energetic hospitality and of the vigour of mind that could write such full and lively letters in the middle of entertaining guests, planning the construction of that Delilah, the house at Abbotsford, finishing the proofs of *The Antiquary* (May), and writing the First Series of *Tales of My Landlord*. His brother, John, the retired Major, died in May, and letters to Tom in Canada set out a full " statement of his affairs which have turned out better than I knew of ".

It would certainly ease the situation if one could prove that the novels were already written and needed only to be taken off the shelf and transcribed by James or John for the press. If there was any such reserve to fall back on, it was clearly unknown to his publishers, for they are constantly in a state of impatiently waiting for work long overdue.[2] If any of these earlier novels was worked up from some fragment of the kind that Scott printed later with his general introduction to the Waverley Novels, one would be willing to accept *The Black Dwarf* as such. " I

---

[1] Which exists only in a ballad forged by Surtees and printed by Scott in *The Border Minstrelsy*.

[2] " We are sadly pestered about the Antiquary and can say nothing as to its progress."—CONSTABLE to LONGMAN & Co., 23rd January, 1816.

" I am terrified beyond measure about Rob Roy. ... Should we not be able to publish this year the loss to our affairs will be most grievous and strikes me with dismay."—CADELL to CONSTABLE, 11th November, 1817.

intended", he writes to Lady Louisa Stuart, " to have written four tales illustrative of the manners of Scotland in her different provinces" [*i.e.*, as the dedication to the First Series shows, *Men of the South, Gentlemen of the North, People of the West*, and *Folk of Fife*]. " But as no man that wrote so much ever knew so little what he intended to do when he began to write or executed less of the little which he had premeditated I totally altered my plans before I had compleated my first volume. I began a border tale well enough but tired of the ground I had tròde so often before I had walked over two thirds of the course. Besides I found I had circumscribed my bounds too much & in manege phrase that my imagination not being well in hand could not lunge easily within so small a circle. So I quarrelled with my story, & bungled up a conclusion " (*Letters*, IV, 292-3). It was in 1797 that he had met David Ritchie, not long after his last visit to Fettercairn and the final dissipation of his hopes, and it is possible that recalling his bitter feelings of that date, as witnessed by the poem I have printed earlier, he was tempted to essay the picture of a misanthrope, made such by the betrayal of a lady whom he had loved and a friend whom he had trusted. The character of Byron, too, as the letters of this year (1816) show, had a strong fascination for Scott even before the publication—too late for any influence on his own story [1]—of the Third Canto of *Childe Harold*, as though

[1] *Childe Harold*, 18th November ; First Series of *Tales of My Landlord*, 1st December, but they were in print early in November. *Childe Harold*, Canto III, was sent to Scott for review, and he writes of it on the 22nd and 26th November to Morritt and to Joanna Baillie : " We gaze on the powerful and ruined mind which he presents us, as on a shattered castle, within whose walls, once intended for nobler guests, sorcerers and wild demons are supposed to hold their Sabbaths. There is something dreadful in reflecting that one gifted so much above his fellow-creatures should thus labour under some strange mental malady that destroys his peace of mind and happiness, altho' it cannot quench the fire of his genius " (*Letters*, IV, 297). " The last part of Childe Harold intimates a terrible state of mind and with all the power and genius which characterizd his former productions the present seems to indicate a more serious and desperate degree of misanthropy."— *Letters*, IV, 300.

there were elements in the younger poet's picture of himself to which Scott could detect a real but suppressed affinity in his own temperament. But an adequate treatment of the theme would have begun with Elshie's earlier life, not recounted parenthetically to explain the later course of events; and such a history of a soul was quite as outside Scott's range as Racine's continuously developed situation was remote from Shakespeare's genius, certainly from his practice.

From any such thought of an introspective study of the development of a misanthrope Scott recoils in his next novel, *Old Mortality*, to the kind of story which was his, and Shakespeare's, normal method of presenting life and character—a broadly delineated chapter of history with strongly marked characters, natural and intelligible, but not too deeply or subtly analysed.[1] " It is ", he writes, " I think the best I have yet been able to execute, although written by snatches and at intervals." " It is a covenanting story, the time lies at the era of *Bothwell Brigg* the scene in Lanarkshire : there are noble subjects for narrative during that period full of the strongest light & shadow, all human passions stirr'd up & stimulated by the most powerful motives & the contending parties as distinctly contrasted in manners & in modes of thinking as in political principles. I am complete master of the whole history of these strange times both of persecutors & persecuted " (*Letters*, IV, 293).

Scott was familiar with the history of the century, though he treats it with the freedom of Shakespeare in the

---

[1] Yet even in *Old Mortality* there is evidence of the influence of Byron. The copy of verses, wrapping a lock of hair in Bothwell's pocket-book, is quite in the spirit of *The Corsair*:

> Since then, how often hast thou press'd
> The torrid zone of this wild breast,
> Whose wrath and hate have sworn to dwell
> With the first sin which peopled hell.
> A breast whose blood's a troubled ocean,
> Each throb the earthquake's wild emotion.

historical plays, telescoping events of different years so as to sharpen and heighten his picture. He thus attributes to Lauderdale's severe but bloodless persecution of Covenanters the cruelties which came with the succession to Lauderdale of the pious and sadistic James, Duke of York, anxious to find justification to raise an army in Scotland which might be useful elsewhere. In like manner he attributes to the Covenanters of these years the temper and excesses of the Cameronians of later years. But these and other unhistorical statements, regarding the use of the Anglican prayer book, the presence of indulged ministers among the rebels at Bothwell Bridge, the too early appearance of Captain (or, as Scott dubs him, " Colonel ") Claverhouse, are of trifling importance, for he was acquainted not alone with the facts but with, weakened perhaps yet not mellowed, the religious temper of Scottish presbyterianism from his own childhood experiences. " Many a sermon have I groaned under at the Tron Kirk." " My mother wd. have written but this being the day of Communion, which is rigorously observed by the presbyterians she has postponed it." " I find that the Coach which leaves Edinr. on Tuesday at Midnight will bring me in to Carlisle on Wednesday Evening. I have agreed with much difficulty to abandon the point of setting out upon Tuesday. It is the fast-day, and the George's Square folks would think me riding post haste to the Devil." Scott was not qualified to enter sympathetically into the religious aspect of the conflict, and indeed it is difficult to comprehend the religious significance of the furious outcry against " that abominable plant of prelacy which is the bane of the throne and the country." When one does come into touch with the devotional element in the Covenanters, it seems to us indistinguishable from the devotional spirit of a devout Roman, or Anglican, Papist or Prelatist : " I have given my hearty consent, good Jesus, to thy coming in and taking possession of my soul, and to the casting out of everything there that stands in opposition to thee. I desire to take thee for my all, to be ruled and governed by thee. . . . Give me thyself and this shall be all my desire." That is the aspiration of every zealous, exalted Christian. But there was a real issue at stake between the Covenanters and Charles, the perennial and insoluble problem of the relation between Church and State, the old conflict between Pope and Emperor, between Becket and Henry, between Hitler and the Church in Germany to-day, alike Protestant and Catholic. What the Covenanters stood for was " the crown-rights of Jesus Christ ", " we must not edge away a hem of Christ's robe-royal ", " no leadership over the spiritual realm bequeathed to Pope or King or Parliament ". In things spiritual the Kirk is absolute, the King is " God's silly vassal ", his duty " to cause all things to be done according to God's word and to defend the discipline ". And in Scotland in the seventeenth century the State was represented by a debauched Government and a brutal soldiery. Scott loved neither the exalted religious sentiment of the Covenanters nor their claim to supremacy in the State, but he did condemn the policy and the methods of the Government. Accordingly, his hero is in much the same position as Edward Waverley in his first novel—a young man who, in agreement with neither side, is, partly by accident, partly by an affair of the heart, drawn into action on one side. He has a better cause, justice and patriotism, than Edward, but it can hardly be said that Scott takes full advantage of it. The interest of the novel is in the various scenes and the subordinate persons— humorous perhaps rather than solid characters, but the best of them with a third dimension, a touch of kindness or good sense or Christian charity that gives them individuality. The whole is a contribution to *la Comédie Humaine* rather than the tragic story it might have been had Scott been able to give the hero a deeper interest in the conflict and been willing to sacrifice the happy ending. As Adolphus, in his *Letters to Heber* (1822) says, it ill becomes the hero, as hero, to be looking on at the trial of his fellow-rebels with his own pardon in his pocket. The balance of Scott's mind, the readiness to discount his own partialities, when he comes to actual portrayal of historical persons, is well brought out by his picture of Claverhouse, for Claverhouse was from youth one of Scott's heroes, and he is one of those heroes, like Mary Queen of Scots, Charles Edward, Montrose, whose aesthetic and romantic appeal has given them an interest out of all proportion to either their real worth or their historical importance. Yet in the novel the charm and gallantry of Claverhouse's character is not more clearly portrayed than his ruthlessness and aristocratic contempt for the common people.

"You are right," said Claverhouse, with a smile; "you are very right—we are both fanatics; but there is some distinction between the fanaticism of honour and that of dark and sullen superstition."

"Yet you both shed blood without mercy or remorse," said Morton, . . .

"Surely," said Claverhouse, with the same composure; "but of what kind ?—There is a difference, I trust, between the blood of learned and reverend prelates and scholars, of gallant soldiers and noble gentlemen, and the red puddle that stagnates in the veins of psalm-singing mechanics, crack-brained demagogues, and sullen boors. . . ."

"Your distinction is too nice for my comprehension," replied Morton. "God gives every spark of life—that of the peasant as well as of the prince; and those who destroy his work recklessly or causelessly, must answer in either case." That is one of the sentences which reveals the keel of not only good sense but right feeling, moral, and I would say, religious, which runs through the novels, disguised as it may be in Scott's letters by the surface of worldiness and the preoccupation with financial activities.

"I say *to you* and to no one else will I even breathe it that

W. S. is not long for this world," Cadell wrote to Constable in November 1817. On 28th February Scott had been seized with so violent a fit of cramp in the stomach—the effect of gallstones—that " I fainted which was quite a novelty to me and truly I thought the grim skeleton was about to take my harp out of the Minstrels hands." [1] But despite these attacks, Scott's activities were allowed a minimum of interruption, and by April he opened the negotiations for *Rob Roy* referred to above. That means, I take it, that the plan of the novel was clear in his mind and possibly some chapters sketched or written. Despite monthly recurrences of the attack, " with unabated violence of pain ", the novel was out by January 1818.

Rob Roy is less of a purely historical novel than *Old Mortality*. Once again Scott turns back on his early and even recent experiences. Francis Osbaldistone is the young Scott, impatient of confinement in his father's office, a poet, a dreamer, and a lover. Not that Di Vernon is a picture of Miss Belsches. She is rather, I suspect, a reflection of the most courageous and unconventional and loyal of his early young women friends, Jane Cranstoun. The differences between Francis and his father recall probably some of Scott's own early family jars ; but in the picture he has drawn of the older Osbaldistone's financial adventures and perils he cannot but be thinking of his own recent experiences " at a crisis so tremendous that " it shook John Ballantyne's soul to recall it : " Accustomed to see his whole future trembling in the scales of chance, and dexterous at adopting expedients for casting the balance in his favour, his health and spirits and activity seemed even to increase with the animating hazards on which he staked

---

[1] To Joanna Baillie, 1st March, 1817.—*Letters*, IV, 394-5. Lockhart dates the first attack on 5th March. In a letter to Joanna on 17th March Scott describes another attack on Tuesday the 4th, after returning from dining at Dalkeith with the Buccleuchs. This was followed on the 5th by the attack to which Lockhart refers. To Morritt, 18th March (*Letters*, IV, 413-5.).

his wealth ; and he resembled a sailor, accustomed to brave the billows and the foe, whose confidence rises on the eve of tempest or of battle." That is Scott as the Ballantynes saw him in the crisis of 1813, when it seemed not unlikely that he would leave Scotland, " for I will not live where I must be necessarily lookd down upon by those who once lookd up to me " (*Letters*, IV, p. 332). " This mixture of necessary attention and inevitable hazard—the frequent and awful uncertainty whether prudence shall overcome fortune, or fortune baffle the schemes of prudence—affords full occupation for the powers as well as for the feelings of the mind, and trade has all the fascination of gambling without its moral guilt." That is a vivid glance of another side of Scott's mind and temperament from that which I have cited from Morton's reply to Claverhouse. It was not in the novels alone as tales of adventure that Scott found a vicarious outlet for his own passion for adventure and action. It was the great adventure of making his genius a source of gain, not for the sake of gain but as affording him the means of indulging his dreams as the owner of land, the founder of a family, the feudal laird. But the end in view was, I think, had he fully realised it, a less attraction than the pursuit,—the excitement of taking risks, the inspiring force of a pledge to be fulfilled by the writing of stories which were still mainly, or wholly, in his brain, the negotiations through the Ballantynes with Constable and Murray and Longman, all the side issues of occasional articles, social undertakings, entertaining guests, planning for his children, Hogg, and Laidlaw, and others—they were all part of the great game of life which he played with that strange blend of romantic glamour, fundamental good sense, and high principle, the very blend which he tried to communicate to his heroes, to Edward Waverley and Henry Morton and Francis Osbaldistone. He failed to communicate his own zest of life and adventure to these heroes partly because it was necessary to give to this zest a definite end, and the prescribed end for the novelist was love—and Scott had no great understanding of love as a passion—partly because in the presentation of the hero he bethought himself—like Milton in writing *Comus*—of those who were to read his work and was anxious to convey a clear impression of the good sense and right feeling which, in the hero's conduct, were combined with their more romantic impulses. He could let himself go more freely in minor and side characters; and he could and did let himself go in the game of his own life as he played it through the Ballantynes and with various disguises which served to protect him from the criticism whether of others or of his own sense and conscience. For the good sense and right feeling he attributes to his heroes were his own. Scott did many things in his reckless playing of the game of life that one may or must judge severely. I have never found any suspicion of his doing anything, or consenting to anything being done, which he felt was dishonest and unworthy.

Even if Scott's temperament would have let him rest, the state of affairs in which that temperament had involved him made it difficult to pause even after such a warning as the attack of cramp in the early spring. *Rob Roy* was planned to meet accruing expenses. " To pay up Hogarths £1050 and other incumbrancies of this month ", he writes to John on 6th September, 1817, " I must raise the wind on the owners of R. R. to the tune of £550 each in addition to the £600 formerly levied. Of this James will apprize you. Your own moiety will be necessary on the 19th. & 20th. You can probably arrange with Constable & Longman to make it easy for you." Yet neither illness nor anxiety about money depressed his ardour. With a view to health and the novel he toured in the West in July:

> " From Ross where the clouds on Ben-Lomond are sleeping
> From Greenock where Clyde to the Ocean is sweeping
> From Largs where the Scotch gave the Northmen a drilling
> From Ardrossan whose harbour cost many a shilling

From Old Cumnock where beds are as hard as a plank Sir
From a chop & green pease & a chicken at Sanquhar
This eve please the fates at Drumlanrigg we anchor."

So he writes to the Duke of Buccleuch from Sanquhar some day before 24th July, on which day he is writing to Joanna Baillie *from* Drumlanrig Castle. By the 27th he is back at Abbotsford and at work on *Rob Roy*, as a letter to Constable shows him inquiring for Richard Burn's *Justice of the Peace* to keep him right about the doings of Justice Inglewood and his clerk Jobson (see chaps. vii and viii of the novel) ; and a little later in the same month to James : " I send you some more of R. R. In a day or two you shall have a larger allowance but I have had attacks of the cramp and am obliged to work piano." From what he has seen of it Constable is proposing to raise the number to be printed to ten thousand. " I hope R. will answer. I will study to make it do it is so much better dealing with Constable than with the other ungracious fellow," *i.e.* poor Blackwood with whom and Murray Ballantyne had trouble in April and May over the printing of the 4th edition of the First Series of *Tales of My Landlord* and the transference of the 5th to Constable. By September Scott is hoping to have *Rob Roy* out in October. The repayment of Hogarth's £1,050 is delayed as Tom has " tipped me bills for £500 ". Nor is *Rob Roy*, which was not off his hands till the end of December, the only work. The long promised Article on Chivalry is taken in hand in September and in course of transmission to Macvey Napier, the editor of Constable's Supplement to *The Encyclopaedia Britannica*. For Murray an article on Scott's own novels, especially *Old Mortality* (which Dr. McCrie has criticised severely), is preparing with the help of Erskine. With all this literary and business activity Scott was entertaining guests throughout the month of August. Lady Byron came some day after the 13th and struck both Scott and Laidlaw by " a great deal of firmness and a certain decision of character (' obstinacy ' is Laidlaw's word) which perhaps is more graceful in adversity than it might at all times have been in prosperity ". After her, I think (though Lockhart says before), came Washington Irving and David Wilkie. The American's picture is more charming than Wilkie's painting—Scott limping actively up the hill to bring him in, the family at breakfast, the dogs, the poet vindicating the nakedness of the heather hills and moors against Irving's expectation of trees : " When I have been for some time in the rich scenery of Edinburgh, which is like ornamented garden land, I begin to wish myself back again among my own honest gray hills ; and if I did not see the heather at least once a year *I think I should die,*" the daughters " bounding lightly like little fawns, and their dresses fluttering in the pure summer breeze . . . Sophia the eldest . . . the most lively and joyous,[1] having much of her father's varied spirit in conversation, and seeming to catch excitement from his words and looks . . . Anne was of a quieter mood, rather silent . . . being some years younger ", Walter " a well-grown stripling . . . Charles a lively boy ". It is the first clear glimpse of the family and the domestic scene since Scott's letters to his wife in 1807 while they were children sitting round the fire with Camp in Castle Street or lamenting the departure of summer at Ashestiel. The stream of life had flowed full and smooth for them even through the troubled events of 1813 and the years that followed, troubles that were not really quite over, nor were ever to be so. Till the final catastrophe Scott's wife and family were ignorant of the dangers that underlay the hospitable, but costly, life at Abbotsford, while the

---

[1] Wordsworth's remembrance of Sophia in 1814 is similar : " Never shall I forget her light figure, her bounding step, her bright eyes, her animated tones, when with a confiding simplicity that was quite enchanting she led my wife and my deceased sister (our fellow traveller) and myself round the precincts of Abbotsford then a small cottage, to every object in which, for antiquarian or other reasons, her father took an interest. This was in 1814 when her father was on his voyage to the Shetlands &c."—WORDSWORTH to LOCKHART, 1838. The " deceased sister " was his sister-in-law, Sara Hutchinson.

"delightful little vine-covered cottage" grew into the Conundrum Castle in grawacky which another American, Prescott, was to describe later.

The negotiations for the Second Series of *Tales of My Landlord* were concluded, as has been described earlier, by 21st November, although it was not in January, as Lockhart believed or would have us believe, but on 25th May that Scott was able to write to the Duke of Buccleuch, returning " the Discharged Bond which your Grace stood engaged in for me and on my account" (*Letters*, V, 153-8).[1] If Scott had died, as Cadell feared, it is not certain that the Duke's bond would have been cancelled at once, though Scott considered it as good as discharged in November 1817. That is, of course, if no MS. had been forthcoming. But, as the letter of 16th April shows, *The Heart of Midlothian* was taking some sort of shape in Scott's mind before *Rob Roy* was itself in final form. One can but wish that the correspondence with William Erskine had survived or other letters given us a clearer clue to the genesis of these, when all is said, wonderful works of creation—*The Antiquary, Old Mortality, Rob Roy, The Heart of Midlothian*, each a buoyant tide of narrative and rich in unforgettable characters. Mrs. Goldie's letter detailing the story of Helen Walker, which is now in the Library of Edinburgh University, was posted on 31st January, 1817. Many suggestions for stories or characters were sent to Scott by correspondents, from the indefatigable Joseph Train to Edward Copleston, Bishop of Llandaff, who in 1829 would have had Scott try his hand on " a Welsh subject even the very topic of Glendower ". Scott took little notice of these suggestions as a rule ; but one can see how the story of Helen Walker, by its dramatic quality, its date,[2] and the connec-

---

[1] Lockhart extracts from this long letter some of the opening sentences and dates them 7th January, 1818. Even from the part he prints there are omissions, but with nothing to indicate them.

[2] The child's body was found in the Cluden in October 1736, the trial of Isobel Walker was on 1st May, 1738. The date of the Porteous Riots was

tion with the Duke of Argyll, may have suggested the bringing together of these thrilling events—the Porteous Riots, the trial, the expedition to London, the appeal to Argyll and through Argyll to the Queen. So exciting were they and so apt to suggest just those characters which Scott was specially able to do justice to, plain country people, a survivor of the days of the Covenanters and Cameronians, the Edinburgh bourgeoisie, a great nobleman and a Queen who was also a woman of character and good sense and feeling, that by 30th January, 1819, Cadell reports to Constable that " the *new Tales of My Landlord* are at press ! ! ! and, what is more, a considerable portion of them". This seems to me absolutely incompatible with the statement by Andrew Lang (*The Heart of Midlothian*, Border Edition, Vol. I, p. ix) that the novel " was not actually taken in hand till shortly after January 15 ". If Cadell is gathering " tracts, pamphlets, etc. . . . about Captain Porteous's mob for the tale, The Heart of Midlothian ", this must have been to check, to correct, and to elaborate what was already in his mind or on paper, composed in the intervals, I would suggest, of waiting for the proofs of *Rob Roy*. The printing must have revealed, too, that the result of the fiery speed with which Scott had told the main story had left him short of the promised four volumes, which may explain why Cadell suggested " that three volumes now and three in autumn would very much increase the interest ", that is, *two* tales as in the First Series. But financial reasons, as Thomas Seccombe sug-

7th September 1736. The MS. of the novel is now in the National Library of Scotland, written in the usual way on the recto of one page with corrections and alterations on the verso of the preceding page. Some further corrections must have been made in proof, but certain errors in the first edition have survived in all its successors. In the motto to the second chapter, from Prior's *The Thief and the Cordelier*, every edition continues to read :

" There the squire of the poet and knight of the post "

where Scott and Prior had correctly :

" There the squire of the pad and the knight of the post."

gested,¹ for Abbotsford was now in process of passing from a cottage to a castle, made him unwilling to throw away on the bargain of November 1817 more than the four volumes promised, so that *The Heart of Midlothian* was extended to the required length by a " coda " which is a sad anti-climax.

The Heart of Midlothian, to the abundant criticism of which I need not add—there is in it no intimate link with Scott's own life—did not appear, as Lockhart affirms, in June, for on 15th July Constable tells William Godwin : " We shall publish 4 new vols. of Tales of My Landlord in a few days," and on the 21st advises a bookseller that " a supply of the New Tales of My Landlord for the London Trade were shipped on board the smack Caledonia which sailed from Leith on Friday 17th". On the 29th of that month the Ballantynes are informed that complaints of the paper on which the Tales of My Landlord, Second Series, were printed continue to such an extent that they must pause before settling Messrs. Cowan & Co., the printers', accounts. In the intervals between the arrival and dispatch of proofs, from January to June, Scott wrote various

[1] " In this book, perhaps his greatest, the fissure is first plainly seen in the mountain of Scott's fame. The artist in Scott was not dead but lulled to sleep when he proceeded to add five hundred pages of sheer padding to his noblest story. The contract was for four volumes—the material barely filled three. But Constable had to be placated. . . . Already Scott, artist, castellan of Abbotsford, was hag-ridden by the necessity of selling nothing as something, and to sweeten the bargain he gave of his best—but not too much. Cruel necessity ! Uncanny insight of Craigenputtock ! "—THOMAS SECCOMBE, *Scott Centenary Articles* (1932), pp, 66-7. " We rather suspect ", writes the reviewer in *Blackwood's Magazine*, August 1818, " that our good friend Mr. Constable wished a fourth volume in the way of trade that he might, with more show of justice, charge the exorbitant price of £1 12s. for a book which in former times would have been sold for *little more* than half that price. . . . We would humbly advise this author, if we may advise one so justly celebrated . . . to be less hasty in publishing ; it is tempting perhaps to take advantage of the public enthusiasm, as we may call it, about his works, not to suffer the ardour of its admiration to cool, or the beneficial consequences of its favour to cease ; but there is some danger of lessening that admiration, and of provoking the censure of the less liberal of among his readers." Whoever wrote the review, I suspect the hand of Blackwood himself in these comments on Scott's popularity and profits.

articles for *The Quarterly Review* and elsewhere—on Sharpe's edition of Kirkton's *Church History*, on Mrs. Shelley's *Frankenstein*, which he attributed to the poet, Walpole's *Letters*, the fourth canto of *Childe Harold*. The third canto he had reviewed (in the previous year) in a way that gave great pleasure to the noble author.[1]

It was in May of this year (1818) that at a dinner party Scott met for the first time his son-in-law to be, the handsome, enigmatical, satirical, very superior person (and, in some respects, genuinely superior), who was busy these same months writing a very superior, not to say snobbish, and sarcastic, picture of Edinburgh society, of Scottish character and education, of Edinburgh personalities, of scenes, real and imaginary, which appeared in 1819 as *Peter's Letters to His Kinsfolk*, a name suggested by the *Paul's Letters* of the man by whom he sat. From Glasgow, Oxford, and Glasgow again, Lockhart had come to Edinburgh in 1815, very conscious of his superior attainments

---

[1] In the autumn of this year someone attempted to do for Scott what Avellaneda had done for Cervantes and pass off on the public a new series of Tales of my Landlord containing *Pontefract Castle* in three volumes. It led to a heated quarrel between Fearman the publisher of the novel and the Ballantynes; but the only important and unfortunate result was that Constable broke once more with Longman & Co., his London agent, and adopted instead the recently established firm of Hurst, Robinson & Co. Longman had quarrelled with Constable so bitterly at an earlier period that he refused to take a share in *Marmion* in 1807. In a letter to Scott of that year Thomas Longman speaks of the " yet unexplained insults we have received from them ". They shared with Constable the first Waverleys up to *Rob Roy*. In the second series of the *Tales of my Landlord* they did not share owing to some misunderstanding, but their name appeared again on the Third Series along with that both of Constable and Co. and Hurst, Robinson and Co. While *Ivanhoe* was printing Constable wrote to Hurst, Robinson and Co. on the 30th of November expressing their surprise " to hear of the countenance given by Longman and Co. to the spurious Tales of my Landlord and I have just received the title page Ivanhoe. . . . We have struck out their firm which otherwise would have stood in the title-page " (*Constable's Letter-Book*). The new firm was not a very satisfactory one to deal with. Cadell complains of their failure to forward as agents books to London customers, and Robinson was a speculator on the stock-exchange. We shall hear of their share in the failure of 1826 and their subsequent conduct. Their attraction for Constable was probably their greater willingness to grant accommodation bills.

in Greek and justly contemptuous of the contempt for that subject, born of ignorance, which prevailed in Edinburgh, and of the disputative, combative aspect of Edinburgh culture due to the predominance of philosophical and legal studies. Scott had no contempt for Greek, but a regret that he had neglected such study of the language as Edinburgh University afforded the opportunity for. But Lockhart had read in other languages in which Scott had also browsed, French, Italian, Spanish, and German ; and it was on Germany (from a visit to which the young and briefless advocate had just returned), Goethe and Weimar, that their first conversation turned ; and on Byron, Burns and Dr. Carlyle, " the grandest demigod I [Scott] ever saw." " As for poets, I have seen, I believe, all the best of our own time and country—and, though Burns had the most glorious eyes imaginable, I never thought any of them would come up to an artist's notion of the character except Byron . . . the prints give one no impression of him —the lustre is there but it is not lighted up. Byron's countenance is a thing to dream of." Lockhart fully shared Scott's interest in Burns and Byron, while, at this time at any rate, he had a passion for Wordsworth that Scott never quite fully shared. The passages which, in *Peter's Letters*, Lockhart quotes from *The Excursion* are an interesting evidence of what that poem meant to many another than Jeffrey, and a reminder, now that its merit has been thrown into the shade by *The Prelude*, how much there is, in the later composed but earlier printed poem, of the essential Wordsworth.

A common love of poetry, a preference of literature and history to metaphysics and law, of anecdote and reminiscence in talk to endless discussion and argument, these were links between Scott and his new friend ; but Scott shared other of Lockhart's leanings, expressed in *Peter's Letters*. Though a patriotic, he was not the complacent, Scot in whose mind truth must take a back seat when things Scottish are criticised, and he did with Lockhart feel that some things were better done in England than here. Dr. Johnson's strictures, he contended to Croker later, though resenting them as evidence of bad manners, had done us good. The English Universities *did* produce a higher, if narrow, type of scholarship than ours could attain to, and gave to those who could afford them a more delightful academic life. For the class into which Scott was moving the English gentleman had become as much the ideal as the English tailor has become since for most European countries. Two of his idols, Pitt and Wellington, were of that class.

There were, however, aspects of Lockhart's manner and character of which Scott was critical. He was not as much at ease in society as he might have been (despite his criticisms of Edinburgh society), being, Lang says, both shy and a little deaf. He had not quite enough *style* for Lady Scott. But Scott's chief anxiety was regarding the vein of satire which, in company with John Wilson (" Christopher North "), Lockhart had begun to give free course to in *Blackwood's Magazine* in the form that monthly took at the end of 1817, a vein of satire in which there is more of sarcasm edged with a touch of snobbery, both social and intellectual. Compare the measure dealt out to poor Keats with that to Shelley and Byron, who, despite their sins or atheistical opinions, are " gentlemen ". Unfortunately for Scott's influence on Lockhart in this direction, he, too, was apt to be at his worst when drawn into political warfare. Even an indirect connection with *The Beacon* disqualified a man as a censor of the excesses of others.

His meeting with Scott in May of 1818 is made by Lockhart the occasion for a delightful digression on the life and manners of his subject in these years when Scott was at the height of his fame and seemingly of good fortune, though his health had received its first rude shock since childhood. We get, accordingly, a picture of Scott in his study in Castle Street with Maida lying beside him, and the cat,

Hinse of Hinsfelt, perched on the topmost step of the Library ladder but descending to take Maida's place if that noble animal left the room.[1] Scott's conversation is contrasted with the endless debates of Edinburgh lawyers —his old-world anecdotes, his *vivid painting*, his good sense, " a still more wonderful thing than his genius." We get a vivid glimpse of his life in Edinburgh, the Sunday dinners with his family and occasional friends—the Skenes of Rubislaw, the Macdonald Buchanans, Joseph Hume, " the well-beloved Erskine," Terry, James Ballantyne, George Thomson the clergyman and artist, Sir Alexander Boswell, Sir Alexander Don of Newton Don (" in all courteous and elegant accomplishments the model of a cavalier "), William Allan the painter. Music was forbidden on Sundays, but Scott read " aloud high poetry with far greater simplicity, depth, and effect, than any other man I ever heard "—Shakespeare, Dryden, Johnson's " Vanity of Human Wishes ", Wordsworth, Southey, Crabbe (" next to Shakespeare, the standing resource "), and Byron, the most potent voice of the hour. On other evenings, when there was no dinner engagement, Scott drove out " with some of his family, or a single friend " in one or other of the directions some of which are still delightful of a summer evening, though the tide of bungalows is rapidly overflowing them—Blackford Hill, Ravelston, Corstorphine, Portobello, by Holyrood, or the overshadowing Castle Rock. " No funeral hearse crept more leisurely

[1] " It was a very melancholy story the death of your two cats. We have a very nice one called Hinsie, the German for Pussy, he is in colour very dark and striped like a tiger, he is very good natured and in short has every perfection that a cat is capable of having. We have got a most delightful dog that Mr. Macdonnel of Glengarrie gave to Papa, it is much taller than any Newfoundland dog, he is between the Spanish wolf-dog and the old highland deer greyhound and with all his beauty and strength he is good-nature itself" (SOPHIA SCOTT to MRS. AGNES BAILLIE, Edinr., 20th May, 1816). " The large one was a stag-hound of the old Highland breed, and one of the handsomest dogs that could be found. He was a present from the Chief of Glengarry to Sir Walter, and was highly valued both on account of his beauty, his fidelity and the great rarity of the breed " (SCOTT to SIR ADAM FERGUSON, 7th March, 1827).

than did his landau up the Canongate or the Cowgate; and not a queer tottering gable but recalled to him some long-buried memory of splendour or bloodshed, which, by a few words, he set before the hearer in the reality of life."

In October of the same year (1818) Lockhart and Wilson visited Abbotsford where they found Scott with Lord Melville and Adam Ferguson, and we get a similar glimpse of Scott's life in the country—walks in the grounds, visits to Melrose and Dryburgh, dinner and dance in the evenings, talk on literary and other topics; and on later occasions, when Lockhart has become a member of the family, we hear of coursing and fishing and field sports and country games. That all the details in these vignettes are strictly accurate is not certain, but the truth of the picture as a whole is attested by the accounts of other visitors in Edinburgh and at Abbotsford. It is to these and Lockhart we must go for the picture of what is lost in the " dark backward and abysm of time ". I have just touched on it to emphasise what I have said of the different facets of Scott's life, each almost hidden from the other. There is this social life, so rich and leisurely and picturesque, Scott with his family and his friends and hosts of visitors, Scott at dinners and assemblies and Highland banquets in Edinburgh, or visiting at Mertoun House, the seat of his kinsman and head of his family, every Christmas, at Dalkeith and Bowhill homes of the Dukes of Buccleuch, at Drumlanrig and Rokeby. Withal there is Scott sitting in the Court of Session beneath the judges for a regulation number of hours every day, or taking his seat as Sheriff in the Court House at Selkirk.

These were the facets that all men might see, but another is that which was known only to himself, to Constable and Cadell and the Ballantynes. Of them, too, Lockhart, in the chapter referred to, gives pen pictures in which the ink is mixed with the gall of satire, and the whole darkened by being seen through the memory of the great disaster.

Letters written before that are in a more friendly tone, though it is doubtful if Lockhart ever loved them or they him. Of this aspect of Scott's life the Letter-Books of Constable, the Correspondence of Cadell with Constable, and the letters of Scott to the Ballantynes supply a more detailed picture than was given by Lockhart, or perhaps could be given. And despite Scott's illness, his recurrent attacks of cramp, there was no relaxation in the negotiations for fresh work. *The Heart of Midlothian* was out in July 1818, and in August Scott visited the Duke of Buccleuch at Drumlanrig and Morritt at Rokeby. But already there were bargains on foot for new Tales and the Ballantynes are negotiating for " slices " for themselves " poor fellows ", with hints of possible dealings with Murray : " I could wish that an arrangement, if it did not involve engagements, could be made before John Murray comes down, as I dread some tampering with him " (*Cadell to Constable, 15th June*). By September Scott is at Abbotsford and at work on *The Bride of Lammermoor* (*To James Ballantyne, 10th Sept.*, 1818, Letters, V, 186, and *To Constable*, 3rd Sept. : " The 3rd Series is announced," *Letters*, V, 181). But withal, and although a History of Scotland has been arranged for, as said above, and bills issued, in November a fresh bargain is concluded for New Travels on the Continent, the author to receive bills for £3,000 to be debited against Scott's final half profits on the whole. Of the other half share John is to get one-third, he apparently finding £1,000 of the £3,000 to be advanced.[1] Moreover, since 1817, negotiations were apparently going on (Scott to his mother, October 1817) for the purchase by Constable of all the copyrights of his works which were in Scott's hands. For these finally Constable paid by bonds £12,000 which, like other advance payments, melted away in the disaster.

[1] " I should have some sort of guarantee entitling me to set the £1,000 advanced by you for History and Travels against the £1070 granted by me for your accomodation."—To JOHN BALLANTYNE, 24th October, 1820.

The third facet of Scott's life is that vivid life of the imagination, which shines for us in the works, and that most genially and spontaneously in these early stories, " the Scotch Novels "—*Waverley, The Antiquary, Old Mortality, Rob Roy*, and those which were just about to follow when Lockhart first dined with Scott—*The Heart of Midlothian, The Bride of Lammermoor, A Legend of Montrose*. How were all these composed amid so many other tasks and distractions? —There were articles for *The Edinburgh* " this for the love of Jeffrey the Editor—the first time this ten years," for *Blackwood's Magazine*, " this for love of the cause I espoused," for *The Edinburgh Encyclopaedia* on " Drama ", " this for the sake of Mr Constable the publisher," for *The Quarterly Review*, " this for the love of myself . . . or which is the same thing for the love of £100 which I wanted for some odd purpose "—so he describes some of his activities to the Duke of Buccleuch to whom, in his final illness, he is writing long letters. In December he has to write more letters, occasioned by the death in India of his never seen brother-in-law, Charles Carpenter, whose will seemed to promise much ultimate advantage to his family; and withal there is a constant succession of visitors at Abbotsford. Lockhart has increased the difficulty of answering this question by speaking in a manner which suggests that the composition of one novel was begun only after its predecessor was finally off the author's hands. Several things suggest to me that the process was more complex, that Scott had more than one novel on hand at the same time. That the composition of the novels fitted into each other more closely than Lockhart suggests seems to me probable from the correspondence, even so far as we have it, of Scott with his publishers and of them with each other. *Guy Mannering* was on the stocks while proofs of *The Lord of the Isles* were passing between author and printer. *The Antiquary* was named and engaged for before *Guy Mannering* was out (24th Feb., 1815), and promised for June 1815, though not actually published till May 1816. But in the

April before this May James has made his offer to Blackwood " of a work in fiction of four volumes &c." (p. 130) of which he has read a considerable portion and knew the plan of the whole, though it was August before Blackwood received the manuscript of *The Black Dwarf*—December (1816) before that and *Old Mortality* were out. The mysterious History of Scotland and *Rob Roy* [1] seem to have divided Scott's attention for some time, but by May *Rob Roy* has it and becomes the chief occupation of the year; yet by September negotiations are begun for what became *The Heart of Midlothian*, and by 30th January, when *Rob Roy* is just out (31st Dec., 1817), Cadell reports to Constable that " the new Tales of My Landlord are at Press ! ! ! and what is more a considerable portion of them ". And, if I may run on with this subject, as it will save some repetitions and present this problem of the how and when of composition in the clearest light, *The Heart of Midlothian* was not out in July 1818 before negotiations were on hand for two more Tales of My Landlord. By September Scott is at work on *The Bride of Lammermoor*, supplying James with copy and receiving proofs (*To James Ballantyne*, 10th Sept., 1818, *Letters*, V, 180). Illness and other engagements referred to in letters to the Duke of Buccleuch (p. 172) interrupt work, but in January he intends " to do great things this summer as the pain in my breast seems quite gone ". But in March 1819 comes a violent recurrence, and Lockhart's *Life* tells of the agonies amid which were dictated " the far greater portion of *The Bride*, the whole of *A Legend of Montrose*, and almost the whole of *Ivanhoe* ".

But there are difficulties of a very puzzling kind in accepting this statement of Lockhart. The autograph of the *Bride*, in Scott's own hand, is now in the Library of the Writers to the Signet and contains all but a small part of

[1] " It will not interrupt the history."—To JOHN BALLANTYNE, April 1817 (*Letters*, I, 514).

the end of the story.¹ But some sheets must have been torn away, for on the verso of the last extant page are corrections of what had been on the recto of the next page, so that it is possible the whole had at one time existed in his own hand. George Huntly Gordon, who was Scott's secretary this year, in a letter of 1855 denies that *A Legend of Montrose* was dictated, saying that he himself transcribed it from Scott's autograph. Of this autograph a portion is now in the University of Edinburgh in a form that also indicates that portions have been torn away, indeed one of the fragments torn away is in the National Library. While Laidlaw, in whom I have entire confidence, confirms Lockhart's account, though disclaiming the dramatic exclamations which the latter attributes to him, he refers only to *Ivanhoe* (*Carruthers's Notanda* appended to the 1871 edition of Robert Chambers's *Life of Scott*). Of that novel portions in Scott's own hand are now in the Pierpont Morgan Library, New York, all written on paper manufactured in 1817. A note appended, by whom I do not know, says: "The greater part dictated, this fragment is all or nearly all which he wrote himself."

The *Bride of Lammermoor* and the *Legend of Montrose* were issued in June 1819. The two novels which followed seem to have run a somewhat neck to neck race, Scott being apparently still pressed for immediate means of meeting expenses. His first thought was a novel on the time of the Reformation in Scotland, and he began *The Monastery*. "I am very glad," he writes to Lady Louisa Stuart on the 23rd of August, 1819, "that your Ladyship found the tales in some degree worth your notice. It cost me a terrible effort to finish them for between distress of mind and body I was very unfit for literary composition.

---

¹ If, as James Ballantyne states, Scott, "when it was first put into his hands in a complete shape, did not recollect one single incident, character, or conversation it contained," it is quite possible that he forgot the circumstances in which he composed it. Otherwise it must be that the dictation was only of the few last chapters. The MS. contains 399 pages of the 500 but there was at least one more page in the MS. now lost.

But in justice to my booksellers I was obliged to dictate while I was scarce able to speak for pain. With better hope I am trying an antiquarian story, I mean one relating to old English times, which is a great amusement to me. I have laid aside a half-finished story on the dissolution of the Monasteries." In support of this last sentence, and leaving the question or mystery of dictation as I have described it, is the fact that the first three chapters and a part of the fourth of *The Monastery* are written on paper with the watermark 1816, the rest on paper bearing the water mark 1817, the same as on the paper used for *Ivanhoe*. *Ivanhoe* is first mentioned, unless it be *The Monastery* that is intended, on 4th July, 1819: " I heartily wish you joy of the success of Jedidiah," so he writes to Constable, " I think I can promise its successor will be as popular. I am thank God able to work and pleased with my labour. I have written to Mr. James Ballantyne whom please to inform when you see him that I wish the present work to be communicated to no person whatsoever out of the office. I wish the world to have an opportunity to debate whether it be by the same author or not." Thereafter *Ivanhoe* is the theme of his letters to the Ballantynes throughout July and August, for Scott is desperately anxious to have it out by September and is sending on MS. just as ready. But there is delay in supplying the paper; and accordingly, in order to increase the amount of promised work on which he may draw bills, Scott writes to John on the 2nd of August that he is to negotiate for " a new novel of the right cast—3 vols.—the subject is quite ready and very interesting; ... I think the first edition should be at least 600—the form that of Ivanhoe and the paper might be got ready against September. Ivanhoe will be out of my hand in four weeks." Longman and Co., it is hoped, will take it and grant bills. The History is to come on after it. By the 19th the novel is called *The Monastery* and " on this Monastery when out I receive (besides £1500 print and paper) £3500—total

£5000 in Longman's beautiful and dutiful bills." " I have finished the second volume Ivanhoe and am determined to let it rest since the paper is not come and take to the other to save time." Longman and Co. appear on the title page of the novel as the first or managing publisher with Archibald Constable and Co. and John Ballantyne, Bookseller to the King, Edinburgh.[1]

How are we to explain these somewhat puzzling facts? One hypothesis, recently mooted, is to push the composition of the novels back into years even preceding *Waverley*. But if this is to be done on the evidence of rapid and overlapping preparation for the press, one must not pick and choose. There is as good evidence for thus assigning *The Antiquary*, *A Legend* and others to this early period as for *The Monastery* or any other. Moreover, though Scott does not tell us much about his composition, and his correspondence with Erskine is lost, we do gather from the extant letters hints of the work he is doing, the sources he is consulting while busy with each of them, and there are long intervals between promised and actual dates for being ready.

My own conjecture is, that the early hours of the morning were given to the " exciting and exhausting form of composition ", as he calls fiction to Cadell—those quiet hours when the house is still asleep and the imagination can range at will, developing and shaping what has passed through his mind as he sauntered with Tom Purdie or

[1] That *The Monastery* is the novel mentioned to Constable on 4th July is suggested by what Scott says about bringing it out under a new *nom-de-plume*, for in October Fearman, the publisher of *Pontefract Castle*, the fraudulent Tale of my Landlord, declares in the Preface : " In addition to the romance called *Ivanhoe* which we last week announced as about to emanate from the pen of the author of *Waverley*, we can assure our readers that the same writer has another work in the Press, entitled *The Monastery*, which is speedily to make its appearance in London. It is supposed that it will be the foundation of a new series of novels which are to be brought forward as the production of some other writer. The Deception will however be soon seen through." If Scott contemplated a new series with the *Monastery* and *Abbot*, this letting out of the project by someone would be fatal to the intention.

another unexciting companion. Letters and occasional articles could be easily taken in hand after breakfast when the post had come and the household was astir. A few chapters of a novel once written, they were bundled off to James Ballantyne for perusal, criticism (perhaps by Erskine also), transcription, and setting up. Such a process would involve pauses, and Scott, who loved to have many jobs on hand at the same time, had hours in which he could turn aside to dream of and plan what would follow this, even writing chapters which Gordon could be set to transcribe till Ballantyne's presses were clear of its predecessor. He did not need to sit down and read up for the purpose (though he did consult books), nor to hire a "devil" to prepare the bricks. For the prolegomena to Scott's novels was his wide reading when a young man, his tenacious memory, his inborn and cultivated gift as a story-teller who had beguiled and delighted his companions in the High School, on the slopes of Arthur's Seat, in Mr. Lancelot Whale's School at Kelso: "Come, slink over beside me, Jamie, and I'll tell you a story." To these early gifts and acquirements experience had brought a knowledge of human nature, if not subtle and profound yet wide and just and sympathetic, more akin in its range and limitations to the genius of Cervantes than of Shakespeare, and the command of a style, careless perhaps and occasionally marred by the traditional melodramatic pomposities of the fiction in vogue, but natural, buoyant, flowing, and at times rising to heights of simple eloquence, and, finally, consummate in Scots dialogue. One need only compare the dialogue of Scott's peasants and shop-keepers with those of Thomas Hardy to realise where the less philosophic but more genial story-teller has the advantage.

My digressions on Lockhart and the question of the composition of the novels has carried me a little ahead, and I must briefly resume events since the meeting with his son-in-law. When that year (1818) closed Scott had actually published, or in the press, or clearly in his mind, all the great " Scotch Novels ", as they were called. He had received the offer of a baronetcy, negotiated the sale of his copyrights, learned of the death of Charles Carpenter with the prospect it brought of securing his children's future and " permitting me to do something for my poor brother Tom's family besides pleasing myself in plantings and policies of biggings with a safe conscience ". In November he concluded through John Ballantyne a bargain with Constable for a set of New Travels on the Continent which, however, was never written, no further visit being made to the Continent till 1831.

CHAPTER IX

> "We shall have to call a halt some day, but we shall ride as long as we can."
>
> SCOTT *to* CADELL, 1823.

WHEN the year 1819 opened Scott was in good spirits, despite occasional attacks of cramp, and hopeful of doing much work. But in March came the culminating attack of the old enemy complicated by jaundice which I have referred to in connection with *The Bride of Lammermoor* and *A Legend of Montrose*. "I am but just on my feet", he writes to Lockhart on 23rd March, "after a fourth very severe spasmodic affection which held me from half past six last night to half past three this morning in a state little short of the extreme agony during which time to the infinite consternation of my terrified family I *waltzed* with Madam Cramp to my own sad music

>   I sighd and howld
>   And groand and growld
>   A wild and wondrous sound

incapable of lying in one posture yet unable to find any possible means of changing it. I thought of you amid all this agony and of the great game which with your parts and principles lies before you in Scotland and having been for very many years the only man of letters who at least stood by if he could not support the banner of ancient faith and loyalty I was mentally bequeathing to you my batton like old Douglas

>   Take *thou* the vanguard of the three
>   And bury me by the braken bush
>   That grows upon yon lily lea."
>
> (*Letters,* V, 321-3).

So far had friendship between the two men developed on the basis of an ardent, in Scott romantic, Toryism. He might not approve of everything in *Blackwood's Magazine*, but he was heart and soul with the young men in their political warfare. " Such principles and such talents must at once attone for errors or extravagancies and command respect where it will not be readily yielded." But this letter and those of the same date to Constable, to Joanna Baillie, and to others reveal how acute were Scott's sufferings and how possible it seemed to him that they might mean the end ; and the illness did bring, as a consequence, effects that were never shaken off. " With its disappearance," Skene wrote in a letter to Lockhart, " although restored to comparative health disappeared also much of his former vigour of body . . . while in personal appearance he seemed too in that short space to have advanced twenty years on the downward course of his life ; his hair became bleached and scanty ; the fire of his eye was much subdued, and his step more uncertain had lost the vigorous swinging gait with which he used formerly to proceed. . . . It was only after this period that I ever perceived that degree of abstraction which he sometimes exhibited when his thoughts had been deeply occupied."

It cannot, I think, be said that the novels which passed the press in this year of suffering show any evident mark of the circumstance in which they were at any rate completed. Lord Tweedsmuir has not unnaturally found in the first and most tragic of Scott's novels " the one novel written during the broken years which is overcast by their shadow. It was not the work of the ordinary Scott, but of a ' fey ' man, living in a remote world of pain. . . . It was the product of a drugged and abnormal condition ". But, as we have seen, Scott was at work on *The Bride* six months before his attacks became acute, indeed while he is able to pay visits to the Duke of Buccleuch at Drumlanrig, to Morritt at Rokeby (breakfasting on the way with the princely Bishop of Durham), to Lord Melville at Melville

Castle, and while at Abbotsford he entertains "visitors chiefly travellers who come to see Melrose". He knows already that the story is "a dismal one" (*To James Ballantyne*, 10*th Sept.*, 1818) which will not bear great elaboration. "Query, if I shall make it so effective in two volumes as my mother does in her quarter of an hour's crack by the fireside?" In fact, if there is a fault in *The Bride of Lammermoor* it is that there is a little too much of an effort to relieve the tragic effect by the humours of Caleb Balderston. These are a little overdone. More interesting is the fact that with these two novels ends, so it seems to me, the genial flow of Scott's creative imagination at work in his own proper field, Scottish history that is not purely history because the spirit which moved in it was not entirely dead for Scott and for many others, whether they looked at it from the same angle as he did or not—the civil war, Montrose and Argyll, the Covenanters, Whig and Tory, Jacobite rebellions, Napoleon's invasion, old family feuds, and the Scottish law courts. Only in *Redgauntlet* was he to recover the genial and convincing naturalness with which he moves among events and characters as real to him as those with whom he lived from day to day—and more interesting.

For in *Ivanhoe*, which followed so closely on the heels of the Second Series, Scott took his first step into the region of history reconstructed from books, in the direction in which his farthest flight into the backward abysm of time was to be the unfortunate *Count Robert of Paris*, and of which the most classical example after Scott is Flaubert's *Salammbo*. The story, as a *Blackwood* reviewer pointed out immediately, "requires to be read with a quite new and much greater effort of imagination," the manners being "unlike anything either the author or the reader of the present times could have had any opportunity of knowing by personal observation". And the result of such effort is twofold. If the reader has made some study of the period, he is more acutely conscious of the errors and anachronisms which Scott so gaily allows himself to make; and, on the other hand, the more completely the novelist succeeds in satisfying the scholar the more remote and artificial the whole picture of life and character becomes. We cannot understand Flaubert's Carthaginians or the fanatical Spaniards of Señor Enrique Larreta.[1]

The popularity of *Ivanhoe*—the first edition was sold out in a week—proves that Scott had not attempted too much, had written what is mainly a good story of adventure for boys. There are not many battle-scenes more thrilling than the siege of Torquilstone Castle as described to the wounded hero by Rebecca. But the greatest success of the book is Rebecca herself, Scott's finest creation of a woman, not only of high principles and steadfast character, like Jeanie Deans, but also refined, cultured, and beautiful. Compared with her the heroines of Scott's love tales are all somewhat insipid, even Diana Vernon is rather a young lover's dream ; nor is the impression produced by Rebecca marred by a conventional happy ending : " a glance on the great picture of life will show, that the duties of self-denial, and the sacrifice of passion to principle, are seldom thus remunerated ; and that the internal consciousness of their high-minded discharge of duty, produces on their own reflections a more adequate recompense, in the form of that peace which the world cannot give or take away." So Scott wrote in the Introduction of 1830. One wishes he had oftener made the conflict in the hero's breast a more real one and, in its effects, more decisive of his fate.

The year 1819 constitutes in more ways than one another era in Scott's life—a definite failure of health, the

---

[1] *The Glory of Don Ramiro, A Life in the Times of Philip II*, by Enrique Larreta, translated from the Spanish by L. B. Walton (J. M. Dent and Sons, London, 1924). The author is or was Colombian Minister at Paris. He writes, as I think Scott never did, from the point of view of one sharing the passions and prejudices of the period, so much so that the sin of which the hero most repents is that he once spared the lives of some Jews. Scott gives to his characters such passions and prejudices but is always ready to stand back and view the actions from the more tolerant and enlightened point of view of his own day.

change of title, the dispersion of his family—and finally in his work as poet and novelist, for the publication of *Ivanhoe* in the end of 1819 marked, as Cadell informed Lockhart, the peak of Scott's popularity as a novelist, at least as measured by the immediate demand for copies by the London booksellers and by the general tone of the reviewers in most of the London periodicals. One cannot but think that the wise course, both for his health and his work, would have been either the contemplated visit to the Continent, on which money had already been advanced by Constable and John Ballantyne, or the History of Scotland as a lighter task at home. But genius and prudence seldom go together, and the engagements into which Scott had entered apparently made any prolonged halt in production impossible. " The Monastery followed—it was composed with great rapidity," Cadell reported to Lockhart, " Mr Scott still depended on the appearance of each new novel for the bills it was to produce." Nothing was allowed to interrupt this labour and the anticipation of profit. " December 1819 saw the completion of *Ivanhoe*—March 20 of the *Monastery*, the *Abbot* in September and *Kenilworth* in the January following " (*Cadell*). And all this was done while the stream of social and family life flowed in increasing breadth and fulness.

His letters in December 1819 are full of the successive deaths of his uncle, Professor Rutherford, his aunt Anne Rutherford, and finally their sister, Scott's own mother, all within a few days and the death of each unknown to the other. Walter's entry on his military career with the 18th Hussars in Cork is the occasion for fresh outlays in " rattletraps ", chargers and allowance ; and also for many long letters of news and advice, the latter given with full paternal authority. But Scott himself is not sure that his own military days are over, and so Walter will return his father's old sabre " cleaned and oiled ", for the " radical scoundrels " are threatening a revolution, and volunteers are to be raised and " the peasantry are clamorous to have me as a leader" (28*th Dec.*, 1819). Long letters to Lords Melville and Montagu in December and January 1820 deal with this scare. Marriages follow deaths, and on 17th January Walter is informed that " Mr. Lockhart has made his formal visits to Mama ", who " would have liked a little more *stile* but she has no sort of objections ". The marriage followed on 29th April, and Sophia becomes Mrs. Lockhart :

> Ah me ! the flower and blossom of my house
> The wind has blown away to other towers.

But, meantime, the old King has died in February, and Scott has joined in proclaiming the Regent as King, and in the end of March he has visited London to be gazetted as a Baronet and kiss hands. Even amid endless social engagements (" if I had three heads like Cerberus I could eat three dinners with them every day and am fairly to be smothered with kindness "), letters to Lockhart about Wilson as a candidate for the Moral Philosophy Chair and about articles for *The Quarterly Review*, he is still attempting literary work in such intervals of time as he can find, and the novel on hand is *The Abbot*, though its predecessor is not yet out (*to Constable, 7th March and 5th April*, 1820), and in London he discovers a number of original Swift letters to enrich a second edition of *The Life and Works of Swift*. While in London he began sitting to Lawrence for a painting and to Chantrey for a bust.[1] The ready money needed for all these things is met by bills from Constable and the Ballantynes on the works that are in process of becoming. The marriage is the chief event on his return, and Lockhart and Sophia are to be settled at Chiefswood when not

---

[1] " That bust which alone preserves for posterity the cast of expression most fondly remembered by all who ever mingled in his domestic circle."
—LOCKHART.

" Excepting the first portrait Lawrence painted of West, and the one he painted of the Duke of Wellington for Sir Robert Peel, all the portraits I have seen by his hand are far surpassed by Chantrey's busts, whenever the same people sat to both."—C. R. LESLIE.

in Edinburgh : " We will be within two miles of each other." " Lockhart is very much what you will like when you come to know him—much genius and a distinguished scholar very handsome in face and person and only wanting something of the usage du monde. I mean there is a little want of ease in his manners in society. He does not laugh as thou doest Anthony—this is however speaking critically for he is neither conceited nor negligent in his manner. His powers of personal satire are what I most dread on his own account—it is an odious accomplishment and most dangerous and I trust I have prevaild on him to turn his mind to something better " (*To Morritt, Letters*, VI, 226). Scott's hope in that direction was not to be fulfilled. Meantime, Lockhart and Scott were putting their full weight into making John Wilson, " Christopher North ", of all things a Professor of Moral Philosophy. His opponent was Hamilton, but of *his* qualifications little was known then beyond the circle of his friends, and the election was a purely political fight between arrogant Tories and complacent Whigs : " It is odd the rage these gentlemen have for superintending education. They consider it as their own province and set their mark on it as Sancho did on the cowheel—then their geese are all swans and the tory swans are all geese and they puff the one and slander the other without mood or mercy " (*To Morritt, July* 1820). And Wilson proved no bad appointment. " His students ", says Sir Alexander Grant, " could forgive in him a thousand irregularities ; they forgave him for not teaching them Moral Philosophy at all ; they drank in his discursive utterances and adored him as a man. . . . It seems impossible to find one of Wilson's students who, on looking back to his lectures from the serene elevation of after life, does not acknowledge that they were beneficial to his mind. . . . Strictly speaking he was out of place in a Chair of Philosophy, but he did a great deal of good in it, and the only harm he did was perhaps to encourage in the future preachers and writers of Scotland a too exuberant style of language " ;[1] and he was a friend to his students as not many Professors have been, reading their essays himself and " his house constantly open to them in unreserved hospitality . . ." Such a Professor was worth many moral philosophers in the eyes of Scott, and of not a few of us. Scott's letter to Lockhart after the appointment is an admirable piece of warning alike to Wilson and to Lockhart himself. " His best triumph, and that of his friends, will be in the concentration of his powerful mind upon the great and important task before him, and in utterly contemning the paltry malice of those who have taken such foul means of opposing him." If Wilson retires, as he should, from his share in the satiric lampoons of *Blackwood's*, " in that case I really hope you will pause before you undertake to be the Boaz of the *Maga* ; I mean in the personal and satirical department, when the Jachin has seceded " (*July* 1820).

Lockhart records two visits to Abbotsford in this year, one week-end (as we should call it now) in February when, with Constable, and John Ballantyne " looking pallid and emaciated as a ghost ", and Tom Purdie, the cottage was visited which was to become Chiefswood. In the August following the election of Wilson, Lockhart and his wife were visitors at Abbotsford for several weeks, and Lockhart takes the opportunity for a fuller picture of Scott's life and hospitality at Abbotsford when at the height of his reputation and of his good fortune to all appearance, entertaining " all sorts and conditions of men " who had any claim on him whether from admiration of his work or from early acquaintance or a Scottish tie of blood. If in the seventeenth century the two men that every important

---

[1] " Wilson's eloquence was of a very brilliant kind, but his speeches sounded better at the time than they appeared on reflection."—SIR ARCHIBALD ALLISON, *Autobiography*, I, 195. For an amusing account of Wilson and the sources of his lectures see *Christopher North* (*John Wilson*) by Elsie Swann, Edinburgh, 1934.

visitor to England wished to meet were Cromwell Protector and John Milton, in the period of the twenties and thirties of the nineteenth century they were the Duke of Wellington and Sir Walter Scott. On the occasion of Lockhart's visit the guests included Sir Humphry Davy, Dr. Wollaston, Henry Mackenzie, William Stewart Rose, and we are given a delightful picture of the setting out on " a clear, bright September morning, with a sharpness in the air that doubled the animating influence of the sunshine " for a coursing expedition when Scott's pet, " a little black pig," interrupted the start by frisking round his pony and having to be led off with a strap round his neck while Scott repeated :

> What will I do gin my hoggie die ?
> My joy, my pride, my hoggie !
> My only beast, I had nae mae,
> And wow ! but I was vogie !

Salmon fishing was interlarded with coursing, and on 28th October took place the great Abbotsford hunt at which neighbours and tenants joined with family and guests, and all was followed by an elaborate dinner at Abbotsford. It was to be able to live his life on this scale of generous hospitality—" generous " is a far fairer word than Macaulay's " ostentatious ", for Scott's pomp burdened nobody, the general tenor of his life was simple enough—that Scott toiled so arduously in the morning hours ; and because he had come late into anything approaching to affluence that he was fain to anticipate the gains which were flowing in. He was thirty-five before *The Lay* and *Marmion* opened the door to fame ; he was forty-four by the time that, escaping from the peril threatened by his rash experiment in publishing, he found himself, after *Waverley*, able to ask and receive whatever prices he chose, and with an income of apparently £10,000 a year and upward. Why should he not spend it in the manner he chose ? And that manner included a lavish hospitality and a

> tear for pity, and a hand
> Open as day for melting charity.

"Nullum numen abest, si sit prudentia" was a motto he often quoted from Juvenal. But genius and prudence go not easily together. His prudence Scott kept for his advice to others and for the conduct of his stories in which he would not allow passion, prejudices, or imagination to run away with him. The spirit in which he lived was closer to that of another favourtie motto :

> Sound, sound the clarion, fill the fife !
> To all the sensual world proclaim,
> One crowded hour of glorious life
> Is worth an age without a name,

using " glorious " as Burns does :

> Kings may be blest, but Tam was glorious,
> O'er a' the ills o' life victorious.

How the money was brought in is hinted clearly by a letter of this same August to James Ballantyne (*Letters*, VI, 250) in which, after telling how he can meet certain bills which are falling due by others which he holds from Constable and John, he continues : "*It is my duty* to tell you that if you do not get to town & finish the book instead of the proofs going through the country in this way we will be in a scrape. . . . I have no doubt you will reply that the matters at P. O. go on even the better for your little jaunt. But that is like the servant in the Clandestine marriage who always shut her eyes when she wanted to keep awake." A letter of four days later to John shows that £2500 had been drawn on the " proceeds of the Abbot ", which was to be out the following month ; and in letters to Constable of 20th August and 10th September we see him hard at work on *Kenilworth* : " The Progresses are doing me yeoman's service, for I am in *progress* myself. . . . What was the name of Dudley Earl of Leicester's first wife, whom he was supposed to have murdered at Cumnor Hall in Berkshire ? ... In Lyson's *Magna Britannia*, or some such work, there is something about this same Cumnor Hall. I wish you would have it copied out for me, and should like indeed to know anything that occurs to you about the village of Cumnor, its situatuon, etc. I like to be as minutely local as I can." Just so he worked when composing *Rokeby* in the critical year of 1812. Clearly *Kenilworth* was *not* among the novels composed before 1814 and just awaiting transcription.

Before I touch on these novels and others that followed in hot haste, driven forward by the ever-pressing demand for money to meet maturing bills and fresh outlay on Abbotsford without and·within, let me briefly sketch the family and social life of the years to 1823 when the financial question threatened again to become critical. To tell the truth, when a man's life is most prosperous in a worldly way it is apt to be the least interesting to read about. Scott was on the top of the wave of social distinction and success, extending and decorating Abbotsford to become the scene of magnificence which was to dazzle Prescott. His family were leaving home, Walter in the army; Charles studying with the Rev. John Williams, Lampeter, afterwards Rector of Edinburgh Academy, in the opening of which Scott took a leading part in 1824; Sophia is married but still near at hand. Anne is at home with her mother. For another Walter, Tom's son, Scott secures the promise of a Cadetship in the East India Company's service and he comes from Canada (1821-2) to train at Addiscombe, and will pay vacation visits at Abbotsford. In January 1821 Mrs. Charles Carpenter, the widow of Lady Scott's brother, returns to England, and after some delay on account of Sophia's health, the cramp with which he had been himself familiar, Scott arrives in London on 15th February to see if arrangements can be made for her coming to Scotland and finds from her lawyers that his children's expectations are not so great as early reports and a sanguine disposition had suggested. But in London he finds more troublesome business on his hands than Mrs. Carpenter's health and her husband's will. For Lockhart had been up in January to challenge John Scott, provoked by attacks on Lockhart's part in *Blackwood's Magazine* made by Scott in *Baldwin's London Magazine*. Lockhart had refused to comply with John Scott's preliminary demand that he should give an express denial of his being the editor of *Blackwood*, and Lockhart had left London (23*rd January*) after denouncing Scott, on Croker's advice, as a liar and a scoundrel, but at the same time issuing a public statement of his complete independence as a contributor to, not an editor of, *Blackwood*, which statement, however, was not in the copy sent to Scott. The result was a duel between Scott and J. H. Christie in which the former was wounded and subsequently died. Sir Walter is not seen at quite his best when denouncing John Scott as a coward, but Lockhart was his son-in-law and Scott was never impartial where his friends were involved. But Sir Walter knew well that the source of the tragedy was not this or that misunderstanding or punctilio or shuffle at the last, but the kind of personal satire in which *Blackwood's Magazine* dealt and to which Lockhart lent the edge of his sarcasm : " You have now the best possible opportunity to break off with the Magazine, which will otherwise remain a snare and temptation to your love of satire and I must needs say that you will not have public feeling nor the regard of your friends with you should you be speedily the heroe of such another scene. Forgive me pressing this. Christie and I talked over the matter anxiously : it is his opinion as well as mine and if either has weight with you you will not dally with this mother of mischief any more. . . . Blackwood has plenty of people to carry on his Magazine, but if it should drop I cannot think it fair to put the peace of a family and the life not only of yourself but of others in balance with any consideration connected with it" (24*th Feb.*, 1821, *Letters*, VI, 363-4). "The peace of a family," for Sophia's first child had been born while John Scott's life was still hanging in the balance (14*th Feb.*), the little delicate grandson who was to be Scott's last great joy and sorrow. In Sophia's occasional letters to her husband when absent in the next two years we get glimpses of that inner family life which was the focus of Scott's affections : " Our little darling is quite well and never was any child so happy or so good. I wish you saw the Unknown saving his egg for him in the morning and playing with him. . . . I am writing with the great Unknown fast asleep on the next chair and snoring most musically." " You may expect to see me with a face like a full moon if eating and sleeping have there [*sic*] usual effect. Mamma absolutely crams me every two hours and the great Unknown sits every evening with his watch *upon the table* for fear by some mistake supper should be delayed beyond half-past nine and the whole family not retired to there [*sic*] rooms by ten. Mamma & Papa are quite delighted with our darling boy." To his own sons Scott writes abundantly during these years, letters full of practical, one cannot say unworldly, advice, letters affectionate but authoritative. They must write home more regularly. Charles is to attend closely to his classical studies and should pick up a little Welsh—Scott is lending to Charles some of his own taste and enterprise. " Sport is a good thing both for health and pastime but you must never allow it to interfere with serious study " (*Letters*, VII, 31). He is glad Charles is " reading Tacitus with some relish. His stile is rather quaint and enigmatical which makes it difficult to the student but then his pages are filld with such admirable apothegms and maxims of political wisdom as infer the deepest knowlege of human nature and it is particularly necessary that any one who may have views as a public speaker should be master of his works as there is neither ancient or modern who affords such a selection of admirable quotations &c." (*Letters*,

VII, 157-8). " The grammar of the learnd languages is the key to every other and when you are possessd of it you have the *Open Sesamum* to all the philological studies which you can desire to know " (*Letters*, VII, 350). Walter as an officer is already in the world and gets more news, public and concerning fresh purchases of land and additions to the house. He is advised concerning his duties as an officer, his studies, his social duties, the need for economy—the more necessary as his father is taking over the education of young Walter from Canada, and Mrs. Carpenter's marriage settlements have reduced the expectations of Scott's family : " I had yesterday the great pleasure of a letter from Sir Thomas Brisbane giving a very good account of your conduct both as an officer and gentleman of which Colonel Murray has reported very favourably to him. Nothing my dear boy which earth has to give me can afford me so much pleasure as to know that you are doing your duty like a man of sense and honour and qualifying yourself to serve your King and Country and do credit to the name you bear " (*Letters*, VI, 213-4). " I am glad you have seen Lady Curran as she wd be civil to you for Lady Abercorn's sake. It is always right to keep the best company you can and evening parties keep young men from sitting late at the mess and other less innocent modes of spending leisure " (*Letters*, VI, 275). But early in 1821 Sir David Baird, coming over to Ireland as Commander in Chief, Walter's regiment is in disgrace because of democratical opinions and gross irregularities in the mess. Scott is righteously indignant and will not listen to Walter's defences : " Men do not become blackguards from one evenings excess in conviviality and the young man who thought of such a brutality as introducing a common prostitute into a regimental mess sitting in their own mess-room although he might have been drunk at the time must I should think have had no gentlemanlike feelings when sober nor can I say much for those who did not turn him & her out of doors as fittest companions for each other. . . . Besides what sort of defence is this of intemperence which you have twice to resort to in order to cover the peccadilloes of your corps?" (*Letters*, VI, 437-8). "A democrat in any situation is but a silly sort of fellow but a democratical soldier is worse than an ordinary traitor by ten thousand degrees as he forfeits his military honour and is faithless to the Master whose bread he eats. . . . If a man of honour is unhappy enough to entertain opinions inconsistent with the service in which he finds himself it is his duty at once to resign his commission and in acting otherwise he dishonours himself for ever" (*Letters*, VI, 426). The regiment was ordered to India and Walter was anxious to go, but Scott will not hear of it. "The ass", he writes to Sophia in his mood of irritation, " wishes to go himself and talks of being absent for five or six years when I will be bound not one of them sees British land again till their beards are grey" (*Letters*, VI, 431). Scott will arrange for his exchange or admission to Sandhurst, and meantime he is shipped off on half pay to Germany for languages and travel.

The public events in which Scott bore his part during these years need little beyond a mention. Sophia's marriage in the end of April 1820 was followed in May by a visit from Prince Gustavus Vasa, the displaced Prince Royal of Sweden, Count Itterburg as he called himself. " When he took leave of me he presented me with a beautiful seal with all our new blazonries cut on a fine amethyst and what I thought the prettiest part on one side of the setting is cut my name on the other the prince's—Gustaf" (*Letters*, VI, 195). More land was bought " adjoining to the Burnfoot cottage so that we now march with the Duke of Buccleuch all the way round that corner ". Among later visitors to Abbotsford came Lord Ashley, the subsequent philanthropic Earl of Shaftesbury, whom he sent on with an introduction to Hector Macdonald Buchanan, his old friend at Ross Priory. " Walter Scott ",

Shaftesbury wrote later, " has contrived to throw an indescribable charm over the whole region. . . . But it is all melancholy to me ; I knew and loved the master mind which is now dead and gone ; and I cannot divest myself here in Scotland of the recollection of him " (*August* 1839). But Morritt came also and William Stewart Rose and Sir Humphry Davy, " who spent some time with us and very merry it was " ; and in November came Joanna Baillie, who writes returning thanks for " daily and hourly kindness shewn us at Abbotsford ".

Throughout 1820 John Ballantyne's health had been failing. His Journal of these years is a record of the oscillations in his health and of recurrent resolutions and relapses : " A friend of mine saw you at the Derby run in very unsuitable weather and to this I have no doubt you owe the cold and inflammation mention'd in Dr. Baillie's opinion. Now really a man who leaves his native country under the impression that a change of atmosphere is nearly absolutely necessary for his malady is scarce likely to find health upon a crowded racecourse and on a very rainy day " (*Scott to John*, 18*th Jan.*, 1820, *Letters*, VI, 210-1). At the end of 1820 John gave up business as auctioneer, " this most disgusting and degrading business." He had planned earlier to retire to Kelso much against Scott's will who still regarded him as a valuable agent : " it is not merely your interference in raising money that is wanted but your advice upon many points as well as explanations of accounts &c. which I am slow in understanding " (28*th April*, 1821, *Letters*, V, 368-9, where the letter is wrongly inserted). On 15th May he writes to him about the arrangements he is making to reassume James as partner in the printing business, and proposing to breakfast with him on the following Sunday. On 1st June John began to spit blood and on the 16th he died. Before his death Scott had undertaken to write Lives for a collected edition of the English Novelists. What Scott's later misfortunes owed, or did not owe, to John's accounting and extravagance it is impossible to say. It is only just to remember that if John got a share in the profits of a novel, it was generally because he had advanced some portion of the bills which were discounted in advance, and that Scott was unwilling to lose his services.[1]

Lockhart and the Christie-Scott duel, with the trouble in Walter's regiment, were not the only anxieties of the year (1821). Before it was out, *The Beacon*, run by some young hot-headed Tories in Glasgow, but for which Scott, Rae, Forbes and Colin Mackenzie had acted as " establishers ", was in trouble over personalities directed against Stuart of Dunearn and Sir James Gibson, later Gibson Craig. The latter threatened a duel, and Lord Lauderdale, an old enemy of Sir Walter's, was to have acted as second. But the fault of the trustees had been want of control, not active part in the campaign. " I feel some unwillingness to think ", writes Colin Mackenzie, " of the degree of personality often scurrilous & often coarse which we have allowed to go on without interference. But now the arrow is barbed by the public knowing & the parties feeling that such things are said in some measure under the Shade of our Names." " Repeated and fruitless endeavours were made to restrain the Course they were pursuing and to make them aware that it was not conformable to our intentions." So Colin Mackenzie, but Scott did not feel comfortable about having started the young men and then backed out, as the " establishers " did. He foresaw more trouble, and had not long to wait for it. The place of *The Beacon* was taken by *The Sentinel*, and a further attack upon Stuart led to a duel with Sir Alexander Boswell in which the latter was shot and died the next day (26th March, 1822). He had just returned from the funeral of his brother, James, the Shakespearean scholar, in London. " I never saw the paper even by chance," Scott wrote to

---

[1] John's slipperiness as an agent and borrower is suggested very clearly by Cadell's letters to him in *Constable's Letter Book*, MS. 789-90, Nat. Lib. Scot.

Heber. " It is some comfort to me that I had remonstrated with all my young friends about continuing this skirmishing war & had kept by dint of authority my son in law out of it."

The great event of 1822 was the exciting and somewhat absurd one of George IV's visit to Edinburgh in which Scott played practically the part of Master of Ceremonies, for which he was formally thanked by the King in a letter from Peel ; but, if Croker be right, His Majesty a little resented the prominence inevitably given to his distinguished and loyal subject. One quaint result of the visit was to make the kilt, etc., the national dress of Scotsmen (and of Englishmen visiting Scotland) which Sir Walter had rejected as the error it is when writing to Haydon on 7th January, 1821 : " In general there is a great error in dressing ancient Scottish men like our Highlanders, who wore a dress, as they spoke a language, as foreign to the Lowland Scottish as to the English " (*Letters*, VI, 331-2). But now Scott blossomed out as a Highlander and that, despite his Jacobitism, in the Campbell[1] tartan, while " our fat friend " appeared " in the full Highland garb,—the same brilliant *Stuart Tartans*, so called, in which certainly no Stuart, except Prince Charles, had ever before presented himself in the saloons of Holyrood." George " did look a most stately and imposing person in that beautiful dress—but his satisfaction therein was cruelly disturbed, when he discovered, towering and blazing among and above the genuine Glengarries and Macleods and MacGregors, a figure (that of Sir William Curtis, a London Alderman) even more portly than his own, equipped, from a sudden impulse of loyal ardour, in an equally complete set of the self-same conspicuous Stuart tartans " (*Lockhart*).

About a week before the King's arrival, George Crabbe, the old poet whose verses Scott had known from his earliest days and with whom he had later corresponded, arrived as a guest and spent some days roaming through Edinburgh

---

[1] Beardie, Scott's great-grandfather, had married a Campbell of Silvercraigs, his only connection with the Highlander.

with Lockhart as guide or a caddy as guardian. The Highland Chiefs surprised and delighted him: " I thought it an honour that Glengarry even took notice of me, for there were those, and gentlemen too, who considered themselves honoured by following in his train. There [at Scott's dinner] were also Lord Errol, and the Macleod, and the Fraser, and the Gordon, and the Fergusson; and I conversed at dinner with Lady Glengarry, and did almost believe myself a harper, or bard, rather—for harp I cannot strike; and Sir Walter was the life and soul of the whole " (*8th August*). But in the midst (14th August) of the functions and celebrations Scott lost a much older and dearer friend than Crabbe with the death of William Erskine, six months after he had been raised to the Bench as the Honourable Lord Kinnedder, one of the Senators of the College of Justice. In Scott's life, as preserved in Lockhart's biography and in the Letters, Erskine remains a strangely shadowy person. In 1796 William and Mary Erskine are the most intimate of all his friends, the confidants of his passion for Williamina, receiving his enthusiastic congratulations on Mary's engagement to Archibald Campbell Colquhoun of Clathick, later Lord Advocate and Lord Clerk Register. Scott, like others when their friends marry, hoped for no breach in their intimacies: " Tell Mary Anne how inconceivably mortified I shall be if I do not retain the same interest in her friendship as formerly—that I expect she will deviate from the fashion so far as to give *petits soupers* as well as *routes*." Like others he found it was not to be so. In time he formed for Clathick, on grounds I have not traced, a positive dislike.[1] Mary Anne grew religious, which meant some coldness towards worldly friends ; and, in a letter to Alexander Young, Scott, deploring a coolness between her and her nieces, Lord Kinnedder's daughters, writes on 5th December, 1827 :

---

[1] " Erskine would have sat there [*i.e.* on the Bench] ten years ago but for the wretched intrigues of that selfish old creature his brother-in-law."— (To JOANNA BAILLIE, 10th Feb., 1822, *Letters*, VII, p. 61).

"It is evident however from the terms of my old friend Mrs. Colquhouns letter that though she is generously willing to assist her nieces necessities it is unhappily without feeling that cordiality of affection which can alone render benefits acceptable or in some cases endurable. I have no doubt that this misunderstanding arises out of circumstances. Mrs. Colquhoun must be much altered from what I once knew her were it otherwise." Words like these imply a long separation from the friend with whom he had once sat " in close divan " over love and marriage. From William, however, there was no separation. Speaking of Kinnedder's shyness, Hay Donaldson declares that " he never was known to ask a favour for himself". He hardly needed to so long as Scott was there to canvass for him. From 1807 onwards a recurring theme of letters to, or about, Erskine is the possibility of finding him better jobs. But the bulk of Scott's letters to Erskine were burned after his death and we have not a line to tell us what Erskine thought either of the poems or the novels, though we are told that he was, with James Ballantyne, Scott's favourite court of appeal. We know from the epistle to him in *Marmion* that Erskine's tastes were classical, and he would have had Scott follow closer in the footsteps of the Ancients :

> Nor ramble on through brake and maze,
> With harpers rude of barbarous days.

But of judgements on the novels, such as were passed so admirably by Lady Louisa Stuart, we have none from Erskine. For Scott's biographers, he counts for nothing.

"I was rather the worse ", Scott writes to his friend John Richardson on 15th September, " of my exertions in the Royal Cause." He was probably saved from more serious effects by the rash which broke out over his body ; but on 10th November (*Letters*, VII, 281) he tells Terry: " I have not been very well—a whoreson thickness of blood, and a depression of spirits arising from the loss of friends [Erskine's death had been followed by that of Hay

Donaldson, his own family lawyer, and agent since 1815 for the Duke of Buccleuch, and of the Solicitor-General, James Wedderburn]. . . . have annoyed me much ; and Peveril will, I fear, smell of the apoplexy. I propose a good rally, however, and hope it will be a powerful effect. My idea is, *entre nous*, a Scotch archer in the French king's guard, *tempore* Louis XI., the most picturesque of all times." The phrase, " smell of the apoplexy " comes, of course, from *Gil Blas* and does not imply anything like an actual stroke, but no one might pursue a life of such tireless activity, literary and social, with impunity. For the novel to which Scott refers in this letter is the seventh since we paused on *Ivanhoe* in December 1819, and this is only November 1822. I shall turn back for a word on those which Cadell names in a previous quotation and their successors.

The shining success of *Ivanhoe* was followed by the first recognised and admitted failure, *The Monastery*, and that was in great part redeemed as far as popularity goes by its immediate sequel, *The Abbot*. But in both Scott had got outside his own range of historical understanding. The Middle Ages were for him the ages of Chivalry. Their animating spirit, that of the Catholic Church, he understood too little to modify the conventional Protestant conviction, in which he had grown up, that it was " a degrading superstition ", the last Abbot of Kennaquhair [Melrose], one " whose designs must be condemned as their success would have rivetted on Scotland the claims of antiquated superstition and spiritual tyranny ". *The Monastery*, as a story, simply breaks down, cumbered by its too solid fairy, the White Lady of Avenel, and the absurd Euphuist, Sir Percy Shafton. Yet it contains a suggestion which a more analytic turn of mind, perhaps a little more time and care, might have made much of, the passionate division in Edward Glendinning's mind when he believes that his brother, Halbert, who is also his successful rival for the love of Mary Avenel, has been killed by the English knight. Did Scott possibly recall something of his own feelings when his friend, " Don Guglielmo ", became the successful suitor of Williamina Belsches ? *The Abbot* is a well-constructed story, as *The Monastery* is not, and the picture of Mary Queen of Scots has been highly praised by greater admirers of that ill-fated princess than the present writer. Yet surely she, in the tragic hour of her life, deserved better treatment than to be merely the good fairy in the love story of two young people, one of them that favourite hero of Scott, the young man with a leaning to both sides in the issue of the day, a foot in both camps, but drawn into the intrigue or combat on one of these sides by a mixture of accident and sentiment, another Edward Waverley. Surely George Douglas should have been the hero and the story a tragedy throughout. But that was not Scott's way, and in *Kenilworth*, which followed in some three months, he regained the level of *Ivanhoe*, and in a novel of the same kind, a brilliant pastiche, concocted from his multifarious reading, of the reign of Elizabeth and the life and character of her showy favourite, the Earl of Leicester. Many literary ingredients gave colour to the picture—from the German poets of his early studies to his lifelong familiarity with Elizabethan poetry, drama, history, and antiquarianism. Goethe's *Egmont* supplied the only love-scene between Leicester and Amy, and Goethe's Mephistopheles is, even more than Iago, the model for Richard Varney. There is enough, and perhaps more than enough, of Elizabethan " tushery " and humours. Historical chronology is treated with a noble contempt. To Leicester's early and public marriage with Amy Robsart is attributed the secrecy of his later marriage to Lettice Knollys, " false wife and widow of Walter, Earl of Essex " (*Froude*). Shakespeare's *Tempest* and *Midsummer Night's Dream* are on the lips of Elizabeth's courtiers in 1575, when the poet was still a

> whining school-boy with his satchel
> And shining morning face, creeping like snail
> Unwillingly to school.

As a picture of the manners of the time, it is worth just as much and just as little as the average historical novel born of books, the best of which are but illusion. Yet of its kind it is a brilliant *tour-de-force*. If *Ivanhoe* made captive readers across the Border, and *Quentin Durward*, later, made a special appeal to the French, *Kenilworth* was for long the novel of Scott's most studied in Germany. *Kenilworth*, and either *The Pirate* or *Nigel*, are probably the two novels which Goethe had just read at Marienbad in 1823, when he told Konrad von Müller that he was at the end with Scott: " he would always amuse me, but I can learn nothing from him. I have time only for the most excellent." Byron was his idol : " Byron alone will I let stand by myself,[1] Walter Scott is nothing beside him."

The Pirate (December 1821), which followed *Kenilworth*, was composed mainly at Chiefswood where Sophia and Lockhart were established in the summer months, and Scott could enjoy re-living some of his own early married life while, at the same time, he pushed on the final transformation and furnishing of Abbotsford. In quest of novelty, he turned back to his visit to the Islands in 1814 and his work on Dryden, which, indeed, he was revising for a new edition. Of the Shetlands his knowledge was of the slightest, and Minna, Brenda, Magnus Troil, Norna of the Fitful Head, Claud Halcro, and Triptolemus have about as much substantiality as the mists that drift across the peat-bogs and the hills of those " naked, melancholy isles ". Yet " this splendid romance ", as Lockhart calls it, had, if some detractors, such well-qualified admirers as Lady Louisa Stewart, Hazlitt, and Senior. To adjust to the last scruple our estimate of each novel to-day is of less interest to the historian than to recover some comprehension of the variety and freshness of appeal which they made to their own day. There had been nothing like it, one imagines, since Shakespeare outshone his rivals on the Elizabethan stage, and of that we have no such contem-

[1] And one of Byron's greatest poems is *The Burial of Sir John Moore* !

porary fulness of evidence as the periodicals of Scott's day supply. "He is Nature's Secretary," cries Hazlitt in reviewing *The Pirate*, but dilating more widely, "he neither adds to nor takes away from her book; and that makes him what he is, the most popular writer living." The changes of scene themselves and the care that Scott took to individualise the background was itself a new and arresting feature: "The charm of Scott derives", Goethe declared, "from the beauty of the three British kingdoms and the inexhaustible variety of their history."

From the Shetlands and the eighteenth century Scott turned back to London in the reign of James I. The first idea was a series of letters supposed to have been discovered, much as the Boswell papers have been of late, in some nobleman's house, which should illustrate the manners of James's reign in city and country, a kind of later-dated Paston Letters. Lockhart prints one of Scott's, and in the National Library of Scotland are preserved those which Scott had set up in type [1] and another in the handwriting of "our dear and accomplished friend Lady Louisa Stuart who condescended to take an oar which she handled most admirably" (*To Lockhart, January* 1832). The letters were in process of setting up while *The Pirate* was in hand, but the scheme was abandoned and for it substituted a romance into the texture of which were woven King James himself, Baby Charles and Steenie, the Duke of Buckingham, George Heriot and other historical figures in a quite unhistorical series of events; the actual course of history is nowhere touched as it is in *Waverley, Old Mortality*, and *A Legend of Montrose*. Scott's cautious and worthy heroes are always rather tedious, and the excesses of Glenvarloch are as awkward as the contortions of Richie Moniplies's limbs, but the latter worthy and King James are in Scott's best manner and in dealing with them

---

[1] With MS. notes in Scott's hand dated 1832 when he was busy reconsidering everything which might be thrown in to help in the work of paying the creditors.

he is able to return to the vernacular. " By the way," he writes to Constable while at work on *Nigel* in the early months of 1822, " did you ever see such vulgar trash as certain imitators wish to pass on the world as Scotch. It makes me think myself in company with Lothian Coal carters—And yet Scotch was a language which we have heard spoken by the learnd and the wise & witty & the accomplishd and which had not a trace of vulgarity in it but on the contrary sounded rather graceful and genteel. You remember how well Mrs. Murray Keith—the late Lady Dumfries—my poor mother & other ladies of that day spoke their native language—it was different from English as the Venetian is from the Tuscan dialect of Italy but it never occurd to any one that the Scotish any more than the Venetian was more vulgar than those who spoke the purer and more classical—But that is all gone" (25*th February*, 1822, *Letters*, VII, 83).

For the picture, more properly the masquerade, of London life, for our contemplation of which the hero is the peep-hole, the magic lantern, rather than a positive interest in himself, Scott drew on another storehouse, furnished by his early reading and capacious memory, the Elizabethan and Jacobean drama, not only Shakespeare but the minors—Ben Jonson, Beaumont and Fletcher, whom he had hoped to edit himself and had then handed over to poor Henry Weber (who had given him real and valuable help in his work on *Sir Tristrem* and romances, introducing him to the German Minnesinger), Massinger, Shadwell, and miscellaneous old plays, dramas the chief interest of which, despite all the eloquence which has been poured out on their poetic and dramatic merit from the days of Lamb and Hazlitt to those of Swinburne, is just this picture they provide of life and manners, that and the fine, careless felicity of their English.

Before *Nigel* was out (May 1822), Scott tells Constable: " I am turning my thoughts to that tumultuary & agitated period of Charles 2ds reign which was disturbd by the popish plot" (25*th February*, 1822), for if Scott was in these years a little carried off his feet by the heady tide of success, and induced to pour novel on the heels of novel with a haste which dismayed the booksellers whose stock of the older ones was not yet off when the new appeared, the publishers were not themselves free of responsibility for the accumulation of bills and the overproduction. Constable, whose health was failing, left Edinburgh in the spring of 1822, and from Castlebeare Park, between Harrow and Kew, sends Scott endless suggestions for editions and novels, editions of Scott's own miscellaneous articles and also of Shakespeare, " an edition of the immortal Bard might be brought out in twelve or fourteen volumes with a selection of readable and amusing notes," novels on possible historical themes: " a Work under the title of '*Pocahontas*' would make the fortune of us all," or King James I's visit to the father of Oliver Cromwell, or the battle of Sheriffmuir, or the period of the Armada in Scotland, or the last Sinclair of Roslin whose connection with the Devil had earned for him the reputation of a man without a shadow. And while suggesting new works, Constable was preparing new editions of the old as he purchased the final copyrights. Early in 1819 he is printing with James Ballantyne a new edition of the Poetical Works in ten volumes, and this is followed by *Novels and Tales* in twelve volumes. These were the works whose copyrights he had purchased for £12,000 in 1818. Now in September 1821 he comes forward with an offer first of £5,000 which, when accepted by Scott, he immediately raises to 5,000 guineas for the copyrights of *Ivanhoe, The Monastery, The Abbot,* and *Kenilworth,* and by November James Ballantyne was preparing estimates for printing " *Historical Romances by the Author of Waverley* in 6 vols.[1] octavo same as *Novels and Tales* ". To all this Constable added *The Poetry contained in the Novels, Tales, and Romances of the*

---

[1] Some of the booksellers complained that these serial issues militated against the sale of the new novels.

Author of Waverley, 1822. He even contemplated, as John Ballantyne's edition proved a failure owing to its disagreeable format, an edition of the British Novelists in the style and manner of the above-mentioned octavo edition of Scott's Tales, etc., with Lives by Scott.[1] All these proposals were, as Lockhart says, "of a nature well calculated to nourish and sustain in the author's fancy a degree of *almost mad exhilaration* near akin to his *publisher's own predominant mood.*" But what of the sober Cadell? Why is his name passed over in silence by Lockhart? For he, too, was art and part, and that in a more purely business spirit than Constable's, in whose mind love of financial enterprise blends with a real enthusiasm for books, art and part in the stimulation of Scott's mind. Cadell's position in these years, 1821-2, is an ambiguous one. He realised more acutely than Constable the want of capital from which the business was suffering, the dangerous amount of paper credit the firm had afloat, the heavy drafts that Con-

[1] This Scott could not undertake as he had promised to continue, for Mrs. John's benefit, the Lives he had begun to write for Ballantyne's Novelists Library of which not Constable but Constable's London agents, Messrs. Hurst, Robinson & Co., were the publishers. Scott had written the Life of Fielding in October 1820, and John dispatched it to London on 17th November. The first volume was issued in 1821, printed "At the Border Press For John Ballantyne Edinburgh", which last words appear in the first three volumes all printed in 1821, but are thereafter dropped. Scott continued to supply the publishers with Lives till 1824 and while the novels from *The Abbot* on to *Redgauntlet* are in progress one must remember that Scott was in intervals of his time composing these delightful critical comments on the works of his predecessors. "Smollett" was finished on 1st June, 1821, a fortnight before John's death. "Le Sage" and "Charles Johnston" (as a preface to *Chrysal*) are dated 20th September, 1822. By the 29th he is sending to James materials for Sterne, Goldsmith, and Dr. Johnson, and these, with Henry Mackenzie, Walpole, and Clara Reeve, were completed by the end of February 1823. "This has something intercepted Peveril," he tells James, adding that he has seen Constable, who had returned to Scotland: "I am convinced he has still that sound judgement and spirit of judicious enterprize which enabled him of yore to make London his washpot & cast his shoe over the Row. One or two of his projects I like hugeously and I am convinced he would have made a better thing of the novels than Hurst." The Life of Richardson Scott dates 1st January, 1824, and Swift, Bage, and Cumberland in December of the same year.

stable and his family were making on the assets; and he twice, in spring 1821 and again in August 1822, would apparently have been glad to sell out his share in the partnership. But of the value of the Author of Waverley and the assistance derived by bills from Ballantyne & Co. he had a shrewd and practical comprehension. No editions of novelists or Shakespeare for him, if these are to interrupt the flow of fiction : " I am so thoroughly convinced of the propriety of his [Scott's] continuing on, on, on, with his works of fancy, that during the last three weeks, wherein I have had the comfort of seeing him almost every day, I have throughout encouraged him by every argument I could think of, and he has taken everything I said with great apparent satisfaction. One day he said—' We shall have to call a halt some day, but we shall ride as long as we can.' On another day he said—' I am wholly against any *hiatus* in these works. I have five or six subjects in my head, and were I either to delay in bringing them out, or something to intervene, the public will expect a finely wrought story, etc., etc., which would work up their expectations, and which there is no chance of their being gratified in ; besides, some other person may step into the arena, and give me a heavy oar to work to make up to him again.' [1] On another occasion he said—' I am now young and healthy and strong ; some two or three years hence it is hard to say how I may be.' . . . I said to Sir Walter, one of these days, ' I would as soon stop a winning horse as a successful author, with the public in his favour ' . . . We have large advances to him for work *to be done* ; so soon as these are accomplished, and he living and well, *then* Shakespeare might do " (5*th February*, 1823, *Archibald Constable and His Literary Correspondents*, III, pp. 238-41, including portions I have omitted). Cadell even attempted a little coup of his own after the manner of Constable in 1808 when *Marmion* was on the stocks. At the request of Joanna

---

[1] As Byron had stepped in and carried off Scott's popularity as the poet of the day.

Baillie (*2nd February*, 1822), Scott had begun to put together a little dramatic piece which outgrew its original purpose and became *Halidon Hill*. Cadell, hearing of it, offered, in the absence of Constable, and Scott accepted £1,000, but Cadell is soon found confessing in his letters to Constable that it is *not* good. In the report which he wrote later for Lockhart, Cadell poses as a restraining influence, at least associates himself with Constable as advocating a pause in bringing out new novels, and deplores the fact that Scott " had got into the lamentably pernicious practice of asking his publishers to engage for novels three or sometimes four deep ". " Would to God you had been as near to him from the beginning," Lockhart replies (3rd Oct., 1833). But the correspondence of these years does not bear this out, nor was it Cadell's way even after the disaster. " *Do not pause*, the more I consider this point I am the more convinced it may turn out a false step," so he writes as late as 21st March, 1828, and goes on to give " a specimen of my opinion on the subject by a pledge to pay to you £4,200 for a Novel in 3 vols by next November—the same sum for one in April or May 1829—and a like sum for one in November of the same year—making £12,600 in 18 months ... this may be thought bold —but I am so thoroughly convinced that the course is your own, that to leave it would be bad, if not fatal, policy". " Your arguments ", poor Scott replies on the 24th, " are prevailing and I will not allow some unpleasant feelings of my own and the unpleasant bodings of our friend James to stand in the way of future novels." To Cadell Scott, before and after the disaster, was a machine for the turning out of novels which brought in rapid returns : " Shakespeare if published to-morrow would only produce some £5000 at from 12 to 36 or 48 months credit and no gain, while one book of three vols will produce nearly £10,000, and great gain, and it is this we require."

There can be little doubt that Constable's was the better

advice, could Scott have taken it. " I like this muddling sort of work," he had said, echoing Dr. Johnson, when engaged on some piece of editing ; and an edition of Shakespeare with a revision of the *Dryden* and *Swift* would have been a happy means of providing a fallow period for his restless mind. Unfortunately his own financial requirements made Cadell's the more prevailing counsel. His meditations on " the tumultuary and agitated period of Charles II's reign ", for assistance in which Constable sends him a long list of sources that might be consulted (24*th March*, 1822) resulted in one of the least happy of all his novels, *Peveril of the Peak*, which saw the light in January 1823. By October 1822 James Ballantyne had begun to have doubts as is shown by a letter to him from Cadell. Cadell will not presume to offer any criticism himself, as James may : " you are differently circumstanced," but he does express an " unqualified dissent to your proposition of extending the work to 4 vols. . . . entirely from commercial considerations, a romance at two guineas will not, I think, be well taken in the present time ". Scott's interest in his work had, however, quickened with the entrance of Charles and the Popish Plot, and the early part was in type and could not be recast. Cadell acquiesced in the four volumes and has later to confess " the success of Peveril in *four* volumes and at *two guineas* ". Nor was any hiatus allowed, for *Peveril* was not out before Scott was hot on a more taking scent, the story " of a young Scotchman going to France to be an archer of the Scots guard tempore Ludovici XImi. You Morritt who study Philip de Comine[s] will easily imagine what a carte de pais I have [before] me " (11*th January*, 1823). In the previous December he is writing to Constable for information as to the site of Plessis les Tours, and *Quentin Durward* was out in June 1823. Nor must one blame Cadell for all this haste. Scott and he alike were running a race with time in the endeavour to secure profits wherewith to meet maturing bills, as is shown by every third or fourth letter to James Ballantyne in which Scott discusses the means of meeting demands ; in October 1822 it is £12,000.

The wonder is, not that the novels thus produced were unequal, but that the best of them were, of their kind, so good. Surveying the list of *Ivanhoe* to *Redgauntlet* one sees relative failures succeeded by relative, and some of them absolute, recoveries. *The Monastery* is retrieved to a considerable extent by *The Abbot*, and *Kenilworth* is, again *of its kind*, that is the romantic reconstruction of the history of a time the life of which lies beyond our ken, a masterpiece. *The Pirate* is but a poor affair, but *Nigel* more than redeems it. *Peveril of the Peak* is the most complete failure of all the novels before the final breakdown, but *Quentin Durward* is full of life and colour, and if in *St. Ronan's Well* one feels that Scott has got off his proper beat, is reviving the "manners" of Smollett and Miss Burney which Jane Austen's and even Miss Ferrier's novels have outgrown, in *Redgauntlet* he is once again the Scott of *Waverley*, *Guy Mannering*, and *The Heart of Midlothian*. Of haste there is evidence enough, of disease I can see none. The sentences which I have quoted earlier from a letter to Terry (*November* 1822) about " a whoreson thickness of blood " and *Peveril* smelling of the apoplexy are taken by Lockhart to indicate that Scott has already suffered some slight shocks of the paralysis which was to overtake him. But Scott's phraseology is literary :— " smell of apoplexy " a recollection of Gil Blas ; " a whoreson thickness of blood " a loose adaptation from Falstaff's " And I hear moreover his highness is fallen into this same whoreson apoplexy.... This apoplexy is as I take it a kind of lethargy, an't please your lordship, a kind of sleeping in the blood, a whoreson tingling." From brain-fag and depression Scott did doubtless suffer, and no wonder, but when apoplexy came it was with unmistakable force and with no merely passing results. No ; if some of the novels written in these years with undue haste are laboured and dull, there is little " smell of apoplexy " about *The*

G.W.S.   O

Abbot, Kenilworth, The Fortunes of Nigel, and *Quentin Durward*. Our novelists may feel that they have, in many ways, outgrown Scott in the portrayal of life and character, but there is none of them who might not be proud to have drawn in succession the portraits of Mary Queen of Scots, of Elizabeth of England ("No historian's Queen Elizabeth", says Thomas Hardy, "was ever so perfectly a woman as the fictitious Elizabeth of 'Kenilworth'"), James I, and the masterly portrait of Louis XI of France.

Scott and Cadell were, I have said, running a race with time and bills, Cadell aware of the insecurity of his firm's credit throughout his whole connection with it, its fatal deficiency in capital (of which apparently Scott had no inkling), and Scott because of the large sums he was expending on the rebuilding and decoration of Abbotsford, the starting of his children in the world, the entertainment of guests, the affording of help to his unfortunate brother, Tom, Tom's children, his old friend Willie Laidlaw, Charles Maturin, and a score of others. One must not think of Scott intent on profits for their own sake. A sharp eye had to be kept on the month's engagements and how to meet them, and it was a pity, so it seemed to him, that John Ballantyne was no longer there to look after the accounts, and that James was often absent from the Printing Office by ill-health, due to "a ticklish stomach ill united with a naturally good appetite and a sedentary disposition". But all that was the business of one corner of Scott's mind. The rest was full of the stories he was composing and of the life he was living as Abbotsford underwent its final transformation and guests in greater or lesser numbers, of greater or less social or intellectual distinction, found their way thither. For the stream of Scott's social life flowed in the years from 1822 to 1825 like a bright and shining river, darkened only by occasional shadows. The notes to James about financial expedients are urgent but have not the sense of imminent danger felt in those of 1813 to 1817. The death of poor Tom in February 1823 was a sorrow but also somewhat of a relief. He had suffered his affairs again, in 1822, to get into disorder, and Major Huxley, Tom's son-in-law, had come to Abbotsford in November of that year to see what help Walter could afford. After Tom's death some oversight or irregularity on his part was made by the War Office a ground for refusing his widow her pension for some time, and a claim for £1,000 was kept in suspense over Scott and his fellow-cautioner, David McCulloch, but the matter was apparently ultimately cleared up.

If the King's visit to Edinburgh was the chief social event of 1822, that of 1823 was a long hoped for meeting with Maria Edgeworth. To her sketches of Irish life Scott acknowledged the indebtedness of an example set and justified. She read *Waverley* on its publication and wrote to express her admiration to the " Author of Waverley ", addressing to James Ballantyne, his printer. Scott replied above the signature of James in his most courtly style : " If I could but hit Miss Edgeworth's wonderful power of vivifying all her persons, and making them live as real *beings* in your mind, I should not be afraid." " He says ", James reports, " you should never be forced to recollect . . . that such a work is a work of fiction, and all its fine creations but of air " (10th *November*, 1814). *The Lord of the Isles* was forwarded by James a little later and there was an interchange of compliments over that and Maria's *Patronage* (1814). Moreover, Maria's didactic father writes to tell how much they had been delighted by the poem which they greatly preferred to *The Lay* : " It has revived my daughter's failing courage, and has convinced her that an author may overcome by subsequent exertion the effect of hasty, unreasonable prejudice." There had been hopes at various times of meeting in London or in Scotland. In April 1822 Maria announced an intended visit in the coming summer, but the death of a relative altered her intentions to Scott's great or gallant disappointment. " I had arranged to stay at least a month after the

12th of May, in hopes of detaining you at Abbotsford, and I will not quit you under a month or two the next year. I shall have my house completed, my library replaced, my armoury new furbished, my piper new clothed, and the time shall be July" (*24th April*, 1822). Sure enough, in June 1823 Maria and her sisters Harriet and Sophy arrived in Scotland. After a brief visit to Dugald Stewart at Kinneil House, near Linlithgow, they drove into Edinburgh on 8th June to Abercrombie Place, where rooms had been taken for them by Margaret, daughter of James Gregory, and wife of William Alison, the Professor of Medicine. There they found a letter from Scott inviting them to dine on Sunday the 10th, but with a double postscript, in the second of which Lady Scott presses them to come round that same evening and hear a Highlander sing boat-songs. Past ten as it was, they set off and " as the coach stopped we saw the hall lighted, and the moment the door opened, heard the joyous sounds of loud singing. Three servants :—' The Miss Edgeworths' sounded from hall to landing-place and as I paused a moment in the anteroom I heard the first sound of Walter Scott's voice—' The Miss Edgeworths *come* !' The room was lighted by one globe lamp. A circle was singing loud and beating time—all stopped in an instant and Walter Scott in the most cordial and courteous manner stepped forward to welcome us : ' Miss Edgeworth this is so kind of you !' " They were quickly drawn into the song and dance, if it can be so called. " ' Will you then join in the circle with us ? ' He put the end of a silk handkerchief into my hand and others into my sisters' ; they held by these handkerchiefs all in their circle again, and the boatman began to roar out a Gaelic song to which they all stamped in time and repeated the chorus which, as far as I could hear, sounded like ' At an Vam ! At an Vam !' frequently repeated with prodigious enthusiasm. In another I could make out no intelligible sound but Bar ! bar ! bar ! But the boatman's dark eyes were ready to start out of his head with rapture as he sang and stamped and shook the handkerchief on each side, and the circle imitated. Followed supper at a round table, a family supper, with attention to us just sufficient and no more. . . . Walter Scott is one of the best-bred men I ever saw, with all the exquisite politeness which he knows so well how to describe, which is of no particular school or country, but which is of all countries, the politeness which arises from good and quick sense and feeling, which seems to know by instinct the characters of others, to see what will please, and put all his guests at their ease. As I sat beside him at supper I could not believe he was a stranger and forgot he was a great man." They visited Roslin with Sir Walter later, and then set out on a Highland tour which finished at Kinross where Maria was laid up with a severe attack of erysipelas. After one day's rest " in your own romantic city ", they arrived on 27th July at Abbotsford to spend a golden fortnight : " her host had always some new plan of gaiety. One day there was fishing in the Cauldshiels Loch and a dinner on the heathy bank. Another the whole party feasted by Thomas the Rhymer's waterfall in the glen—and the stone on which Maria sat . . . was ever afterwards called *Edgeworth's stone*. A third day we had to go further afield. He must needs show her, not Newark only, but all the upper scenery of the Yarrow where ' fair hangs the apple frae the rock '—and the baskets were unpacked about sunset beside the ruined chapel overlooking St. Mary's Loch—and he had scrambled to gather bluebells and heath flowers with which all the young ladies must twine their hair—and they sang and he recited until it was time to go home beneath the softest of harvest moons. Thus a fortnight was passed—and then the vision ended." So Lockhart writes, looking back wistfully across the gulf of the disaster. At the time he could write more satirically : " Miss Edgeworth is at Abbotsford . . . a little, dark, bearded, sharp, withered, active, laughing, talking, impudent, fearless, outspoken, honest, Whiggish, unchristian, good-tempered, kindly, ultra-Irish body. I like her one day, and damn her to perdition the next. She is a very queer character.... She, Sir Adam, and the Great Unknown, are 'too much for any company'" (*To John Wilson, July* 1823). To Croker he writes on the 3rd August from Chiefswood : " I have not seen Scott for a few days but he is at Abbotsford in great vigour where I hope to dine with him to-day. He has got with him your countryman Maria Edgeworth and two of the junior progeny of the old Pentegunis and I have seen very little of the celebrated lady. She seemed very angry one day when she was here on discovering that my wife drove in the gardenchair two donkeys by name Lady Morgan and Hannah More but I cannot say which of the godmothers had her sympathy." It is these little portraits of each other that are now the interest of the episode—Scott " not so heavy in appearance as I had been led to expect ... more lame than I expected, but not unwieldy ; his countenance ... benevolent and full of genius without the slightest effort at expression, delightfully natural ". Lady Scott " must have been very handsome—French dark large eyes : civil and good-natured " ; " Lockhart—very handsome, quite unlike his picture in *Peter's Letters*—reserved and silent, but he appears to have much sensibility under this reserve." Sophia, " a slight elegant figure and graceful simplicity of manners. There is something most winning in her affectionate manner to her father ; he dotes upon her." Young Walter " excessively shy, very handsome, not at all literary ... his younger brother Charles ... has more easy manners, is more conversible, and has more of his father's literary taste ". To Scott Maria in " external appearance is quite the fairy of our nursery tales, the Whippity Stourie who came flying in through the window to work all sort of marvels ". Anne Scott, whose mind had some of the satiric turn of Lockhart's, likes " her very much, though she talks a great deal, and does not care to hear others talk. There was a dreadful scene at parting. The great Maria nearly went into fits; she had taken such a fancy to us all".

In the same month came John Leycester Adolphus, whose *Letters to Richard Heber* on the common authorship of Scott's poems and the Waverley Novels, the finest piece of analytic criticism to which the latter had been subjected, appeared in 1821, and Lockhart reproduces his interesting memoranda with their vivid description of Scott's conversation, " the sweetness and abandon with which it flowed —always, however, guided by good sense and taste; the warm and unstudied eloquence with which he expressed rather sentiments than opinions; and the liveliness and force with which he narrated and described; and all that he spoke derived so much of its effect from indefinable felicities of manner, look, and tone, and sometimes from the choice of apparently insignificant words that a moderately faithful transcript of his sentences would be but a faint image of his conversation." " Not only was he inexhaustible in anecdote but he still loved to exert the talent of dramatising." " Never did a man go through all the gradations of laughter with such complete enjoyment and a countenance so radiant."

" He has indeed ", Maria wrote from Abbotsford, " such variety of occupations that he has not time to think of his own works : how he has time to write them is the wonder." *Quentin Durward* had been going to James for transcription all the spring : " I am very glad you like the sheets—they will improve as they go on and the story shall be simple & intelligible yet with much bustle & event " (*March* 1823). A third of Volume IV is despatched to him on the 29th, and Cadell is preparing to advertise on the 31st, and by the middle of May is dispatching copies to London and Dublin. Scott meantime turns aside to write short Lives of Henry Mackenzie, Horace Walpole, and Clara Reeve. In January and February he had helped to found the Bannatyne Club, correspondence about which with David Laing goes on to the end of his life, and he had been admitted, not in *propria persona*, but as the Author of *Waverley*, to the older London bibliographical club, the Roxburghe.

But the reception of *Quentin Durward*, though admitted by readers and reviewers to be an excellent story, was in London disappointing, and Cadell was brought to share Constable's view that there should be some intermission in the stream of novels, and Scott admits that " if . . . it is thought necessary to leave greater intermission betwixt these affairs . . . we must keep the mill going with something else " (18*th June*, 1823). In March Scott had suggested to Ballantyne as a means of raising " £1000 & upwards " to " purchase Walter into the army again ", " a curious little dialogue (in character) on popular superstitions . . . I mentiond this in a late letter to Constable." Constable offered £500 for the copyright, but that was not enough, and by May Scott had got under way with a new story—" Sir Walter has just been here in great glee—has begun the New—it is a Scotch story. I have just seen Ballantyne. I fear the boggles [*i.e.* bogles=ghosts] are dormant in the meantime " (*Cadell to Constable*, 13*th May*, 1823). " ' I dare say we will just do that some day but I find no such profitable way of employing my time as the present trade ' " (*Scott as reported by Cadell to Constable*, 19*th May*, 1823). So in July apparently (the letter is undated) pages of *St. Ronan's Well* are transmitted to James : " I have thoughts of making the tale tragic, having ' a humour to be cruel '. It may go off, however. If not, it will be a pitiful tragedy filled with the most lamentable mirth " (*Letters*, VIII, 29). By November, when the Edgeworths, Adolphus, poor Hartstonge, " the quintessence of bores—the best humoured of all Irishmen and the dullest of created beings," Hogg who " found his lair at Abbotsford on Friday, Lockhart bringing him here like a pig on a string for which the lady of the mansion lent him little thanks "—when these & other " heavier birds of passage " are flown, the last proofs are dispatched to

James : " I was pretty well aware that the inclosed is either a hit or a miss. I am glad you think it the former." In December it is out, and on 1st January Scott finished and dated his Life of Richardson for the Ballantyne Novels.

" A pitiful tragedy filled with the most lamentable mirth " is not an altogether unjust description of *St. Ronan's Well*, though I myself prefer it to many of the historical romances where sentiment and manners are all alike unreal. Scott had not Shakespeare's sense of how comedy and tragedy may mingle. The comic must take colour from the tragic. The humorous strain in *Hamlet, King Lear, Macbeth*, and *Coriolanus* is very different from the comedy of Falstaff, Fluellen, Dogberry, Verges, Benedick and Beatrice. Meg Dods is admirable, and MacTurk, Mrs. Blower, and some others possible, but the Smollett-like vein is not in harmony with the tragedy of poor Clara, for a tragic figure she is and, to my mind, a rather lovely one if the story be read in the light of the end as Scott composed it before Mrs. Grundy, in the person of James Ballantyne, intervened and made of her suffering and her interviews with Tyrrel " a tale of little meaning though the words be strong ". Incest had a certain fascination for the romantics, Byron, Shelley—for Scott only as a tragic *impasse*. He had told Lockhart and Laidlaw a tale of incest and crime in his own neighbourhood just as he was contemplating his novel. He was one of the few who knew the truth of the Byron separation : " there was a reason, *premat nox alta*."

Few of the novels after the first ' Scotch novels ' have much root in Scott's own experience, but in *St. Ronan's Well* there are fleeting reminiscences of recent troubles and experiences. " No, John," replied his sister, " it is not of such men as these that I have any fear—and yet cowards are sometimes driven to desperation and become more dangerous than better men "—it was so Scott had spoken, not quite justly, of John Scott and of Stuart of

Dunearn. The Lives of the British Novelists, too, which he wrote with delightful understanding and sympathy, had a little too much carried him back to the manners and humours of an outworn fashion. If he could have drawn more directly from the people he knew at first hand and made them more natural, less melodramatic and less of the picaresque type, poor Clara's story might have been the centre of a better harmonized whole. But nothing is more instructive of what I have called the separate facets of Scott's life, that not only is his composition kept a secret but that the tales themselves touch so slightly on his own experience, and that almost entirely the experience of his early years. Except for the reference to the financial ventures of Frank Osbaldistone's father in *Rob Roy* the drama of trade and finance never enters the world of Scott's creation. What a novel Balzac could have made of Scott's ambitions and negotiations and reckless expenditure and labours, and the careless ease and expansion of the social life he was to all appearance chiefly interested in—and then the failure and the tragic end.

CHAPTER X

"On with the dance, let joy be unconfined."
BYRON.

For by August 1823 the financial question was again raising its head. The lag in the sale of *Quentin Durward*, or some other cause, had quickened Constable's anxiety over the number of bills which were afloat bearing the names of James Ballantyne and Co. or of Archibald Constable and Co. either as drawer or acceptor, and on the 8th Constable wrote to Scott on the subject. On the 19th details were furnished showing that the current bills " amount just now to about £30,000". Into the full history of the negotiations I need not enter. Their significance is only clear when to the letters between Constable and Scott one adds those which Cadell was writing to his partner, for these reveal, what Scott was not fully aware of, the extent to which the affairs of the two parties were interlocked, their fortunes mutually dependent. Cadell's anxiety was lest Scott should be in any way alarmed by too great awareness of the actual circumstances. " What can be the reason of your neverfailing remarks about Ballantyne's bills is a mystery to me but the utter ignorance of the absolute wants of your concern being as great if not greater than those of J. B. and Co. I say ours are greater than theirs—their bills to us I know are sooner cashed than ours to them—do you suppose I have no alarms—I have many but it is not for Ballantyne *it is for A. C. and Co.* . . . As long as A. C. and Co. are solvent there is no fear of Jas. B. and Co. . . . without them and the bills and books A. C. and Co. would not, in all likelihood have existed. I am therefore most grateful to them . . . so far from making any attempt to beat down their bills I shall do my utmost to keep them on smoothly, as I tell you honestly *we need them* and *must have them*—the greatest fear I have in this quarter is James Ballantyne's death." What seems to me clear from these and other statements is, what Scott, ignorant of the actual financial position of Constable and Co., its want of sufficient capital, could not suspect, that on the anticipated profits from his works depended not only his heavy outlays on Abbotsford then at their height (" this is my last year of heavy expense " *To James Ballantyne* 29*th March*) but the entire credit of Constable and Co. Any break in the flow of these, any doubt as to their sufficiency, might precipitate the failure of both.

At Cadell's instance, accordingly, Constable confined his request for reduction in the number of outstanding bills to the accommodation bills, the mutual loans, making no reference to the bills for work done or to be done. Scott's reply was, first, a desire to know " whether the cause of your present correspondence arose merely out of the extent of these pecuniary transactions, which I am as desirous as you to abridge or whether the deficiency of the sale of Q. D. has diminished your general confidence in this sort of literature and inclined you to restrict on all points our hitherto very extensive concerns " (*Letters*, VIII, 76). Reassured on this latter point by Constable, Scott makes a statement as to his own efforts to reduce : " With this purpose I have adopted and maintained a system of retrenchment which has reduced £6000 since April last as will appear from your books " (*Letters*, VIII, 79), and he goes on to suggest that when *St. Ronan's Well* is out—in October he hopes, as a fact it was not till December—another work should be contracted for, the bills for which should be used to " retire the same value of accommodation bills ". But apparently Scott was deceiving himself as to the reduction affected, if we may believe Cadell who states in a letter which apparently he had not the courage to send to Scott : " The writer would respectfully observe that the sum appears to him to have greatly increased within that period " [1]—*i.e.* April to August. The proposal which Scott makes for the future is that the bills for a work *to be written* might be discounted and used to retire accommodation bills. As Cadell saw, Constable could not afford to risk any breach with Scott : " Nothing is so clear ", his London agent had written in 1822, " as that the Author of Waverley should hold his hand for a year or two ; but this, I fancy, cant be attempted without great danger that he might be induced to offer some new work to Murray or Longman." There was the danger. Constable had staked too much on Scott to be able to do without him, and for that reason was forced to grant bills both for work to be done and by way of loans to an extent that no other publisher, Murray, Blackwood, Longman, could or would have done. And if Scott and James Ballantyne were extravagant, so, it is clear from Cadell's letters, was Constable.

[1] The sums involved were of two kinds. There were the bills " for value received " *i.e.* Constable's bills for (1) the copyrights which they had bought outright, (2) the reserved shares in *Quentin Durward* and *Peveril* which they had bought from Ballantyne and Scott, (3) Printing Accounts, and (4) some other small items amounting to from £4,000 to £5,000. Altogether the value engagements at this date came to about £35,000. Besides these there were the accommodation bills or loans between the two firms. It was for these that there were always counter-bills granted and Cadell states quite frankly to his partner that those granted by Ballantyne and Co. were more easily negotiated than those of their own. Scott too writes to James Ballantyne about 1818 : " I fancy Constable's people find our counter-bills convenient which makes them preserve five of the renewals." The bills of this kind amounted in 1823 to about £27,000. In addition Constable had advanced in cash £11,000 for novels to be written so that their obligations or advances in connection with Scott's affairs came at the time to over £70,000. Cadell was not unnaturally afraid of the effect on Scott's mind of a realisation of the full truth. The value engagements, of course, worked themselves off in course of time as the novels sold. It is not certain, Mr. Glen thought, that Cadell was right in stating that Scott deceived himself. A contract for a new novel would have reduced the accommodation bills and their counter-bills but Constable and Co. would have had to provide cash which Cadell did not wish to contemplate.

I say James Ballantyne, for a further financial complication for Scott had been occasioned by his reassumption in 1822 of James as a partner in the printing business of which he had been since his marriage a salaried manager. Into all the complexities of the mutual debts and credits of Scott and James it is impossible to enter even were the present writer better qualified as an accountant, impossible for the full figures are unobtainable ; but the result of Mr. Glen's examination of such as are preserved in the Writers to the Signet's Library convinced him that to James's extravagance is due a proportion of the accommodation bills standing in the name of J. B. and Co.

But the threat of trouble passed and the year 1823 flowed merrily out to the sound of revelry in the new Library of Abbotsford : " We had a dance of neighbours which began without music and ended at five in the morning without light—the whole stock of gas being burned out just as the company broke up " (*Letters*, VIII, 159), that is the oil-gas with which the enlarged house was equipped. " You will hardly know my premises when you see them again, and I begin to think I have flung away a good deal of money which might have been as well saved. But having had all my life certain visions respecting a house I could not resist the temptation of realising them, so now like Christabel's phantom guest the place is

A thing to dream of not to tell."
(*To Miss Clephane* 23.1.24 *Letters*, VIII, 159.)

" If you have seen little Russell he will tell you how our Christmas gambols came off gaily and how they danced till moonlight and starlight and gaslight were one. The entrance hall with its blazonry, carved oak panels and huge freestone chimney-piece with such pieces of old armour as can be handsomely stor'd therein will be quite baronial. The outer court with its screen and carved work looks very antique " (*To Terry* 5th Feb., 1824). " I have gambolled a little in the entrance hall which is a Dalilah, as Dryden says of some of his flights, of my own imagination which I knew was not in very good taste when I did it, but why should a gentleman not be a little fantastic as Tony Lumpkin says ' So be he is in concatenation accordingly'" (*To Lady Louisa Stuart 4th April*, 1824).

The outlay on Abbotsford was not over in 1823,[1] as the letters show, and in the year that followed Scott was not only purchasing Walter's return to the army, providing his allowance, and educating Tom's Walter at Cooper's Hill, but he was preparing to drop the Indian appointment for Charles which Lord Bathurst had promised him in 1820, and to send that young man to Oxford in the sanguine but illusive hope that he would prove a scholar. But the great family event of 1824 was the securing for Walter a well-endowed bride. The negotiations were opened in a letter to the unsuspecting Walter early in March announcing in a cryptic way, by a reference to the first scene of *The Merry Wives of Windsor*, in which Walter is to see himself as Mr. Abraham Slender, a proposal by Sir Adam Ferguson and his wife with regard to their niece Miss Jane Jobson (the Anne Page of the reference), the daughter of a deceased merchant who in 1813 had purchased an estate in Fifeshire, by name Lochore, and of his rather more aristocratic and very evangelical wife Rachel Stewart. Scott ascertains that the marriage should afford the young couple an income of from £1500 to £2000 a year, and as for her connections with trade " I would just have you remark that we are but cadets of Raeburn who are cadets of Harden and therefore, though gentlemen, are much like what the French call gentillatres and the Highlanders Duniewassells. In the present day there is no

---

[1] " Abbotsford has cost me a mint of money without much return as yet. But after all it is the surest way of settling a family if one can do without borrowing money or receiving interest. Said Abbotsford has thrust its lofty turrets into the skies since you saw it. . . . In fact I have nearly completed a sort of vision which I always had in my mind."—To JOHN RICHARDSON, 1823, *Letters*, VIII, 129.

aristocracy so strong as that of wealth or talent and no one thinks [anything] of making some sacrifices of the prejudices of birth to acquire the former. Witness the valiant knights and squires now laying siege to Mrs Anne Page. I would not therefore have you take up poor Anne's follies who rather makes herself ludicrous by some affectations of superiority" (*To Walter, 2nd April*, 1824, *Letters*, VIII, 239).

Walter accordingly meets the young lady, apparently for the first time, in September when she is on a visit to the Fergusons at Huntly Burn. "It is clear that your coming down here must be considered as entirely experimental and not binding on Anne Page or you" (*2nd April*). "I think you have done very sensibly to propose coming down—ones own eyes alone are to be trusted" (*13th April*). "You should ascertain as far as possible whether she has the thoughts and sentiments of a lady and that can only be in the course of a little time. . . . I have some reason to believe that Mrs Anne's best qualities are those which are not most intrusive" (*21st April*). "Sir Adam cannot receive the visit he expected untill about the 12th August. . . . Putting the matter off would have the great inconvenience of throwing the scene into the *médisance* of Edinburgh whereas here the intimacy of the families and the retired state of the country may permit such a thing to glide on—or off—without attracting any observation" (*25th July*). These and other letters dispose, I fear, of the little fairy-tale of a previous meeting and unsuspected mutual or one-sided attraction which Scott got up for the benefit of Lady Louisa Stuart and Morritt. Walter arrived in September but he was not the only visitor. Mrs. Hughes—the strong-minded wife of a canon of St. Paul's and vicar of Uffington, whose acquaintance Scott had formed in his early Princess Caroline days—had come in May on a tour through Scotland and recorded in her diary her admiration of Abbotsford : " So admirably *old* (in appearance) so finely finished in every part according

to the Gothic style . . . so many towers and turrets and pinnacles and bartizans and all that I ever read of in ancient story . . . ceilings, passages all encrusted with roses, leaves, fruit, groups of figures imitated in plaster like oak with such exactness that it is impossible to detect it from the finest oak-carving without scraping it &c. &c."
" Abbotsford is the Paradise of dogs—they abound in it and have free quarters in every room. . . . Sir Walter is seldom without a four-footed follower."

In September even Sir Walter has to acknowledge that he is " harrassed with company "—the Countess of Compton, her mother and two sisters (the Clephanes) . . . Mr. and Mrs. Terry . . . Lady Alvanley and her two daughters . . . " and late in the evening came Mrs Coutts attended by a lady, a secretary, a doctor, and I dont know how many servants ". Mrs. Coutts was the *quondam* actress Harriet Mellon subsequently mistress, wife, and widow of the great banker. She did not stay long on this occasion, for, provoked by the deference which Scott showed her by postponing dinner till her arrival, Lady Compton with aristocratic rudeness ruffled her wounded spirit so much that, despite Scott's intervention with his previous ward, and her attempts to propitiate, Mrs. Coutts departed the next morning. " However, I could not help the matter, so e'en let rank and wealth fight it out their own way." Sir John Malcolm was also a guest this autumn, at what exact date I cannot say : " I was two days there " , he wrote to his daughter, " and most delighted was my friend Sir Walter to see me. We walked together over all his estate, and looked at all his fine castle. We had a large party and many a tale, and Sir Walter declares that I best him in legends. But his is the wizard's art of giving them the shape that delights the world."

More interesting than these vanished shades, aristocratic and plutocratic, are the reminiscences of the American artist C. R. Leslie, a friend of Coleridge, Lamb, Constable and many others, who had already met Scott in London at the Dumergues amid a large company which included James Boswell, the Shakespearean scholar. This autumn he came to Abbotsford, selected by Constable to paint a portrait commissioned by Ticknor, the Boston professor [1]: " I have had three sittings from Sir Walter . . . during one of them there came on a thunderstorm, and as the peals followed more closely the flashes of lightning Scott became uneasy, and at length rose from his chair saying, I must go to Lady Scott, she is always frightened when it thunders." " I am painting in the Library. When Sir Walter is seated I always place a chair in the direction in which I wish him to look which is never long unoccupied by some one of his visitors who is sure to keep him in conversation. At the other end of the room there is generally a group round the harp or piano. Imagine how delightful these sittings are to me." " I remember Rose saying he had never known anybody who had read Voltaire's *Henriade* through. Scott replied, ' I have read it *and live*, but indeed in my youth I read everything '." " He talked of scenery as he wrote of it—like a painter ; and yet of pictures as works of art, he had little or no taste, nor did he pretend to any. To him they were interesting merely as representing some particular scene, person, or event. . . . There were hanging on the walls of his diningroom things which no eye possessed of sensibility to what is excellent in art could have endured. In this respect his house presented a striking contrast to that of Mr Rogers in which there was nothing that was not of high excellence . . . in music also Scott's enjoyment arose chiefly from the association called up by the air or words of a song." " His conversation was enriched with quotations often made highly humorous by their application . . . comparing the sound

---

[1] Who had made Scott's acquaintance in 1819, in Edinburgh and Abbotsford, where he was a guest for two days but was then compelled to leave by one of Scott's attacks of " violent spasms in his stomach, which could be controlled neither by laudanum nor bleeding."—*Life, Letters, etc., of George Ticknor*, London 1876, I, 280-284 ; and see *Letters*, V., 321 f.

of the dinner-bell, for which he said he had a very quick ear, to

> the sweet south
> That breathes upon a bank of violets
> Stealing and giving odour.

" There was more benevolence expressed in Scott's face than is given in any portrait of him," and Leslie notes his kindness to his deaf secretary, George Huntly Gordon, seating him always by his own side at the table, and dropping into his ear-trumpet any good thing that was said.

Among the guests expected was Canning, but his visit was prevented by the death of the King of France. Lady Alvanley was taken ill shortly after leaving Abbotsford and died at an Edinburgh hotel early in January 1825. On Scott as the only intimate friend in Edinburgh fell " many painful duties . . . and particularly the duty of supporting the two affectionate girls who were in a state of absolute distress and desolation ". In a juncture such as that the veneer of worldliness which wealth had induced, and which is apparent in Walter's marriage, disappeared, and there emerged the Scott who in youth had been the one friend faithful to the disinherited Kerr of Abbotrule. In November his letters are full of the great fire in the High Street which destroyed the steeple of the Tron Church and spreading endangered the " Courts of Justice and the Advocates more than princely Library. By great exertions it was prevented approaching this public building and Sir William Forbes's Bank also escaped. But all the other houses in the Parliament Square are totally destroyed, and I can conceive no sight more grand or terrible than to see these lofty buildings on fire from top to bottom, vomiting out flames like a volcano from every aperture, and finally crashing down one after another into an abyss of fire which resembled nothing but Hell, for there were vaults of wine and spirits which sent up huge jets of flame when ever they were called into activity by the fall of these massive fragments—Between the corner of the Parliament Square and the South Bridge all is destroyed excepting some new buildings at the lower extremity, and the devastation has extended down the closes which I hope will never be rebuilt on their present, I should say *late*, form" (*Letters*, VII, 427-8).

At Christmas Walter was home again, Charles commanded to remain at Oxford and pursue his studies. Walter put his fortunes to the touch in an Abbotsford more finished and decorated than in the previous winter, and " lighted with gas ", Captain Basil Hall reports, "in a style of extraordinary splendour" and at "a larger party than the house could ever before have accommodated " (*Lockhart*). Walter was accepted by the young lady, but her mother had scruples about giving her daughter to an officer of dragoons, belonging to a family of " episcopal principles ", and the son of a man of " poetical renown ". It may be she had some doubts as to Scott's financial position, prosperous as that might appear: " You have the rent-roll of Abbotsford ", Scott writes to Sir Adam on 11th January, " and may consult agriculturists about it if you will—it rates altogether £1680 which in the present day might sell for upwards of £50,000. I know it has cost me more than the same. My very successful literary undertakings engage me in cash transactions of considerable extent but from these I have made large sums of money and I have no doubt that I will add greatly to the landed property which must support my name and the rank with which my sovereign honoured me before I am called to part with it. I should also say that my younger children have a provision of about £5000 under life-rent of their maternal aunt and that I have insured my life for £10,000 and upwards in case of sudden death. . . . Besides this Walter has £5000 alongst with the others and his commission which, including £2037 lying at Coutts for purchase of the first troop vacancy, may amount to as much more, £10,000 in all independent of me entirely" (*Letters*, VIII, 473-4). So Scott contemplates his own position as in a kind of sanguine dream. Cadell who knew the insecurity of the position—Scott thought of profits to come as already there, much as Coleridge thought of works he dreamed of as already written—the insecurity of both the firms, had refused in 1821 to allow Constable, his father-in-law, to appoint Scott one of his marriage trustees : " I am clear, connected as he is with James Ballantyne and Co. and engaged as we are in bills with him and them, Sir Walter would never do as a trustee." Other business men with whom Mrs. Jobson may have had contacts through her husband's friends must have known something of the bills which were afloat in such large numbers, even if they did not know all that Cadell did. However Mrs. Jobson's scruples, whatever they were, religious or financial, were overcome. She was " silenced if not convinced ", later " quite subdued and reconciled ". " Settlements are preparing and the marriage is to take place next week " (*To William Laidlaw*, 25th *Jan.*, 1825).

But I have run ahead and must turn back for a word on the work of this, Scott's " last year of undisturbed prosperity " (*Lockhart*), the work done while he, with Tom Purdie, thinned the now growing plantations, with Gordon arranged his books, and with the help of Daniel Terry in London, and neat-handed carpenters and tailors and house-painters from the village of Darnick, furnished the growing house. " I should like the mirrors handsome and the frames plain ; the colour of the hangings is green with rich Chinese figures. On the side of the table I intend to have exactly beneath the glass a plain white side-table of the purest marble on which to place Chantrey's bust. A truncated pillar of the same marble will be its support, and I think that besides the mirror above there will be a plate of mirror below the table. . . . I am much obliged to Mr. Baldock for his confidence about the screen. But what says Poor Richard, Those who want money when they come to buy are apt to want money when they come to pay. Again poor Dick observes :

> That in many you find the true gentleman's fate
> Ere the house is complete he has sold the estate.

So we will adjourn consideration of the screen till other times, let us first have the needful got and paid for. The stuff for the windows in the drawing-room is the crimson damask silk we bought last year "—and so on, and so on. What is " needful " is a relative thing, hard to define, nor are things fully paid for, at least to the relief of the payer, by discounted bills on profits not yet realised.

In September 1823 Cadell had visited Scott at Abbotsford and found him, to his great relief, " in the best health and in no respect offended with me or at our late correspondence. . . . St. Ronan's advances and the next after it is already chalked out—it is to contain the Goblins and to be called the Witch, the materials for which in his extraordinary head are abundant." This projected story, which was apparently to embody some of the material for the Bogles or Goblins, that is the later *Demonology*, " was destined never to appear " (*Cadell to Lockhart circ.* 1833). The later months of 1823 and the early part of 1824 were given to completing an article on Romance for Constable's *Encyclopaedia Britannica*, the *Life of Richardson* for Ballantyne's Novels, a revision with much new material of the edition of Swift's Works : " Many thanks for the Witchcraft book " he writes to Constable in September, " ' A'thing helps ' as the wren said when it bestowed the superfluities of its person upon the sea. As you request I have put Swift in full progress." But *Redgauntlet*, at first called " Herries ", was also in full progress. It had been contracted for, Cadell told Lockhart, as early as May 1822 and, on the same authority, was begun " the moment *St. Ronan's Well* was finished ", that is, I take it, by November when the final proofs of the latter were going to James. But by December another scheme was already being outlined, something to follow *Redgauntlet*, " for ", says Cadell, " I was in Ballantyne's Printing Office " [the P.O. of Scott's letters] " when Sir Walter came in. *St. Ronan's Well* was just then out of his hands and the conversation turned on the subject of the next, for there was at the time four works contracted for. He said on the moment ' give me the pen. I shall make Josiah Cargill speak ' and wrote the following memorandum to be appended to the Novel of St. Ronan's Well as an advertisement. Which was done : ' Per Mess. Constable and Co. in one volume 8o. in the press and will speedily be published. being a specimen of the author's General History of the Crusaders, an account of the Siege of Ptolemais by the Reverend Mr Josiah Cargill Minister of the Gospel at St. Ronan's '." This was a mere *jeu d'esprit* though it *was* appended, with some few variations, to the first edition of the novel. What it shows is that the Tales of the Crusaders were already floating in Scott's mind. Indeed in February 1824 Scott tells Terry : " My present labours comprehend " [by which he means, I think, they are among the projects in view. The word need not imply that he is actually at work on them] " two narratives in about two volumes each they may perhaps intrude on volume 3. I intend that you shall have this which I think will be highly dramatic as soon as printed and as nothing can come out till the other volumes are both written and printed you will have ample time to dramatise it before any intruder can possibly interfere ". Douglas in *Familiar Letters* refers this to *Redgauntlet* and *The Betrothed*, but it was never intended that the former should be linked with another narrative in the manner of the first *Tales of my Landlord* and the later *Tales of the Crusaders*. It is to these last that Scott is referring, I must think. But Douglas has left out some words just before " my labours comprehend " [the original I have not seen], and it is possible that by the word " this " Scott does mean

Redgauntlet, on which he is at work, while prospecting the later Tales, for *Redgauntlet* was in fact dramatised [1] and acted in Edinburgh in the end of May 1825. The novel was issued in June 1824, and by July copy for *The Betrothed*, the first of the *Tales of the Crusaders*, was going to James : " I send some copy. I am a little downhearted about it but am getting on. When I do not please you or myself how can I please other folks. However I will get on " (*Letters*, VIII, 336).

That *Redgauntlet* was one of the early novels kept in cold storage, as Dame Una Pope Hennessey has suggested, is a tempting thought when one considers the crush of work which Scott was carrying through in these years, and also notes the surprising degree to which early memories re-blossom in the story and the characters as compared with the novel's immediate predecessors. But the MS. is extant in Scott's own handwriting, written as usually on the recto of each page with corrections and additions on the verso of the preceding page, and all on paper manufactured by Cowan in 1822.[2] This also must be accepted as a product of the early morning hours in these crowded years. " What time do you work? " Maria Edgeworth had written after the Abbotsford visit (12th October, 1823) and Scott's reply was : " Two hours rising in the morning before the rest of the family are active makes the greatest possibly difference between

---

[1] Whether by Terry or not I do not know. " Mr Murray respectfully informs his friends and the public that his benefit is fixed for Saturday Evening May 28, 1825, when will be performed for the first time in any theatre a Dramatic Sketch in Three Acts, interspersed with Music, founded upon the celebrated Novel called REDGAUNTLET &c."—Theatre Royal Edinburgh Play Bills, N.L.S. The songs included " The Minstrel Boy," " Go where glory waits thee," and other incongruous verses.

[2] The novels were sent to the press, transcribed and set up just as they were written, apparently without any waiting for the completion of the whole in MS. To a publisher, wishing to see sheets in advance, Constable writes : " We observe what you say as to the transmission of the early sheets of the Author of Waverley and would gladly amend it were it in our power, but we dont see how it can be done, and the difficulty being with

leisure and want of it. This space resolutely employed will serve in the usual case to despatch much of the business which is necessarily pressed upon every man." Captain Hall in his Journal of the visit in December-January 1824-5 discusses the same question: " In each page of *Kenilworth* there are, upon an average, 864 letters. Now I find that in ten days I have written 120 pages which would make about 108 pages of *Kenilworth*; and as there are 320 pages in a volume it would at my rate of writing this Journal cost about twenty nine and one half days for each volume or say three months for the composition of the whole work. No mortal in Abbotsford-house ever learned that I kept a Journal. I was in company all day and all the evening till a late hour—apparently the least occupied of the party; and I will venture to say, not absent from the drawing-room one quarter of the time that the Unknown was. I was always down to breakfast before any one else, and often three quarters of an hour before the Author of Kenilworth—always among the very last to go to bed—in short I would have set the acutest observer at defiance to have discovered when I wrote this Journal. I dont say it cost me much labour; but it surely is not too much to suppose that its composition has cost me, an unpractised writer, as much study as Kenilworth has cost the glorious Unknown." And occasionally Hall did get a glimpse of Scott at work: " Jan. 9. We saw nothing of the chief till

---

the author and the way in which his MS. goes to the Printer any change is almost impossible when we mention to you that the MS. goes in all cases to the Printer as it is written without waiting for the completion of a chapter or volume and is set up as soon as received so that at the completion of the third or last volume the work is in types as soon as he could get the MS. copied, you will at once see that we can afford you no facilities in this respect and it often happens that the last part of one of these works is all at press within a few days of the completion of the MS. by the author, even the whole three or four vols put into our hands is in ordinary cases complete. We could wish that we could treat with you on a different footing but our great author takes his own way and we must conform."—*Constable's Letter-Book*, 16th September, 1825.

luncheon-time between one and two, and then only for a few minutes. He had gone out to breakfast, and on his return seemed busy with writing. At dinner he was in great force, and pleasant it was to observe the difference which his powers of conversation undergo by the change from a large to a small party. On Friday when we sat down twenty to dinner it cost him apparently an effort to keep the ball up at table; but next day when the company was reduced to his own family with only two strangers (Fanny and I) he appeared to be delighted to be at home, and expanded with surprising animation, and poured forth his stores of knowledge and fun on all hands. I have never seen any person on more delightful terms with his family than he is. . . . Even the youngest of the nephews and nieces can joke with him, and seem at all times perfectly at ease in his presence—his coming into the room only increases the laugh, and never checks it—he either joins in what is going on or passes. No one notices him any more than if he were one of themselves."

No; if *Redgauntlet*—which like *The Antiquary* and *Quentin Durward* was not received with immediate favour—has become for many readers, like the late Lord Oxford, a novel with the freshness of the first " Scotch Novels ", it is because the author is once more upon his native heath and breathing the same historic air. Once again, too, there are, not casual references to recent experiences, but a revival of older and deeper rooted memories and emotions. The opening of the story in epistolary form may have been suggested by his preoccupation with the novels of Richardson during these same months; but he was also recalling his own early correspondence with Charles Kerr of Abbotrule when that young man, cut off by his family, was wandering through England to London, thence to the Isle of Man, and so to that Mecca of impecunious Scots in trouble, the plantations of Jamaica. Scott's own letters have disappeared but Kerr's are in the National Library; " I shall keep your letters as proof of an honest heart ". " God bless you for your past friendship, receive my warmest thanks—would to God I had more to offer." " The letters of Ker ", Lockhart wrote to Cadell in 1834, " have enabled me to convert Redgauntlet into almost a perfect picture of the life of two friends about 1788-9." The lighter tone of the letters in the novel, lighter than those of Kerr, explain why in the *Life* Lockhart claimed Clerk as the original of Darsie Latimer, but from what we know of Clerk he was not the irresponsible person that Kerr and Darsie show themselves. Alan Fairford is Scott as he remembered himself in those past days, at least one side of himself,—douce and prudent but a loyal friend ready to stick at nothing when his feelings are roused : " As for Mr Scott, mayhap you may take him for a poor lamiter but he is the first to begin a row and the last to end it " ; so a young midshipman had said of Walter, and Darsie's first letter fills out the picture : " Are you not my only friend . . . You taught me to keep my fingers off the weak and to close my fist against the strong." And Alan's father is the old W.S. who had warned his son to " have nothing to do with Charles Kerr ". " He offered, if I preferred his own profession immediately to take me into partnership with him . . . but he did not disguise his wish that I should relinquish the situation to my younger brother and embrace the more ambitious profession of the bar." But he was distrustful of friends who might seduce his son into idleness or other interests than the law. The " Green Mantle " is certainly not Miss Belsches but may well be Miss Jane Cranstoun who had followed his ride in 1796 to Aberdeen with such sympathy, for that too is recalled when the Baillie would have made Alan a freeman of the town of Dumfries had he been " a year aulder ", for so had Aberdeen done to Walter in recognition of his father's services. In none of the novels do we breathe so much the air of Scott's early life, which is no proof that it was then written, for it is when seen through the casement of the years that our past experiences take on a mellow and enchanting hue. Even the picture of the Quakers has its source in an old interest in his own Quaker ancestors on both the Scott and the Swinton side.

In the April before the publication of *Redgauntlet* Lord Byron died: "I have been terribly distressed", Scott writes in early June to Lady Abercorn, " at poor Byron's death. In talents he was unequalled, and his faults were those of a bizarre temper arising from an eager and irritable nervous habit rather than any depravity of disposition. He was devoid of selfishness which I take to be the basest ingredient in the human composition. He was generous, humane and noble-hearted when passion did not blind him. The worst I ever saw about him was that he liked indifferent company rather than that of those whom he must, from character and talent, have necessarily conversed with most upon an equality" (*Letters*, VIII, 292). " Nothing can interest me more than the last verses of poor Byron born as he was for something so noble and only prevented from attaining the highest point in public esteem by the faults which I think flowed from a morbid temperament which like the slave in the triumphant chariot so often accompanies genius to humble her and her triumphs " (*Letters*, VIII, 338). Scott's review of the third canto of *Childe Harold* in the *Quarterly* had evoked from Byron a letter of almost passionate gratitude. " I owe to you more than the usual obligation for the courtesies of literature and common friendship—for you went out of your way in 1817 to do me a service when it required not merely kindness but courage ; to have been recorded by you in such a manner would have been a proud memorial at any time but at such a time when ' All the World and his Wife' (or rather *mine*) as the proverb goes were trying to trample upon me was something still higher to my self-esteem " (28*th March*, 1822). To Scott as to Goethe, if in a very different way, indeed to almost everyone capable of feeling, Byron was, whatever the artistic faults of his poetry, a force, an event not to be forgotten by anyone who had experienced it, a force whose impact one might resent and resist or welcome, but the general effect of which could not be ignored, a disturbing and disintegrating but also a releasing, emancipating effect alike in politics, in morals and in poetry. Finer poets at their best had gone down, unnoticed for the time being by the world, or lived on unregarded. Yet even for the right appreciation, the enjoyment of their poetry—Wordsworth, Shelley, Keats—it was Byron and Scott who, in a measure, supplied the ferment.

Byron's life did not illustrate the only way in which the temperament of genius might humble its possessors and their triumph, as Scott was soon to learn. The stream of his family and social happiness rose to its highest level in the early part of 1825, but so did his expenses. " The real road to ruin ", he writes to Tom's widow, " 1st is to have an improveable estate with a taste for building—2ndly to have your son marry a wealthy heiress and call on you for outfit and marriage presents, and if over and above you can manage to have a troop to buy for him in a crack regiment of cavalry you will find the bottom of the purse with a vengeance. But there is always balm in Gilead for Clerks of Session whose quarterday is always coming round in its due time " (*Letters*, IX, 123). Alas! the salary of a Clerk of Session would by itself go but a small way in encountering such a sea of expenditure. In the marriage contracts of the young couple Scott settled Abbotsford on Walter reserving the right to borrow £10,000 on the estate, less, of course, the £3000 existing mortgage on Kaeside. For Walter's captaincy he advanced the sum of £3500 which his son was to regard as a debt. To Jane, the new daughter, Scott not only sent gifts but wrote her, during the next few months, some of the happiest of all his letters : "Here I ought to stop for I have twenty letters to write. But like all old papas I would rather write nonsense to my children than play *genteel, sensible* and *clever* with half the world beside." " On the other hand remember it is our bargain that you are never to mend a pen when you write to me or think a moment either about subject or about expression. Sometimes perhaps I shall suggest topics as I did in my last which you answered so faithfully from Abbotsford " (*Letters*, IX, 17). " My daughters who deserve all the affection a father can bestow are both near me and in safe guardianship. . . . For my sons I have taught them, and what was more difficult, I have taught myself, the philosophy that for their own sake and their necessary advancement in life their absence from my home must be long and their visits short. . . . But for you my dear Jane who have come among us with such generous and confiding affection my Stoicism must excuse me if I am more anxious than becomes a philosopher or a hackneyed man of the world who uses in common cases to take the world as he finds it " (*20th March*, 1825). So he writes to her while the newly married couple move to London to visit the Dumergues and others, and thence to Ireland where he warmly commends them to the kindness of the Edgeworths; and to Ireland he determines himself to go in July, his first move abroad since he was in Paris in 1815. In these ten years he had written eighteen novels in addition to *Paul's Letters*, the historical portions in some numbers of *The Edinburgh Annual Register*, biographies of novelists, to say nothing of contributions to such works as *Provincial Antiquities*, the *Encyclopaedia*, the *Quarterly*, &c. I say eighteen novels, but might say nineteen including *The Talisman*, for before 1824 was out, *The Betrothed*, first of *The Tales of the Crusaders*, was completed, and by James pronounced a failure : " I am very apprehensive of finding some remedy for the failure which you very justly announce but I greatly doubt your recipe. What has happened may happen again under the same circumstances. Constable, I fear, had more shrewdness than either of us when he recommended a *fallow*. But we will talk over this. In the meantime be assured that sincerity is the quality I most value in a friend or critic and though I think you are sometimes fastidious about trifles I never fail to consider your opinion as completely authoritative upon general results especially when as in this present case it completely coincides with my own, for you must not think that, as Dorax says to Sebastian :

> Thou hast dared
> To tell me what I durst not tell myself."
> (*To James Ballantyne*, 11th Nov. 1824).

But Scott soon rallied to James's advice to try another. *The Betrothed* was laid up in James's office, and by April 1825, the marriage functions over, Scott is sending back proofs of the early pages of *The Talisman*, composing the story as printing goes on : " I think I have a good plot with two surprises in it. If I suceed I may make a sort of continuation bringing home Richard and giving an account of his captivity. Perhaps the tale is threadbare " (*Letters*, IX, 88). By May the work " approaches its end. Pray do you gentlemen proprietors intend the same politeness by me as on former occasions viz. to pay me the copy money of Vol. 4th? If Walter makes his purchase of a troop this will be convenient for me—if not I had as lief it goes to account of cash received for future labours and so diminishes my debt with you " (*Letters*, IX, 113-4). In June accordingly " The *Tales of the Crusaders* were put forth ; and as Mr Ballantyne had predicted, the brightness of *The Talisman* dazzled the eyes of the million to the defects of the twin story. Few of these publications had a more enthusiastic greeting " (*Lockhart*). " I cannot help writing you a line to say ", thus Lady Louisa Stuart on 2nd July, " how much I like the Crusaders. Your long pause has been *se reculer pour mieux sauter*, for they soar far above their immediate predecessors and approach the height of *Ivanhoe*, especially *The Talisman*. . . . I had no suspicion of the Saladin either in the Emir or the Physician, he burst upon me quite by surprise. Both are wonderfully well managed; the desert too—the fountain that refreshes as one reads—Denys Morolt—Archbishop Baldwin and many other things in the Betrothed have great charms in my eyes. And I am particularly glad of the ballads addressed to Ahriman &c. having gone without any verse for a great while."

Even before the *Tales* were out there was a great meeting at Abbotsford of Scott and Constable at which the latter developed with all his expansive eloquence the popularisation of literature by the issue of cheaper books, " Constable's Miscellany ", " this is the cleverest thing that ever came into the head of the cleverest of all bibliopolic heads " (*Scott to Lockhart*, 5th *May*). For this Scott, who had so often been besought to get on with the twice promised History of Scotland, and whom James's adverse judgement on *The Betrothed* had somewhat persuaded that " the vein of fiction was nearly worked out ", undertook to write " the most wonderful book which the world ever read—a book in which every incident shall be incredible, yet strictly true—a book recalling recollections with which the ears of this generation once tingled, and which shall be read by our children with an admiration approaching incredulity. Such shall be the Life of Napoleon Bonaparte by the Author of Waverley." So the two Napoleons " of the realms of print " were to combine on a venture bearing the name of the man who, Byron had said, made past fame dubious and future fame impossible. They were an extraordinary couple, Scott and Constable, a difficult team for the sober and canny Cadell to drive and keep in the middle of the road; little wonder that when they stumbled and fell he was eager to clear the traces of the " bookseller " and gain exclusive control of the " bookmaker ".

For Scott Napoleon had the same attraction as Byron. Politically he had no sympathy with either, and Napoleon he had hated as every British patriot felt it natural and right to do. But both appealed to his imagination as in their different ways the most extraordinary men of an extraordinary age. To write of Napoleon was, too, as in the best of his novels, to blend history with personal memories. He had lived through the Revolution and the career of Napoleon, been at least a volunteer when invasion was threatened, known what it was to have all the foundations of society breaking or threatened. Before June was over he had written the greater part of the Introduction on the Revolution.

And then, with two novels just published and a new work on hand, he set out in July for his holiday in Ireland : " I expect to be able to set out for Glasgow on Saturday 9th July " (he writes " June " but the 9th July is the date of the postmark on the letter). " Next day we will go to the Kirk like good bairns and spend the day with Dr Lockhart and set off next day by steamer for Belfast. So with any luck of a tolerable passage Anne Lockhart and I will be in St. Stephen's Green " [where Walter and Jane were housed] " in the evening of the 12th or morning of the 13th July." It was on the 8th, according to Lockhart, they left Edinburgh, more probably the 10th as Scott is dating letters from Edinburgh on the 9th. His earliest letter from Dublin is dated the 15th, on which day Lockhart writes to Sophia : " we reached Dublin yesterday (thursday)."

For the details of Scott's triumphant reception in Ireland one must go to Lockhart—the receptions and dinners and honorary degree at Trinity, the visit to Wicklow where despite his lame leg he " climbed into the stony bed from which Saint Kevin precipitated the fair Kathleen into the lake " and then to Edgeworthstown and a tour with Maria to Killarney, going and coming by different routes. Scott's heart had been early drawn to the Irish, not sufficiently to make him support any movement likely to endanger Britain : but he loved the Irish wit and warmth of feeling and he more than suspected the injustice from which they had suffered and still suffered. He came to accept Catholic emancipation, though on purely opportunist grounds, for he maintained that had the penal laws been continued for another half-century Popery would have been all but extinguished, and he was urgent with Lockhart later not to give Southey a free hand in the *Quarterly* to oppose Wellington's policy in 1829. But he did not believe that the root of the trouble was religious : " I suspect, however, it is laying a plaister to the foot while the head aches and that the fault is in the landlords' extreme exactions not in the disabilities of the Catholics or any more remote cause " (*To Walter, 4th April,* 1825). And if Scott had a regard for the Irish they had welcomed his works as warmly as the English or Scots. The novels are dispatched to Dublin by Cadell on issue as promptly as to London. When poor Tom's wife was stranded in Cork in 1813 expecting a baby, the mention of her brother-in-law's name secured for her and her family every attention : " I am sure seven or eight people sent me the newspaper when the present of your native city was mentioned—in short I think they have an uncommon degree of politeness or rather real kindness." So the visit of a month was an ovation and a picnic : " I well intended to have written from Ireland ", he informs Joanna Baillie in October. " But alas! Hell, as some stern old divine says, is paved with good intentions. There was such a whirl of visiting and laking and boating and wandering and shouting and laughing and carousing, so much to see and so little time to see it, so much to be heard and only two ears to listen to twenty voices, that upon the whole I grew desperate and gave up all thought of doing what was right and proper upon post-days . . . I have not the pen of our friend Maria Edgeworth who writes all the while she laughs, talks, eats, drinks, and I believe, though I do not pretend to be so far in the secret, all the time she sleeps too. . . . We had Lockhart to say clever things, and Walter with his whiskers to overawe postillions and impudent beggars, and Jane to bless herself that the folks had neither houses, clothes nor furniture, and Anne to make fun from morning to night,

   And merry folks were we."

(*Letters*, IX, 237-40.)

 Lockhart's note on Miss Edgeworth's ready pen is more sarcastic : " We have been kept in motion so continually that no one but Miss Edgeworth could ever find a moment for penwork. She, to be sure, is a being by herself as to that matter, and well might Joanna Baillie say she would be scribbling at Almack's. I dont think we ever stopped ten minutes but she was at it—what, why, or to whom, God only knows."

But if both Scott and Lockhart enjoyed the expedition and appreciated the wit and humour of the peasantry, even political prejudice could not disguise from them the misery of an ill-used country. " But ever and anon, as we moved deeper into the country, there was a melancholy in his countenance and, despite himself, in the tone of his voice. . . . The constant passings and repassings of bands of mounted policemen armed to the teeth . . . the rueful squalid poverty that crawled by every wayside and blocked up every village where we had to change horses with exhibitions of human suffering and degradation such as it had never entered into our heads to conceive—and above all the contrast between these naked, clamorous beggars . . . and the boundless luxury and merriment surrounding the thinly scattered magnates who condescended to inhabit their ancestral seats, would have been sufficient to poison those landscapes had nature dressed them out in the verdure of Arcadia. . . . It is painful enough to remember such things . . . such widespread manifestations of the wanton and reckless profligacy of human mismanagement, the withering curse of feuds and factions, and the tyrannous selfishness of absenteeism." North Wales seemed a Paradise after Ireland.

For the holiday was not over with the departure from Ireland on the 18th of August. They returned by Holyhead and Chester; and, after a visit to the Ladies of Llangollen, described by Lockhart in his most sarcastic manner, and to Wilson at Elleray on the banks of Windermere, Scott, Lockhart and Anne joined a party at Storrs, the seat of John Bolton, a Liverpool merchant, a party which included Canning and Wordsworth. "There was high discourse," writes Lockhart, "intermingled with as gay flashings of courtly wit as ever Canning displayed, and a plentiful allowance on all sides of those airy transient pleasantries in which the fancy of poets, however wise and grave, delights to run riot when they are sure not to be misunderstood. There were beautiful and accomplished women to adorn and enjoy this circle. There were brilliant cavalcades through the woods in the mornings, and delicious boatings on the lake by moonlight," and he goes on to describe the procession of fifty barges when " the bards of the Lakes led the cheers that hailed Scott and Canning ". So in the *Life*: in a letter at the time his usual sarcasm has freer play: "Wordsworth is old and pompous and fine and absurdly arrogant beyond conception—evidently thinks Canning and Scott together not worth his thumb.... He is well where he ought to be, would he only drop a little of his airs, and his preaching above all for that is the devil, particularly where two such anti-preachers as your Papa and the Secretary are in the room." "Here is this beautiful lake" writes Scott to his daughter-in-law, "lying before me as still as a mirror reflecting all the hills and trees as distinctly as if they were drawn with a pencil. I wish you were with us Love for we expect a grand show upon the Lake.... Tomorrow I go down to Keswick to see Southey who is unwell. Wordsworth I saw yesterday much the worse for wear—he looks so old that I begin to think I must be getting old myself—a secret which I am by no means fond of prying into." From Storrs they passed to Rydal where Scott and

Wordsworth vied with one another in quotations from Wordsworth's poetry, mutually silent on Scott's; and to Southey " pale and sickly—stung by a venomous insect in the Netherlands"; and then, unaccompanied by Wordsworth, the Scott group visited Lowther Castle. He was at Abbotsford on the 26th August : " I am here once more stationary. . . . I want to get to work again as soon as possible for idleness does not suit me. I cannot however call myself idle since I am busy reading and making notes. . . . J. Ballantyne is also very hungry for business and I beg of you to lend him a shove just now which we may pay back another day in some equivalent piece of kindness." So he writes to Constable on the 9th of September, telling him also that he has booked him as the publisher of a collected edition of Charles Maturin's poetry and novels.

So ended Scott's last real holiday. The stream of his life, literary and social, was to flow for some months yet, full but tranquil. *Napoleon* is pushing on, Constable sending books as required, including a " set of the Moniteur commencing in June 1789 and continued to December 1823 in 70 volumes" (*Constable to Scott 20th September*). The *Lives of the Novelists* are continued, at least a Life of Charlotte Smith is sent to James in September though her novels were not ultimately included in the Ballantyne series. Very soon we hear that *Woodstock* is in preparation : " I have begun Woodstock—your doubt about the title may be supplied by an additional one" (*To James B., 6th November*). The full title was ultimately *Woodstock or the Cavalier. A Tale of Sixteen Hundred and Fifty-one.*" Of visitors there was the usual coming and going : " Lord and Lady Ravensworth and their son Mr Liddell is staying here, they are all very pleasant" (*Anne Scott to her cousin Walter at Chatham, 20th September*). " We have a large houseful just now, Lord and Lady Gifford, Lord Chief Baron and Lady Shepherd, besides two friends of Lord Sidmouth. . . . There is the Solicitor too by the way. . . . We have the Russells with us for ten days"

(11*th October*). "John Richardson has been here looking at an old domain within five miles of us and left us in the earnest determination to buy having caught a basket of trout in the stream he is to call his own" (12*th October*). "My dear Captain and Mrs Hall ... I lose no time in saying that you and Mrs Hall cannot come but as welcome guests any day next week which may best suit you. If you have time to drop a line we will make our dinner hour suit your arrival, but you cannot come amiss to us" (13*th October*). "We expect the great Mrs Coutts today bringing in her train the duke of St. Albans and his sister—the former the newspapers will have it is slave to her *beaux yeux* or more properly the *beaux yeux de sa cassette*. I think she is scarcely such a fool as to marry him but to be a Duchess is a pretty thing" (25*th October*). "Here is Mrs Coutts good lady has taken possession of my home and kicks up a row which would be less troublesome at any other time" (26*th October*). Among these departed great ones came—*after*, I think, not as Lockhart says, *before* Mrs. Coutts—the great little Irish poet and biographer of Byron, Tom Moore. "Here has been Mrs Coutts with &c." (5*th November*). "Thomas Moore is here and in grand feather. In these ticklish times I dare not ask you to leave headquarters. I would have otherwise been glad you had met him" (*To James Ballantyne, 6th November*). Of Moore's impressions a few are recorded by Lockhart, much of the same tenor as those of others.

CHAPTER XI

"I can no longer have the delight of waking in the morning with bright ideas in my mind, haste to commit them to paper and count them monthly as the means of planting such groves and purchasing such wastes; replacing my dreams of fiction by other prospective visions of walks by
> Fountainheads, and pathless groves,
> Places which pale Passion loves."
>   SCOTT, *The Journal*, December 18, 1825.

"There is no period of his life at which he inspires a more affectionate, a more reverent interest than when he wrote under the incubus of pecuniary distress. It is an interest that quenches criticism, and extinguishes pity and sorrow, in admiration and gratitude."
>   EDWARD EVERETT, *The Mount Vernon Papers* (1860), p. 141.

BUT, as the letter to James indicates, the times were growing ticklish. Some omens of what was coming are touched on in earlier letters: "The people are all mad about joint-stock companies", he had written to Maria Edgeworth as early as 23rd March, " and the madness which possesses John Bull has caught his speculative brother Sawney. No man can commit the extremity of folly with so grave a countenance and under the influence of such admirable reasoning as a Scotchman. The whole nation indeed deserves the character given to the sapient Monarch of old, the wisest fool in Christendom." In the facetious introduction to *Tales of the Crusaders* he had enlarged on the paradox by which a man by membership of Joint Stock Companies might be both buyer for and seller to himself, when, as Lockhart comments, " he was just about to see the apparently earth-founded pillars of his own worldly fortune shattered in ruins because, not content with being the first author of the age, he had chosen to be also his own printer and his own bookseller."

The advent of the crisis in Scott's financial affairs is closely connected with Lockhart's own activities at this juncture. To obtain for his son-in-law some well paid berth that might make him less dependent on *Blackwood*, with its temptations to satiric warfare, had been one of Scott's chief preoccupations during the autumn following his return to Scotland. He was always an active canvasser for his friends—William Erskine, Archibald, brother of Mungo Park, Joseph Train, poor Henry Weber, George Thomson, " the guider of my boys ... nearer Parson Adams than any living creature I ever saw—very learned, very religious, very simple and extremely absent," William Laidlaw (" But for you ", writes Laidlaw's brother, " my brother would have been reduced to depend for the necessaries of life upon his grudging creditors."), Charles Maturin, James Bailey, B. R. Haydon, Archdeacon Williams, his brothers Daniel and Tom and their children, were, with others, all indebted to Scott's indefatigable efforts for their welfare. " I wrote myself blind and sick last night about poor Williams," he tells Lockhart as late as 1828, when the rector of the Edinburgh Academy had too hastily thrown up his post to accept a professorship in the episcopally anathematized University College, London. If nothing more could be done, a Bank of England note was enclosed to Haydon in the King's Bench, or a bill on Constable to Maturin. What could be got for Lockhart was a thought never absent from Scott's mind now and to the end of his life. To the Countess of Stafford he writes in June to promote his candidature for a Sheriffdom—Caithness or Sutherland. But Lockhart's own thoughts were turning in another direction. Gifford, who was old and never had been strong—he died in 1826—laid down the editorship of *The Quarterly* in 1824. Scott suggested Southey as a possible editor (*To Southey* 26*th September*, 1824), but, mainly at Southey's instance, John

Taylor Coleridge, a nephew of the poet, had been appointed by Murray for the time being. Southey hoped that in his hands there " would be none of that injustice and cruelty (for example) which was shown towards Keats ". But before Gifford's retirement Lockhart made two journeys to London in 1824 with, I think, a view to his own succession. Croker, on whom he relied as a dominant influence in the *Review*, without discouraging Lockhart nevertheless failed to mention his name to Murray.[1] But by the autumn of 1825 Murray, growing doubtful of Coleridge as an editor, or of his remaining in view of his growing work at the bar, approached Lockhart, without consulting Croker. He did so at first in connection with quite another venture, the establishment of a new morning paper, for which the impetus came from a young man of twenty-one. On the 27th of September there appeared at Chiefswood, to the surprise of Lockhart who had expected an older man, " a sprig of the rod of Aaron, young d'Israeli. In point of talents he reminded us of his father for sayth Mungo's garland

    Crapaud pickanini
    Crapaud himself

which means a young coxcomb is like the old one who got him " (*Scott to Rose*, 12*th October*). The proposal, of which Lockhart had been advised in advance by his friend Wright, was that Lockhart should become either editor or, as it might be called, " adviser ", of *The Representative* and " take a superintending part not as laborious editor or contributor but rather that you should take a place connected with it of the highest rank that a paper established on a great scale can ensure you. For this Murray will guarantee for three or four years a salary of £1000 a year

---

[1] " As for the matter personal to myself of which I spoke to you, I can only say I left it in Croker's hands."—LOCKHART to WILSON, 2nd January, 1825. " During all my consultations on the former occasion [*i.e.* when Coleridge was appointed] he [Croker] never mentioned your name."— MURRAY to LOCKHART, 24th November, 1825.

with a reasonable prospect of making two thousand or upwards ". " All minor arrangements have been settled and there has been considerable communication with Mr Canning on the subject but I presume he does not come forward so as to take any personal responsibility." So his friend Wright had written to Lockhart as early as the 12th September, and it was to lend the support of his ardent temperament and persuasive eloquence that Benjamin Disraeli had come north, for in announcing that Disraeli " will wait on you in a day or two " Wright says not a word about *The Quarterly*. *The Representative* and the possibilities of its leading to work at the bar and even a seat in Parliament are the themes on which he and Disraeli expatiated, but Wright with caution and suggesting a visit to London before committing himself. " Do not make Disraeli acquainted with the contents of this letter, he is Murray's right hand in settling arrangements in this new scheme and promises are bright." It was Wright's talk of " Disraeli " without the " Benjamin " that led Lockhart and Scott to expect an older man : " Mr Lockhart had conceived it was my father who was coming " (*To Murray*). Wright's letter reached Lockhart on the 17th and he wrote to Disraeli in Edinburgh. The latter arrived at Chiefswood, as stated, on the 27th, and Scott came to breakfast on the 28th, " and afterwards we were all three closeted together. ... The Chevalier entered into it excellently. ... He agrees with me that M. [*i.e.* Lockhart] cannot accept any official situation of any kind as it would compromise his independence, but he thinks *Parliament for M. indispensable* and also very much to *our interest*." So the young Dizzy to Murray while he is busy persuading Lockhart that all the great interests are behind the scheme and that " he is coming to London to be not the Editor of a Newspaper but the Director General of an immense organ and at the head of a band of high-bred gentlemen and important interests. ... Of [Lockhart's] capability, *perfect, complete capability* there is no manner of doubt ... you are dealing with a *perfect gentleman*" (*To Murray*).¹ Scott and Lockhart were charmed with the enthusiastic young man, and he with them, as also with " the beauty and unique character of Abbotsford."

But that Lockhart should be the actual editor of a daily paper was not to Scott's taste : " This department of literature may and ought to be rendered more respectable than it is at present, but I think this a reformation more to be wished than hoped for" (*Letters*, IX, 250). Accordingly the two younger men went up to London together in the second week of October, Lockhart carrying a letter from Scott to Constable who had travelled up a week earlier on the business of his " Miscellany ". In London a new bargain was struck and Murray writes to Scott on the 15th October : " I have proposed to Mr Lockhart to come to London as the editor of the Quarterly —an appointment which I verily believe is coveted by many of the highest literary characters in the country, and which of itself would entitle its possessor to enter into and mix with the first classes of society. For this, without writing a line, but merely performing the duties of an editor I shall have the pleasure of allowing him a thousand pounds a year ; and this with contributions of his own might easily become £1500." In *The Representative* he is to have a share, the profit of which should amount to another £1500. It is possible that Murray contemplated regaining a share in Scott's interest. He made some tentative efforts after the disaster, but treated Scott always with great generosity. There was not entire satisfaction in London either with the way in which Coleridge had been dropped or with the choice of a *Blackwood* man to succeed him.²

¹ The references throughout are to the *Life of Benjamin Disraeli, Earl of Beaconsfield* by William Flavelle Monypenny, Vol. I, 1804-37. London 1910.

² " I am afraid that Murray has been behaving very absurdly in not communicating to Mr Coleridge what he *did* about the Review when I was in town up to the time when you receive this. I think I have secured that this nonsense shall not go on any longer. Mr Coleridge, if it should, would have just reason to complain and it is even probable that I who have had

Croker, that somewhat ambiguous friend of both Scott and Lockhart, Barrow of the Admiralty, and others, perhaps Southey, expressed their uneasiness, and Disraeli had to rush down to Scotland again to see Scott who wrote a long defence of his son-in-law to Murray (17th *November*) and somewhat of an apologia to Southey (22nd *November, Letters,* IX, 284-8, 297-9).

Long afterwards[1] Disraeli recalled his visits to Abbotsford and early sight of Scott and Constable. " I remember him quite well, a kind but rather stately, person: with his pile of forehead, sagacious eye, white hair and green shooting-coat.... I have seen him sitting in his armchair in his beautiful library ... with half-a-dozen terriers about him: in his lap, on his shoulders, at his feet. ... He would read aloud in the evening or his daughter, an interesting girl, Anne Scott, would sing some ballad on the harp. He liked to tell a story of some Scotch chief, sometimes of some Scotch lawyer." " As I came down to dinner " [on his second visit] " Sir Walter was walking up and down the hall with a very big, stout, florid man, apparently in earnest conversation. I was introduced to him before dinner as Mr Constable—the famous publisher of the *Edinburgh Review* and the Waverley Novels, the authorship not then acknowledged. It struck me that I had never met before such an ostentatious man, or one whose conversation was so braggart. One would think that he had written the Waverley Novels himself; and certainly that Abbotsford belonged to him. However, he seemed to worship Scott and to express his adoration.... He informed me that he intended to build a new wing to Abbotsford next year, and you would have supposed from

nothing to do with the matter may be blamed by him.... I understand Mr Barrow and Mr Hay (of the Colonial department) being *consulted* by Murray have advised him against doing a thing which in fact; and as he ought to have told them, *is done* . . . they consider me as a man of squibs and of squibs only . . . a sort of connection with Blackwood which has had no existence."—LOCKHART to CROKER, 16th November, 1825.

[1] " Written nearly forty years later." Monypenny, *op. cit.* I, 77-8.

what he said that Sir Walter had only commenced developing a new Eldorado." The Eldorado in Constable's mind was his projected "Miscellany".

It was while all this was going on that to Lockhart at Chiefswood came news in a letter from Wright which he passed on to Scott, who had left Abbotsford for Edinburgh on the 11th of November. The letter is not now extant, but Scott's reply of the 18th indicates clearly what were its main contents. Lockhart had returned from London on 22nd or 23rd October, leaving Constable still there. Constable returned to his home at Polton on the 7th of November, and informed Scott of his return by a letter of the 11th. What Lockhart now communicated to Scott, on the strength of the letter he had received, was that Hurst, Robinson and Co. (Constable's London agents) were in a precarious condition, and that Constable himself had left London hurriedly because his banker had thrown up his book. Scott was shaken, and at once reported what he had heard to Cadell, without mentioning the source.[1] Cadell reassured him, saying among other things " that they had no engagements either present or future that they were not amply prepared to fulfill. I think the report has originated in the difficulties of the money markets which even the greatest houses must feel a little and in the bankruptcy of a great bookseller lately which always sets on foot similar reports of failure . . . and Constable may have had some pinch for the moment" (*Scott to Lockhart, 18th*

[1] I have not retold the story of Scott's drive to Polton to see Constable after Lockhart had brought, as he says, to Abbotsford from Chiefswood the report that Constable had left London hastily because a " London Banker had thrown up his book ". I cannot bring myself to believe the story. Constable left London early in November and reached home on the 7th, as he reported in a letter to Scott on the 11th, which he need not have done had they already met. Scott had himself returned to Edinburgh on that day, and it was on 18th November that he received from Lockhart the letter in which Wright announced the report about the Banker which Scott immediately conveyed to Cadell who, as I have said, reassured him. A letter of Cadell to Constable shows that he suspected Lockhart was the source of the story as far as Scott was concerned, and bitterly resented it. See *Times Literary Supplement*, Sept. 29, 1932, *Correspondence*, p. 691.

November). This indicates clearly what I have said earlier of Scott's confidence in the solidity of Constable and Co., his unawareness of that deficiency of capital of which Cadell made continual complaint in his letters to his partner.

Three days after his visit to Cadell, and his reassuring letter to Lockhart, Scott began to keep a journal, moved thereto by what Moore had shown him of Byron's journals: " I have bethought me, on seeing lately some volumes of Byron's notes, that he probably had hit upon the right way of keeping such a memorandum book by throwing aside all pretence to regularity and order and marking down events just as they occurred to recollection. I will try this plan." Two months later Scott knew himself a ruined man, and his connection with Constable and the Ballantynes was public knowledge. The authorship of the novels was an open secret, though not acknowledged till two years later. Accordingly the element of secrecy in Scott's life disappears, that compartmental arrangement of his interests and activities to which I have referred was over. The three streams, social, literary, commercial, united, flowed on openly for such as cared to know, and for posterity in the *Journal* and letters. There are no more difficult problems to discuss; and I propose to trace the events shortly with a good deal of omission of detail, endeavouring rather to bring into relief the aspects of Scott's character and mind which the searching experiences of these years served to heighten or emphasise. Nothing in the novels or the letters reveals so clearly as the *Journal* the acuteness and depth of his sensibility. He had not been prone to wear his heart upon his sleeve though it might reveal itself at moments when some happening broke through the surface of stoicism and worldliness—the tears to which he confesses in communicating to Clerk the encouraging letter from his first love, his outburst to Jeffrey when the Whig lawyer spoke lightly of changes in Scottish law and custom, his horror when one of the Commissioners made a gesture as if to place the recovered crown of Scotland on the head of a young lady. Scott's deepest feelings sought expression and relief in action, whence his numerous acts of kindness. Lockhart " mentions poor Southey testifying much interest for me, even to tears. It is odd. Am I so hard-hearted a man? I could not have wept for him, though in distress I would have gone any length to serve him. I sometimes think I do not deserve people's good opinion for certainly my feelings are rather guided by reflection than impulse. But everybody has his own mode of expressing interest, and mine is Stoical even in bitterest grief. *Agere atque pati Romanum est.* I hope I am not the worse for wanting the tenderness that I see others possess, and which is so amiable. I think it does not cool my wish to be of use where I can. But the truth is I am better at enduring or acting than at consoling. From childhood's earliest hour my heart rebelled against the influence of external circumstances in myself and others. *Non est tanti* "—deep sensibility; the impulse, born at once of such acuteness of feeling (as a protective instinct) and of pride, to disguise feeling or let it find relief and expression in action rather than words or tears ; personal and social pride with an entire absence of vanity ; a sanguine temper and love of life that had kept, " usually veiled under an air of worldly seeming," the heart of a boy and a boy's love of action and of dreaming : " Since I was five years old I cannot remember the time when I had not some ideal part to play for my own solitary amusement." " My life though not without its fits of waking and strong exertion has been a sort of dream spent in

> Chewing the cud of sweet and bitter fancy.

I have worn a wishing-cap—the power of which has been to divert present griefs by a touch of the wand of imagination and gild over the future prospect by prospectives more fair than can ever be realised." " The love of solitude was with me a passion of early youth ; when in my teens I used to fly from company to indulge in visions and airy castles of my own, the disposal of ideal wealth and the exercise of imaginary power"—so Scott contemplates his own life and character in the hours of awakening that followed the disaster. Never perhaps had he dreamed more uninterruptedly than between 1818, when Constable and Cadell became his settled publishers, and the end of 1825, when novels were streaming from his pen, Abbotsford was rearing its towers and pinnacles without, and being decorated and lighted within. With Walter's marriage to a wealthy heiress he seemed to be securing the foundation of a landed family: "Walter Scott Esq. bridegroom apparent—of the King's Hussars by grace of God and the Horseguards Lieutenant—younger of Abbotsford and expectant of Lochore and a Baronet in posse to boot of all that." Such is the superscription of the note Walter carries to Constable, who is to supply him with "the needful", two days before the marriage.

But now the awakening was come. The alarm of 18th November died down on Cadell's assurances though Cadell was quite as much alarmed as Scott, but before the month ended Scott signed a bond with Constable for £5000 to give relief to Hurst, Robinson and Co. The Lockharts left for London on 5th December: "Left us early and without leave-taking; when I arose at eight o'clock they were gone. This was very right, I hate red eyes and blowing of noses.... I have lost some of the comforts to which I chiefly looked for enjoyment—Well I must make the more of such as remain—God bless them. And so I will unto my holy work again which at present is the description of that *heilige Kleeblatt*, that worshipful triumvirate, Danton, Robespierre, Marat." But his heart was heavy within him—the uncertainty of the business world, his wife's illness, his own health. No one could work so hard for ever without penalty. There had been warnings, in sudden attacks in April, and later in Ireland. On 11th December he notes "a touch of the *morbus eruditorum* . . . a tremor of the heart, the pulsation of which becomes painfully sensible—a disposition to causeless alarm—much lassitude—decay of vigour of mind and activity of intellect. The reins feel weary and painful, and the mind is apt to receive and encourage gloomy apprehensions and causeless fears ". On the 14th December he resolves to borrow £10,000 on Abbotsford which will enable him to pay off the incumbrance of £3000 to old Moss's daughter and £5000 which he had borrowed from the Misses Ferguson, Sir Adam's sisters,[1] but he is still confident that he is well to windward of any possible disaster and full of resolves for the future.

It was on the 18th of December that the full force of what was to come broke on him followed by a temporary, deceptive lull in the threatening storm. " Ballantyne called on me this morning. *Venit illa suprema dies.* My extremity is come. Cadell has received letters from London which all but positively announce the failure of Hurst, Robinson so that Constable and Co. must follow and I must go with poor James Ballantyne for company. I suppose it will involve my all. . . . I have been rash in anticipating funds to buy land, but then I made from £5000 to £10000 a year and land was my temptation. I think nobody can lose a penny—that is one comfort. Men will think pride has had a fall.[2] Let them indulge their own

---

[1] When this was done later at Cadell's instance the £7,000 available, after the mortgage was paid, went to help J. B. and Co. (£4,000) and A. C. and Co. (£3,000). The debt to the Misses Ferguson remained with all the others, but Scott arranged with Walter that he should make himself ultimately responsible for it, if necessary. When in 1827 an instalment was paid to them, as to other creditors, Scott had great difficulty in persuading them to accept it : " When it occurd to the benevolent Colonel that you might want it for your purchase, and without a word to any one he went and offerd it to Mr. Bayley [Walter's lawyer] : there really are good people in this world when one can light on them " (*To Walter, Letters,* X, 349.)

[2] When in 1813 rumour announced the failure of Ballantyne involving that of Scott, Morritt wrote : " What your sins are I know not but upon my soul I believe that such is the envy and malignity of mankind that hundreds who have not even the slightest knowledge of you would be glad of any illluck that befell you merely because you have been successful and happy."

G.W.S.　　　　　R

pride in thinking that my fall makes them higher or seem so at least. I have the satisfaction to recollect that my prosperity has been of advantage to many and that some at least will forgive my transient wealth on account of the innocence of my intentions and my real wish to do good to the poor. This news will make sad hearts at Darnick and in the cottages of Abbotsford which I do not nourish the least hope of preserving. It has been my Dalilah and so I have often termed it.... I have half resolved never to see the place again. How could I tread my Hall with such a diminished crest? How live a poor indebted man where I was once the wealthy, the honoured?... My dogs will wait for me in vain. It is foolish but the thoughts of parting from these dumb creatures have moved me more than any of the painful reflections I have put down.... Poor Will Laidlaw, poor Tom Purdie! this will be news to wring your heart, and many a poor fellow's besides to whom my prosperity was daily bread."

Poor Scott! his life had been a dream—the making of money, the buying of land, the building of Abbotsford, the entertainment of guests and the lending a helping hand to the less fortunate had all been a game, a dream, and now it was all breaking round him as he sat in the small back-room in 39 Castle Street where he had written so much—and sat alone. "The magic wand of the Unknown is shivered in his grasp. He must henceforth be termed the Too-well-Known. The feast of fancy is over with the feeling of independence. I can no longer have the delight of waking in the morning with bright ideas in my mind,

---

When failure did come the most eloquent of those who justified Morritt's forecast was S. T. Coleridge, now the eminent Christian philosopher: "My judgement is in perfect coincidence with your remarks on Sir Walter; and when I think of the wretched trash that the Lust of Gain induced him to publish for the last three or four years, which must have been manufactured for the greater part, even my feelings assist in hardening me. I should indeed be sorry if any ultimate success had attended the attempt to unite the Poet and the Wordling."—*Unpublished Letters of S.T.C.*, ed. E. L. Griggs (1932), II, 402.

haste to commit them to paper, and count them monthly as the means of planting such groves and purchasing such wastes, replacing my dreams of fiction by other prospective visions of walks by

> Fountainheads and pathless groves
> Places which pale Passion loves."

Nothing could reveal more clearly than that last sentence the character of Scott's dreams—how remote with all his faults he was from miserly rapacity, social ostentation, or ambition for power. Like Shakespeare apparently, or Balzac, unlike Jonson or Milton or Flaubert, he used his talents as a means of realising, not literary immortality, but certain worldly aims of which he had dreamed from youth. "Sir Walter", writes the rather complacent Whig lady Mrs. Fletcher, his contemporary, "was one of those great men who had an undue estimate of the Pride of Life. He did not care for money, but he cared much for baronial towers and aristocratical distinction; and yet this taste was unaccompanied by haughtiness of disposition or manners. It was rather the romance of his character that had led him to add acre to acre and to found the family of Scott of Abbotsford; for there was nothing sordid in his nature; he was frank and kind-hearted, as much beloved by his poor neighbours as he was admired and courted by the great" (*Autobiography &c.*, 1875).

Before the evening was out James brought better news and there was a brief lightening, deceptive because Hurst, Robinson and Co. and also Constable and Cadell were all busily engaged in that desperate measure of the threatened —raising money from their friends by assertions of confidence in their resources, measures which in the end extend the range of the disaster. It was on this ground that the Banks later were unwilling to grant Cadell's discharge. On the 21st of December Scott dined with James to meet Mathews the comedian whom he had met twice before, once in company with Sir Alexander Boswell and once in

1815 along with Lord Byron,[1] old and unhappy associations : " I could not help thinking, in the midst of the glee, what late gloom was over the minds of three of the company—Cadell, J. B., and the Journalist's. What a strange scene if the surge of conversation could suddenly ebb like the tide and [show] us the state of people's real minds ! Savary[2] might have been gay in such a party with all his forgeries in his heart :

> No eyes the rocks discover
> Which lurk beneath the deep.

Life could not be endured were it seen in reality." On the 24th nevertheless he left for Abbotsford "with a light heart".

It was when he returned to Edinburgh on the 16th January 1826 that the final blow fell, that the apprehensions of December were realised : " Came through cold roads to as cold news. Hurst and Robinson have suffered a Bill of £1000 to come back on Constable which, I suppose, infers the ruin of both houses. We will soon see. Constable it seems who was to have set off in the last week of December dawdled here till in all human probability his going or staying became a matter of mighty little consequence. He could not be there till Monday night and his resources must have come too late.[3] Dined with the Skenes."

[1] " Poor Byron lunched or rather made an early dinner with us at Long's, and a most brilliant day we had of it. I never saw Byron so full of fun, frolic, wit and wisdom ; he was as playful as a kitten. Well I never saw him again."

[2] " Henry Savary, son of a banker in Bristol, had been tried for forgery a few months before." Douglas's footnote.

[3] Cadell had also been urgent with Constable to go to London and was so as late as 13th January. " Oh that you had been in London now as first intended—had it been so this could not have happened. Do not delay long at Polton, and once on the road oh, get on—it is fine moonlight in the early part of the evening." (MS. 323, N.L.S.). He arrived in London on the 16th and left again on the 19th having in vain endeavoured to get the Banks to support Hurst, etc. Lockhart's account of Constable lingering on in London in a state bordering on insanity is mythical. In a later letter to the younger Sir Walter, Isaac Bayley expresses his suspicion that Constable had delayed in Edinburgh to persuade Scott to advance the £10,000, but this was done at Cadell's instance on the 13th December.

It is idle to attempt now to decide whether Constable could have done anything effective by arriving earlier in London, or indeed to attempt to unriddle what has been called the enigma of Scott's failure, even if I were an accountant and all the accounts were accessible. To anyone who has followed the story as I have tried to envisage it, there is little mystery about it. The habit of living on anticipated profits, helped out by occasional loans, even if the profits do ultimately accrue, as Scott's eventually did to the benefit of his creditors and of Robert Cadell, must mean that any temporary failure to meet maturing bills might spell disaster. Scott's frequent notes of reminder and exhortation to the Ballantynes show how clearly he was aware of this. The general financial crisis of 1825, the speculative activities of Robinson to which Constable refers in a letter of January 1825, brought about just such a crisis in the affairs of all three of the interlocked businesses; and then there gradually became clear, what Scott had never realised or suspected, that Constable and Co. had no reserves. For months after the first announcement of the failure Scott's view of his own position and his chances of recovery is coloured by his hopes that the other two companies must be able to pay a substantial dividend and so lighten the claims upon himself.[1] The hope was a delusion; and ultimately Scott had to work to pay a debt of which at least £40,000 was not his debt but that of Constable and Cadell. What small dividend came in

[1] "I look at my affairs on the worst side and I believe there is good cause for, though I would not have you say it to Robinson or anyone whose business it may be to look out for themselves, I do believe such a concern as Constable's never occurd before—A large and flourishing establishment carrying on the most thriving speculations with great returns of profit—never having met with any loss of the most trifling consequence—yet making so poor a comparative return of assetts, without book-debts, without stock, without almost anything but copyrights and many of these unpaid for. Hurst and Robinson owe them £70,000 however, if that is paid it must make an alteration in their affairs."—To LOCKHART, 2nd February, 1826.

"Who could have suspected Constable's timbers to have been rotten from the beginning?"—*Journal*, 9th February, 1826.

from Constable's estate was seized later by the creditors to pay a portion of the interest still due when Scott's executors had paid twenty shillings in the pound.

For the position in which he found himself Scott could not but blame his own rashness : " I had a lesson in 1814 which should have done good upon me, but success and abundance erased it from my mind." " I have been rash in anticipating funds." But it is hard for any of us, not least for a proud man as Scott was, to accept the whole blame for a great error ; and it was not unnatural that he should feel he had been deceived by Constable, though why Cadell should have been exempted is a little hard to understand. The explanation of their difference in treatment which Lockhart gives is not just to Constable, for the borrowing of £5000 to help Hurst and Robinson was done at Cadell's instance jointly with Constable and Ballantyne, and it was Cadell, not Constable, who advised Scott to borrow £10,000 on Abbotsford. " Constable paid well and promptly but, devil take him, it was all spectral together, moonshine and no merriment. He sowed my field with one hand and as liberally scattered the tares with the other." So Scott told Skene ; but that applies to the firm, Constable and Cadell. It was Cadell not Constable who offered Scott £1000 for *Halidon Hill* which he had never seen, paying in bills discountable at three and six months. When Constable in 1823 grew alarmed at the number of outstanding bills, it was Cadell who restrained him from putting all the facts before Scott. When Constable wisely suggested a " fallow " to be got by an edition of Shakespeare or a History of Scotland or a Demonology, it was Cadell who was urgent for the quicker profits of the novels, and he was to preach the same policy later.

No ; if Scott turned on Constable somewhat harshly and unjustly it was because, consciously or unconsciously, he felt in Constable something of his own too sanguine temperament, a reinforcement of his own enterprising nature. In blaming Constable he is blaming himself. He had needed a counteractive rather than a stimulant. When Constable made it clear after the fall (24*th January*) that " he was utterly ruined without my connection ", and that he wished to go on without Cadell, Scott's comment is : " I certainly will befriend him if I can but Constable without Cadell is like getting the clock without the pendulum, the one having the ingenuity, the other the caution of the business." What Scott had needed was just what he had sought to avoid by the policy of secrecy, the restraint that would have come from the criticism of friends.

It was into something like a partnership with Cadell that Scott passed as, surrendering to a Trust his actual property and the profits of work done and to be done, but retaining with consent his official salary of £1600 a year, the house at Abbotsford and home farm, he settled down with heroic resolutions of work and economy, the first of which he found more easy to maintain than the second : " My pleasure is labour and varied by a walk with Tom Purdie I have little wish beyond it. In Edinburgh I must be lonely and my heart sinks a little at the idea of leaving poor 39 Castle street with its diverse easements so suited to our wants and wishes. But a man who falls out of a three pair of stairs window has reason to thank God if he escapes with a *dirl* on the elbow." Economies are to be rigid : " One thing was to give up farming which I detest. . . . I expect to make a fortune by the time I shall spare from useless visitors at Abbotsford as it is our purpose to refuse all strangers. As to our few real friends we will be like the man in Parnell's *Hermit* whose gold cup was stolen :

> Still we'll welcome but with less of cost.

I daresay my kind friends of Buccleuch will not quarrel if they find port and sherry instead of claret and champagne. Yet hang it we will rummage the cellar when you come for all that has come and gone yet " (*To Lord Montague, 6th February*). But economy does not come easily to one who has never practised it. There were still children and friends to help. To refuse hospitality, even to strangers if they came with introductions, was not easy after the first shock was over. His work on *Napoleon* necessitated a visit to London and Paris in 1826, and a visit to his daughter and friends gave him a well-deserved holiday in 1828. It was with the help of advances from his publisher, payments for occasional articles, and the retention of the profits of some of the side-pieces of work, that he met current expenses and paid off some of the small personal debts. Even so he had added before his death some £3000 to £6000 to the debt.

Against this is to be set the enormous work he did for, and sums he brought into, the Trust. When the blow fell he was deep in *Napoleon*, and it was from a table surrounded by the books he was consulting that he rose on the morning of 17th January to tell Skene "This is the hand of a beggar. Constable has failed and I am ruined *de fond en comble*. It's a hard blow but I must just bear up; the only thing which wrings me is poor Charlotte and the bairns." *Napoleon*, manuscript and proofs, was to occupy him for the next two years. But *Woodstock*, begun in November or earlier, was also carried on during the first troubled days. "We dined of course at home," he writes on 19th January, "and before and after dinner I finished about twenty printed pages of Woodstock but to what effect others must judge. A painful scene after dinner and another after supper endeavouring to convince these poor dear creatures that they must not look for miracles, but consider the misfortune as certain and only to be lessened by patience and labour." By the end of March *Woodstock* was finished, the question then being who was to be publisher. Hurst, Robinson and Co. were pressing, for they still claimed that they would be found solvent, and if that should prove so, it was better to retain all the novels in the same hands; and they offered apparently £8,400. But John Gibson, agent for the Trust, required unshakeable security or cash down, and the result of the negotiations was to reveal the completeness of their and Constable's failure. Murray and Longman were both offerers and ultimately the latter became publisher, paying £6,500 for 7,900 copies. "Hurst and Robinson, the Yorkshire tykes, have failed after all their swaggering and Longman and Co. take Woodstock." The clear profit to the Trust was £6075. The title page bore the inscription " Printed for Archibald Constable and Co., Edinburgh, and Longman, Rees, Orme, Brown, and Green, London."

But before March, Scott had found an outlet for his repressed feelings and irritation of mind in an assault upon the English policy of contracting the powers of the Scottish Banks to issue notes and thereby make credit more easy. Croker, as might be expected, represented to the Duke of Wellington that Scott's action was determined by gratitude to the Scottish Banks, and Lord Tweedsmuir seems to accept this ; but the impulse came from a deeper source. After all, the Banks in what they did for Scott were looking after their own interest, as Banks always do. They had threatened to take harsh measures, to reduce Walter's marriage settlement and to sell Abbotsford. Scott's offer to work for his creditors was likely to give a much better result. Even the later paying off of Abud, the obdurate Jew who held a bill of Constable's, was for the creditors a self-protective measure. No ; Scott had long resented the purposeless changing of Scottish legal customs and practice by the English government ; and now that government was threatening what he knew from experience to be an active agent in the development of the country's trade and commerce. So, beginning temperately, in a series of *Letters from Malachi Malagrowther* he launched out, as he went on, into a passionate appeal to the spirit of the Scottish people and to that "feckless" body, the Scottish members of Parliament, the "time-serving *faineants* who call themselves the Representatives of Scotland". He sent round the fiery cross, and even appealed to the Irish members to bethink themselves of what might happen to Ireland if the fundamental law of the Union between Scotland and England were to be thus lightly violated, the express condition that none of the laws of Scotland was to be changed except it were shown that " the alteration proposed was for the evident utility of the subjects of Scotland ", whereas the change contemplated now was sought merely on the ground of a wish for uniformity of practice. But Scott was not Swift. He appealed also to the candour and fairness of the English people, and went on to deplore, as has often been done since, the fairness of the English when dealing with individuals from another country, their thick-skinned insensibility to the *national* feelings of other peoples. Scott's letters gave mighty offence to many of his own political friends—Canning, Melville, Croker ; but he gained his point, and none of the ill-will excited proved enduring.

Woodstock arranged for, Scott turned back to *Napoleon*, to the relief of James (28th March), who had been struggling with the " tautologies and inaccuracies " of the sheets to hand : " every one sheet costs me 5 hours labour, if it costs me five minutes." The transcription from Scott's own autograph, which had been the practice with the novels (whence the cleanness of the Scott autographs), was now abandoned as unnecessary. But in March Scott, who had left 39 Castle Street for the last time on the 15th, received two premonitions of the blows that Fate was preparing for him. His beloved grandson " is visibly losing strength, that its walking becomes more difficult and, in short, the spine seems visibly affected. . . . Here is my worst augury verified.[1] The bitterness of this probably impending calamity is extreme. The child was almost too good

---

[1] " Evening spent in talking with Sophia on their future prospects. God bless her, poor girl. She never gave me a moment's reason to complain of her. But O my God, that poor delicate child so clever, so animated, yet holding by this earth with so fearfully slight a tenure—never out of his mother's thoughts, almost never out of his father's arms when he has but a single moment to give to anything. *Deus providebit.*" *Journal,* 2nd December, 1825.

for this world, beautiful in features and, though spoiled by every one, having one of the sweetest tempers as well as the quickest intellect I ever saw. . . . The poor dear love had so often a slow fever that when it pressed its little lips to mine I always foreboded to my own heart what all, I fear, are now aware of." On the 19th a letter from Anne, who with her mother had stayed on in Edinburgh, announced the beginning of his wife's last illness : " her asthmatic complaints are fast terminating in hydropsy as I have long suspected." The first blow was to be postponed for some years, but the second fell very soon. Lady Scott followed to Abbotsford on the 23rd and with various ups and downs, " the same harrassing state of uncertainty," lingered till May. Tom's daughter, Anne, came down at Scott's request to help her cousin. On 10th May Scott's legal duties recalled him to Edinburgh, and on the 15th Lady Scott died. The *Journal* records his feelings and I have no desire to join in the rather ghoul-like task of dissecting these records to measure the degree of Scott's heartlessness. All that he says seems to me to his credit and to hers, to show that he had been a kind, if perhaps both over-indulgent and at the same time masterful, husband, and that she, whatever her limitations, had been a good wife to him : " I wonder how I shall do with the large portion of thoughts which were hers for thirty years : I suspect they will be hers yet for a long time at least." " The solitude seemed so absolute—my poor Charlotte would have been in the [room] half-a-score of times to see if the fire burned and to ask a hundred kind questions." " When I had come home from such a business I used to carry the news to poor Charlotte who dressed her face in sadness or mirth as she saw the news affect me." " I have often deserved a headache in my younger days without having one and Nature is, I suppose, paying off the scores. Ay, but then the want of the affectionate care that used to be ready with lowered voice and stealthy pace to smooth the pillow—and offer condolence and assistance—gone—gone-for-ever-ever-ever." Like the hero of Crabbe's *Parting Hour* Scott had loved in early days and lost, and the scar left by that early betrayal, as he regarded it, was never healed entirely. But Crabbe knew more of the human heart than many psychologists and biographers; and when in the end of the day the parted couple are united as friends it is not to her and those early days that his dreams in sickness go back, but to the wife and children with whom he had shared the active years of his life:

> And now his Judith lays her knitting by,
> These strong emotions in her friend to spy;
> For she can fully of their nature deem—
> But see! he breaks the long protracted theme
> And wakes, and cries—" My God! 'twas but a dream ".

Scott was not the man to live thirty happy years with a woman and not to feel her death : " But it is not my Charlotte, it is not the bride of my youth, the mother of my children, that will be laid among the ruins of Dryburgh which we have so often visited in gaiety and pastime—no, no—she is sentient and conscious of my emotions somewhere—somehow—*where* we cannot tell, *how* we cannot tell—yet would I not at this moment renounce the mysterious yet certain hope that I shall see her in a better world for all that this world can give me." " Lonely, aged, deprived of my family—all but poor Anne—an impoverished and embarrassed man, I am deprived of the sharer of my thoughts and counsels who could always talk down my sense of the calamitous apprehensions which break the heart that must bear these alone. Even her foibles were of service to me by giving me things to think of beyond my weary self-reflection."

Returning to Edinburgh after the funeral, to Mrs. Brown's bug-haunted lodgings, Scott settled down to steady labour at *Napoleon* for which Longman in October agreed to pay ten thousand five hundred guineas. The work entailed a visit to London and Paris in the months of

October and November. He visited Morritt at Rokeby on the way, breakfasted and dined with Rogers and others in London, and at Windsor with the King: " His Majesty received me with the same mixture of kindness and courtesy which has always distinguished his conduct towards me. There were no company besides the royal retinue—Lady C[onyngham], her daughter and two or three ladies. . . . He is in many respects the model of a British monarch—has little inclination to try experiments in government otherwise than through his ministers, sincerely I believe desires the good of his subjects, is kind towards the distressed, and moves and speaks every inch a king. I am sure such a character is better fitted for us than one who would long to head armies or be perpetually intermeddling with *la grande politique*." In Paris he was fêted and saw *Ivanhoe* as an opera, but he was glad to escape. In London again he sat to Lawrence for the completion of the picture begun in 1820. Sir William Knighton secured for him the promise of a post in the Foreign Office for Charles. He saw an early friend, Lydia White, " on a couch . . . unable to stir, rouged, jesting and dying " ; he breakfasted with Allan Cunningham, and was introduced by Rogers to " Madam D'Arblay the celebrated authoress of *Evelina* and *Cecilia*—an elderly lady with no remains of personal beauty but with a gentle manner and a pleasing expression of countenance." She, who had been the friend of Johnson, Reynolds, Boswell and others of a past epoch, told him now that she had wished to see two people—Canning and Scott. At Peel's he dined with " Lord Liverpool and the Duke of Wellington . . . the conversation very good—Peel taking the lead in his own house, which he will not do elsewhere". At Oxford he dined with Charles and his young friend Surtees, and breakfasted next morning with Charles at Brasenose : " How pleasant it is for a father to sit at his child's board! It is like the aged man reclining under the shelter of the oak which he has planted." So it might have been had all gone well, but Charles and others were still dependent on his labours and influence. Oxford had lost its charms since the happy days with Reginald Heber, " now dead in a foreign land " and with other " able men all entombed ". On 27th November he was home, no longer at Mrs. Brown's but in a furnished house in Walker Street, and next day he heard of the death by his own hand of Colonel Huxley, the husband of Tom's eldest daughter : " Awaked from horrid dreams to reconsideration of the sad reality ; he was such a kind, obliging, assiduous creature. I thought he came to my bedside to expostulate with me how I could believe such a scandal—and I thought I detected that it was but a spirit who spoke by the paleness of his look and the blood flowing from his cravat " (*29th November*). One pays a price for the too vivid imagination of the poet.

Meantime Cadell was manoeuvring to procure a composition with the creditors of the firm, to slip Constable, and to start on his own with Scott as his chief asset : " I am seriously contemplating making a composition in person for A. C. and Co. . . . I am doing this independent of Mr Constable, he does not seem to like my procedure and I daresay it will be troublesome to get rid of him . . . the Trustee [Cowan] is very favourable . . . it requires 9/11 [of the creditors] to carry the measure—a discharge is almost impossible without this—the weight of the Banks is so overwhelming." He is " to recommence as a publishing bookseller in November". James Ballantyne had backed this ambition of Cadell from the moment of the failure : " Rely on it that months hence when this business is settled, as settled it must be one way or another, you if you choose it will be the publisher of Sir Walter Scott." So he had written on the day after the fatal 16th of January 1826. James had reason afterwards to regret his haste to substitute Cadell for Constable, for Cadell was first and foremost a man of business, always ready to seek a reduction of James's prices, and quite willing on any pretext to employ other printers. James had more than once to appeal to Scott for intervention on his behalf. But for Scott's purpose, of working himself to death to reduce his debt, he could not have had a more pushing, shrewd, long-headed publisher.

A discharge was not, however, obtainable easily and at once, the Banks objecting that Cadell had " gone about to the last moment declaring that no insolvency was to occur and thereby obtaining sums from individuals down to the very day when payment was stopped " (*Wm. Bell to Scott, 31st December,* 1828). It was only in 1829 that, at a stormy meeting, the Bank granted a discharge, and it was done mainly at Scott's instance, anxious as he was that Cadell should be free to carry on the publication of the collected and annotated edition of his works, the *Magnum Opus* of which we shall hear later. Scott thus became solely responsible for the £40,000 which was not his debt but that of Constable and Cadell, jointly and severally. And meantime Cadell, with the help of a brother and friends, purchased a " lump of the stock " of A. C. and Co. and set up as Cadell and Co. To secure Scott as an asset he made a skilful manoeuvre. The sickness and funeral expenses of Lady Scott, and other charges, were making it apparent that Sir Walter could not do the work he had undertaken to do if he had to depend entirely on his official salary. Before October, while *Napoleon* was still on the stocks, Scott arranged with Cadell for a new novel, or series of stories, to be called *Chronicles of the Canongate or the Traditions of the Sanctuary by the author of Waverley*. For this Cadell was to pay Scott £500 for so many copies, and thereafter for the whole 8,000 copies the Trustees were paid £2,228 7s. 6d., Cadell paying also the expenses of paper and printing : " The relationship I bear to my friend Chrystal Croftangry is of that nature that you will give great allowance for a warm attachment to him on my part. I feel myself engrafted on him, what with delivery of paper, orders for what is required, advances of many friends, and the hope that my first work would be a successful one—to see him therefore under other parentage would be ... a severe stroke." (*Cadell to Scott*, 21st August, 1826). In *Napoleon* Cadell also acquired an interest so that when the nine volumes, to which the work had grown by stages, appeared in the end of June 1827 it bore the inscription : " Printed by Ballantyne and Co. for Longman, Rees, Orme, Brown and Green, London, and Cadell and Co. Edinburgh." The first series of *Chronicles of the Canongate* followed in November. But before that was out Cadell was arranging for an immediate sequel. "A good thought came into my head," Scott writes on 24th May, " to write stories for little Johnnie Lockhart from the History of Scotland like those taken from the History of England. I will not write mine quite so simply as Croker has done. I am persuaded both children and the lower class of readers hate books which are written *down* to their capacity and love those that are more composed for their elders and betters. I will make if possible a book that a child will understand yet a man will feel some temptation to peruse should he chance to take it up." But evidently the thought was older than the 24th, for on the same day Cadell writes : " I send Mr Croker's book. ... I hope you do not intend the proceeds of this little book for Mr Gibson's money-bags—it would be both a sin and a shame, permit me to say, to let the amount travel such a road after having done such wonders this year already." On the 30th he made an offer which included £500 to Gibson but in the end, after talking it over, Cadell paid to Scott seven hundred and fifty guineas for ten thousand copies, a similar sum to be paid if ten thousand more were wanted. In 1831 the Trustees record : " Tales of a Grandfather, History of Scotland for Lardner's Cyclopaedia and Letters on Demonology were kept by Scott for current expenses and this the Trustees have passed over." The *Tales* appeared in four successive series during 1827-30. In March 1828 he writes : " With my usual delight in catching an apology for escaping the regular task of the day I threw by the novel of Saint Valentine's Eve, [*The Fair Maid of Perth*] and began to run through and correct the Grandfather tales for the press. If I live to finish them they will be a good thing for my younger children. If I work to the amount of £10,000 a year for the Creditors I think I may gain a few hundreds for my own family in bye-hours" (*Journal, 23rd March*).[1]

I have thought it well to state the facts concerning these books and the dealings with Cadell, for they do perhaps lay Scott open to criticism. Strictly speaking, I suppose, everything beyond the £1,600 of official salary should have gone to the Trust. Against this is to be set: (1) Scott did not think of himself for a moment as a dishonest defaulter working penitently to expiate his sins. It was the failure of others that had ruined him by depriving him of money he had earned and been, as he thought, paid in bills, which bills had not matured through the fault of Constable and Co.[2] That left him legally a debtor and feeling himself bound in honour to pay off that debt. But he had also a debt to his children whom, more than any creditor, he had wronged. (2) He believed and affirmed that he had, from the beginning, insisted that he must have elbow-room in which to work, that he was not a toiling Samson, "eyeless in Gaza, at the mill, with slaves." "You will remember", he wrote to Gibson, agent for the Trust, to whom he wished to repay a sum he had borrowed at the moment of the failure for the equipment of his nephew, "that I requested a clause to be struck out of the Trust

---

[1] In his Will, Scott left the profits of the *Tales* and other small works, after paying some personal debts, to the Trustees for behoof of the Creditors.

[2] "Jeffrey has also lost a great deal I am told. But I shall be the great sufferer having left bonds in their hands which should have been paid off by them many years since, but which they, not very fairly, kept up, paying the interest regularly so that I never knew of their existence."—To WALTER, 26th January, 1826. To what this refers I do not understand except it be the bills for the copyrights purchased, which Scott discounted but Constable did not take up.

Deed by which it was declared that I should convey such future literary property as I should create or acquire [1] and which was taken out accordingly. By my own sense of justice and expedience I am nevertheless bound to afford the Trustees ... the full advantage of my time and exertions to clear these matters. Accordingly suppose Bon. sold at the sum at all proportional to Woodstock I will have realised £20,000 and upwards in one year and will do as much as possible the next. But then in order to have the ease of mind necessary to labour so hard it is essential that I should have no encumbrance on my mind, and this debt *is* such an encumbrance." [2]

Tales of a Grandfather were not far advanced before Cadell was asking " what is to follow Chronicles and Tales : I have no hesitation in stating that a three-volumed novel would be well received after this—something on the theme of Louis XI which has been so successful in Quentin Durward " (*Cadell to Scott, 2nd August*). But " I omitted to mention Shakespeare which will I trust before long come into play " (*Cadell to Scott, 6th August*), or, for Cadell has been reading the *Tales* so far as the death of Bruce, " there must be many subjects for your pen in the periods of the History of Scotland ... there must be much in Lord James of Douglas which would permit three volumes most delightfully " (*Cadell to Scott, 6th August*). Thereafter might follow " a second series of the Chronicles". Cadell's cry was ever for novels which brought in quick profits, and James roared for chivalry. It is in this same letter that Cadell makes an

---

[1] What Scott did convey was his lands, and houses in town, and the two works approaching completion and already bargained for, *Woodstock* and *Napoleon*. The others are covered by a statement of intention : " I the said Walter Scott have resolved to employ my time and talents in the production of such literary works as shall seem likely to be most likely to promote the ends I have in view, the sum arising from which works I am also desirous to devote to the payment of the debts owing by me as a partner of the said company and as an individual."

[2] August 5, 1826. *Letters*, X, 86 f. See the whole letter.

offer, as cited earlier (p. 207), for three novels in advance, one in March next, another in the following November, and a third in the Spring of 1829. " Had a packet from James—low about the novel but I have another from Cadell equally uppish. He proposes for three novels in 18 months which would be £12,600—Well, I like the Bookseller's predictions better than the printer's. Neither are bad judges, but James who is the best is not sensible of historical descriptions and likes your novel style out and out " (*Journal*, 22*nd March*, 1828). Nothing could daunt Scott's sanguine temper.

No successor to *Quentin Durward* was attempted, but by April 1828 Cadell reports to his London agent that the *Chronicles*, second series, *The Fair Maid of Perth*, will be out immediately, and to Scott in March of the same year his cry is still for " a steady flow of novels . . . the enthusiasm in the public mind in favour of your writing, I do maintain, is unabated—no sooner is one book done than we receive orders for the next although not named—and then a universal cry, ' if this is not so good as its predecessors it is far, far beyond anything else. . . .' I have a dread that a pause might coincide with the abatement of the public interest " (21*st March*, 1828).

Was ever willing horse so driven? Nor do *Napoleon*, the *Tales*, the *Chronicles* exhaust the labours of these years. They include articles for *The Quarterly* on Mackenzie's *Life of Home* (*Q.R.*, June 1827), On Planting Waste Lands (*Q.R.* October, 1827), On Landscape Gardening (*Q.R.* March 1828). He even turns aside from his own labours to write for the spendthrift and impecunious R. P. Gillies articles for *The Foreign Quarterly*, on the Novels of Hoffman (*F.Q.* No. I, July 1827), on Molière (*F.Q.* 1828). The first of these was a gift ; for the second he kept the £100. " In my own pocket it may form a fund to help this poor gentleman or others at a pinch ; in his I fear it would be only an encouragement to a neglect of economy." But Gillies got from him further financial assistance. Two sermons were in like manner composed to relieve from debt his deaf secretary, George Huntly Gordon, in the closing weeks of 1827, and brought that young man £250.

But new novels, histories, biographies and articles were not Scott's only resource or Cadell's only device. Everything was to be thrown in, even old experiments in drama like *The Doom of Devorgoil* and *Auchindrane*. The miscellaneous prose works were got together, edited and published in 1827; but alas! Lord Newton assigned them to Constable's trust on the ground that he had bought them though paying for them by bills which were dishonoured and which had become a charge on Scott's estate. The law is a strange and mysterious process. But there was a larger plan in Cadell's mind. The copyrights in Scott's earlier novels, which Constable had also purchased, were now to be sold by his trustees. These were valued at some £4,000, and Cadell, with Scott's backing, persuaded Gibson and his fellow trustees to allow him to borrow the sum he had undertaken to pay for the second series of the *Chronicles*, some £4,000, and with this to purchase these copyrights. As a fact they went for over £8,000 and the trustees had to step in and buy one half of them for the Trust. Thereupon Cadell began to arrange for a collected edition with illustrations [1] by the best artists includ-

---

[1] Here again Cadell reaped where Constable (and Scott) had sown. In a letter of the 22nd December, 1825, when disaster was in the air, Constable wrote to Scott from Polton: "The objects which I should wish to accomplish by my projected Journey to London encrease in number and importance the more I think of them—there is one in particular which I will take the liberty of submitting to you. A splendid edition of the Novels, Tales and Romances of the Author of Waverley—from Waverley to Woodstock enclusive—the whole would extend to about 32 volumes. The new feature which I would propose for this edition to consist of Notes and Illustrations of the leading circumstances or subjects in the various works—such as I believe I formerly took the liberty of suggesting to you—they would give new and great additional interest to the different Works and would, I am much inclined to believe, render the almost immediate sale of an impression of 2000 copies perfectly secure. . . . There should be engravings, vignettes, portraits through the whole, properly selected and executed in a superior manner, the letterpress to be superbly printed by Ballantyne, to be sold at a Guinea

ing Turner who, after some difficult negotiations with Cadell, came to Abbotsford in 1831. It was while Turner was sketching at Smailholm that Scott told Skene, who was sitting with him awaiting the completion of the sketch, " how the habit of lying on the turf there among the sheep and lambs, when an infant, had given his mind a peculiar tenderness for those animals which it had ever since retained " (*Lockhart*). A large part of Scott's work became the supplying of fresh introductions and notes for which Scott received £100 a month paid by joint concern, the trustees getting £50 regularly from Cadell. For his management Cadell had an allowance, the amount settled by a reference to Adam Black, confidential agent to the Trust. (*Report by Trustees, February*, 1831),

a volume and brought out periodically, five volumes at a time . . . and it would probably require a period of not less than three years to bring out the whole. It may appear a large undertaking . . . but I am convinced there are purchasers in the Country to take up the edition at once. . . . It would be a standard library book and I am quite convinced would not interfere with the sale of the different editions of the works at present existing &c."—*MS. Edinburgh University Library.* Constable's fertile brain was busy with every scheme that might persuade the banks and creditors to give time for the two firms to recover their footing. Lockhart accuses Constable of a mad proposal about a guarantee for £20,000 and states that Mr. Cadell's frank conduct in warning Ballantyne and Scott against this produced a strong impression in his favour, and led to the later connection. But this, as Mr. Glen has shown, is unjust to Constable : " Constable's proposal, which however did not mature and . . . came too late was that while his firm assigned their copyrights Scott should join by granting his personal obligation for £20,000 in an endeavour which was being made to obtain a loan in London on the footing that £40,000 or £45,000 was to be available for the purposes of A. C. & Co and J. B. & Co. . . . If some such arrangement could have been effected in time, and the money applied by each of the two firms in taking up £20,000 of the bills for which they were respectively primarily responsible, then, even if bankruptcy had ultimately taken place, Sir Walter's estate would have been saved from a ranking of £40,000 of bills and benefited to the extent of £20,000."—*Letters of Sir Walter Scott*, I, xciii.

CHAPTER XII

"La fin est toujours sanglante."
Pascal.

"Life could not be endured were it seen in [its] reality."
SCOTT, *The Journal.*

INTRODUCTIONS and notes, history and biography, articles for periodicals, were all tasks Scott was able to make interesting. George Ellis had commented on his power, shown in *The Minstrelsy of the Scottish Border*, of making even notes interesting. But Cadell's insistence on a flow of novels was becoming an *idée fixe* in Scott's mind, and home from a two months' holiday in 1828 he was at work again, not only on notes for the Collected Edition, articles for *The Quarterly*, and *Tales of a Grandfather*, but on a new novel, *Anne of Geierstein*,[1] which, checked for a little by James's criticism, was out in 1829. In February 1830 came the beginning of the end, the first unmistakable stroke. Still he carried on. *Count Robert of Paris*, after a very rough passage with James and Cadell, the latter of whom told him with brutal frankness that it was likely to injure the whole collected edition (the *Magnum Opus*), was got out in 1831. *Castle Dangerous*, an attempt suggested probably by Cadell's remarks on possible subjects which I have quoted above, appeared in the same year. Even

---

[1] "I shall soon be done with the second of *Anne of Geierstein*. I cannot persuade myself to the obvious risk of satisfying the public, although I cannot so well satisfy myself. I am like Beaumont and Fletcher's old Merrythought who could not be persuaded that there was a chance of his wanting meat. I never came into my parlour, said he, but I found the cloth laid and dinner ready; surely it will always be thus. Use makes perfectness."—*Journal*, 27th January, 1829.

from the Mediterranean he writes to Laidlaw : " I have been turning the siege of Malta into one of the best romances I ever wrote in the beginning of the 17th century."

It is a strange picture of human nature, and of the wonderful way in which our great industrial system with its credits and bankruptcies works, that is presented by bringing together the record of Scott's work in these years —Scott, with Cadell and Ballantyne to guide and advise, labouring to pay off a debt, which was theirs as well as his, Cadell's to the extent of some £40,000, while laying by his efforts the foundations of a fortune for the latter which, at his death, was in the neighbourhood of £100,000 :

" Sic vos, non vobis, mellificatis apes."

How long Cadell supposed the success could be maintained by " a steady flow of novels " I do not know. He was quick to take alarm if Ballantyne gave any signs of hesitation, for he had no confidence in his own literary judgement. The first jolt came with the second series of *Chronicles of the Canongate* : " had a formal communication from Ballantyne enclosing a letter from Cadell of an unpleasant tenor. It seems Mr Cadell is dissatisfied with the moderate success of the 1st Series of Chronicles and disapproves of about half the volume already written of the Second Series obviously ruing his engagement" (*Journal, 11th December*, 1827). Scott was quite ready to recognise that his popularity could not last forever, that the talisman must some day be broken : " This far from taking me by surprise or giving me annoyance I was sure the day *must* come and therefore no way disconcerted on being informed that it *has* come for I am not conscious that any degree of pains which I can bestow is like to mend the matter. A whip may make a lazy horse move, but ten ell of whipcord could not make a foundered or tired one put out more strength than he has, and it is just so with authors and criticism. For the books I have only the defence of Burns' patriarch :

> I wrote them as I wrote the lave
> And night and day I'm busy."

(*To James B.*, *12th Dec.* 1827, *Letters*, X, 330, See note).

So Scott, who had bitterly resented Blackwood's strictures on *The Black Dwarf*, accepted meekly the judgement of James and the apprehensions of Cadell. Two of the stories, " My Aunt Margaret's Mirror " and " The Laird's Jock " were cancelled, but the " two learned Thebans . . . deprecated a fallow-break as ruin ". *The Fair Maid of Perth* was pushed on : " They are good specimens of the public taste in general, and it is far best to indulge and yield to them unless I was very *very* certain that I was right and they rank [*sic*.]." (*Journal*, 12th December, 1827). A similar shock came with *Anne of Geierstein* : " I got a note from Cadell in which Ballantyne by letter enclosed totally condemns Anne of Geierstein—three volumes nearly finished—a pretty thing, for I will be expected to do it all over again. Great dishonour in this as Trinculo says, besides an infinite loss " (*Journal, 8th March,* 1829). The final blow was given to *Count Robert of Paris* in May 1831 : "Here is a precious job. I have a formal remonstrance from these critical persons Ballantyne and Cadell remonstrating against the last volume of Count Robert which is within a sheet of being finished. I suspect their opinion will be found to coincide with that of the public, at least it is not very different from my own. The blow is a stunning one I suppose for I scarcely feel it. . . . I have suffered terribly that is the truth, rather in body than in mind, and I often wish I could lie down and sleep without waking. But I will fight it out if I can. It will argue too great an attachment of consequence to my literary labours to sink under [*two words illegible*]. Did I know how to begin I would this very day, although I knew I should sink at the end. After all, this is but fear and faintness of heart, though of another kind from that which trembles at a loaded pistol. My bodily strength is terribly gone, perhaps my mental too " (*Journal*, 6*th*-8*th May*, 1831).

Of Scott's character and feelings during these years the abiding record is the *Journal*, but the stories, too, reveal in a refracted manner the nature of his reactions to the disaster which had overtaken him. The severest blow was to his pride, that the Great Unknown had become the too-well-known. " I went to the Court for the first time today and like the man with the large nose thought everybody was thinking of me and my mishap. Many were undoubtedly and all rather regrettingly, some obviously affected. . . . Some smiled as they wished me good day as if to say 'Think nothing about it, my lad, it is quite out of our thoughts'. Others greet me with the affected gravity which one sees and despises at a funeral. The best bred —all I believe meaning equally well—just shook hands and went on." But pride dictates repression of feeling and, as Maria Edgeworth wrote to Lockhart in 1838, Scott paid the penalty of his unwillingness to tell all that he must have felt, even to himself in the *Journal* : " I much regret that his stoical pride and disdain of pity, or his belief that no one could sympathise with him sufficiently . . . prevented him from opening his mind thoroughly to any of his friends—even to Morritt." It was the price Scott had to pay for never having told them the whole truth in his lifetime. It explains the relief it gave him to write the Malachi Malagrowther letters in 1826; and later, in 1827, when Marshal Gourgaud threatened a duel over Scott's account of his treacheries to Napoleon in St. Helena, the thought of meeting him was a relief to the same repressed feelings of anger and injured pride : " Received from James B. the proofs of my reply to General Gourgaud with some cautious Balaam from mine honest friend alarmed by a Highland Colonel who had described Gourgaud as a *mauvais garcon*, famous fencer, marksman and so forth. I wrote in answer, which is true, that I would hope all my friends would trust to my acting with proper caution and advice ; but that if I were capable in a moment of weakness of doing anything short of what my honour demanded I would die the death of a poisoned rat in a hole out of mere sense of my own degradation" (*Journal*, 17*th September*, 1827). " In a moment of weakness "—for Scott's courage was not that of insensibility. I have suggested that in his youth, in the years of early delicacy, he had known what it was to be capable of fear, with his vivid imagination a thing hardly to be escaped. His courage, like that of the young Swinburne when he climbed the cliff, was the courage of a pride and strength of will that threw fear behind him as a shameful thing. But the overwork of these years had brought back at moments a tremulousness of sensibility, " the morbus, as I call it, aching pains in the back, idle fears, gloomy thoughts and anxieties which if not unfounded are at least bootless" (*Journal*, 11*th April*, 1826). It was this strain in his feelings, I imagine, the fear of fear, that led his mind back to poor Daniel, that "beautiful child" who had messed his later life, and in an hour of peril in Jamaica had " shown the white feather ", and so Scott told the story of Conachar in *The Fair Maid of Perth*. And even in *Chronicles of the Canongate* there seems to me to be a refracted image of his own experience If R. P. Gillies, a fellow victim of the depression, is in part the model of the spendthrift Chrystal Croftangry, yet in the story of that hero's return to the property he had gambled away and the reception he met with from the old servant of his mother, Scott passed sentence on the folly of conduct that had been the ruin of more than one young laird brought up to idleness, but also on his own feudal dreams. The new manufacturer who had bought the property had proved more of a benefactor to the tenants than the old feudal laird : " Mair regretted, mair missed ? ... How should they be mair missed than the Treddleses? The cotton mill was such a thing for the country! The mair bairns a cottar body had the better ;

they would mak their awn keep frae the time they were five years auld; and a widow wi' three or four bairns was a wealthy woman in the time of the Treddleses."

"But the health of these poor children... their education and religious instruction?"

"For health," said Christie, looking gloomily at me, "ye maun ken little o' the warld, Sir, if ye dinna ken that the health o' the poor man's body, as weel as his youth and his strength, are all at the command of the rich man's purse.... But the bairns were reasonably weel cared for in the way of air and exercise, and a very responsible youth heard them their carritch [catechism], and gied them lessons in Reediemadeasy. Now, what did they ever get before? Maybe on a winter day they wad be called out to beat the wood for cocks and sichlike, and then the starving weans would maybe get a bite of broken bread, and maybe no, just as the butler was in the humour—that was a' they got." And even for the failure of the Treddleses there was an excuse which Scott felt was his own: "there was some warrant for a man being expensive that imagined he was making a mint of money."

In the October preceding the publication of the *Chronicles* Scott received letters and a request from one who belonged to a chapter in his life which had closed in the autumn of 1796, the mother of her from whom he had taken farewell, as it proved, in verses written on the Hill of Caterthun on the 5th of May of that year. Williamina had died in 1810. Her husband was now at the head of the Bank which was Scott's greatest creditor. Lady Jane Stuart was living in Maitland Street, opposite Shandwick Place, where, in the house of Mrs. Jobson, Scott had taken up his abode in November for the winter. A young cousin of Lady Jane was setting up as a publisher, and she wrote to ask permission for him to print, in some Miscellany he was meditating, certain old poems, not of Scott's composition, but which Scott had copied for Williamina in a "Book which I would with pleasure convey to you as a *secret* and *sacred* treasure could I but know that you would take it as it is given without a drawback or misunderstanding of my intention".

To Scott in his sensitive condition " the recurrence to these matters seems like a summons from the grave. It fascinates me. I ought perhaps to have stopped it at once but I have not nerve to do so. Alas! Alas! But why alas? *Humana perpessi sumus*". In November, when at work on the Second Series of the *Chronicles* and threatened with a prosecution by Mr. Abud, " the same Jew broker who formerly was disposed to disturb me in London," he called on his old friend and " fairly softened myself like an old fool with recalling old stories till I was fit for nothing but shedding tears and repeating verses for the whole night. This is sad work. The very grave gives up its dead, and time rolls back thirty years to add to my perplexities ". And then, in a way which does not seem strictly relevant to the occasion but betrays the suppressed irritability of his mind, he breaks out : " I dont care. I begin to grow over hardened, and like a stag turning at bay my naturally good temper grows fierce and dangerous." As his brain wore out that irritability increased and grew querulous. In the picture of Chrystal's old friend, as Chrystal found him after his long absence, Scott was drawing on the memory of his father's last illness, and in that picture Lockhart saw too close a resemblance to Sir Walter's own last days.

But before this last stage was reached the financial success of *Napoleon* and *Woodstock*, the welcome extended to *Tales of a Grandfather*, and the starting of the great scheme of the Collected Edition did much to revive Scott's spirits. Twice, in 1826 and 1827, the Trustees expressed their appreciation of the gigantic efforts he had made, and on the second occasion made a present to him of his library, antiques and furniture, which was estimated to be equivalent to an additional two shillings in the pound. In April and May of 1828 he enjoyed a final holiday, a kind of St.

Luke's summer, for the last visit to the Mediterranean was a hopeless pursuit of the unobtainable. With Anne for his companion he visited Carlisle, where the keeper of the castle was anxious to show them the cell where Fergus MacIvor had been imprisoned, Penrith, Derby, Kenilworth, Warwick—" Warwick Castle is still the noblest sight in England. Lord and Lady Warwick came home from the Court and received us most kindly,"—Stratford on Avon—" We visited the tomb of the mighty wizard. It is in the bad taste of James the First's reign, but what a magic does the locality possess! There are stately monuments of forgotten families; but when you have seen Shakespeare's what care we for the rest?" Charlecote and Edgehill followed, and on 9th April they were in London with Sophia, Lockhart, the babies, and Charles, now a clerk in the Foreign Office. Old friends were visited, " dining is the principal act of the day in London." At a dinner given specially in his honour by Rogers, which Scott attended with the Lockharts and Anne, Fenimore Cooper whom Scott had met in Paris was present and, like Wordsworth and Washington Irving and Ticknor, was charmed by Sophia: " She is eminently what the French call *gracieuse*, and just the woman to have success at Paris by her sweet simple manners. . . . I thought her quick of intellect and reflective of humour." Scott's fellow guest at a dinner given by Sotheby was " that extraordinary man Coleridge " who, " after eating a hearty dinner during which he spoke not a word," discoursed upon the Samothracian Mysteries, and then on Homer " whose Iliad he considered as a collection of poems by different authors at different times during a century. There was, he said, the individuality of an age, but not of a country. Morritt, a zealous worshipper of the old bard, . . . gave battle with keenness, and was joined by Sotheby our host. Mr. Coleridge behaved with the utmost complaisance and temper but relaxed not from his exertions. 'Zounds, I was never so bethumped with words'." He breakfasted with

Haydon, who made a sketch of his head, and seems to have thought he would gain favour by denouncing his old friends of the Cockney School, Hunt and Keats, a line of conduct which did not appeal to Scott. To Haydon he seemed depressed. Johnny was ill again, and the Lockharts had taken flight for Brighton. "He told some admirable stories, but still was quieter than before. ... I started ghost stories quoting Johnson's assertion in *Rasselas*. He told us some curious things, affecting to consider them natural, but I am convinced he half thought them supernatural. Walter Scott has certainly the most penetrating look I ever saw except in Shakespeare's portraits." What portraits of Shakespeare Haydon referred to I do not know. Praise of his genius Scott waved aside: "Ah, Mr. Haydon, we wont say a word about that. At any rate I have amused the public and that is something." He sat to Northcote also, "the old wizard Northcote. He really resembles an animated mummy." Northcote disillusioned him regarding Reynolds "whom from the expressions used by Goldsmith, Johnson and others I used to think an amiable and benevolent character". But Northcote assured him that he was "cold, unfeeling and indifferent to his family".[1] Chantrey executed a second bust to take the place in his studio of that of 1820 which was presented to Scott as an heirloom.[2] He dined with the King, and later was "presented to the little Princess Victoria—I hope they will change her name—the heir apparent to the Crown as things now stand. ... She is fair like the Royal Family but does not look as if she would be pretty".

On 27th May Scott set out on his homeward journey. "It has cost me a good deal of money, and Johnnie's illness has taken away much of the pleasure I had promised my-

---

[1] It was not thus that Northcote spoke of Reynolds in his conversations with Hazlitt.

[2] "The expression is more serious than in the two former Busts, and the marks of age *more* than eight years deeper" (*Chantrey to Peel, 26th January,* 1838).

self." But he had achieved certain ends. He had helped to put Lockhart on a good footing with influential persons, mainly Sir William Knighton, the King's private secretary, and Sir Robert Peel. He had taken steps to recover for his family the money settled on his wife's mother long ago, to which I have referred in an earlier chapter. He had got a commission for a son of Skene, two cadetships for sons of Allan Cunningham, and a post in India for the son of Shortreed. Withal he had been able to render material assistance to poor Daniel Terry who, he found, "was ruined horse and foot, all owing to the carelessness which I dreaded from the first, and letting small debts grow into great ones by accumulation of interest and expenses."

Scott returned to the life of labour I have described. On 17th May, 1829 he notes : " I never stirred from my seat all this day. My reflections as suggested by Walter's illness were highly uncomfortable, and to divert it I wrought the whole day save when I was obliged to stop and lean my head upon my hand. Real affliction, however, has something in it by which it is sanctified. It is a weight which, however oppressive, may like a bar of iron be conveniently disposed on the sufferer's person. But the insubstantiality of a hypochondriac affection is one of its greatest torments. You have a huge featherbed on your shoulders which rather encumbers and oppresses you than calls forth strength and exertion to bear it." Walter's lungs were threatened, and it was difficult to persuade him to obey doctor's orders. Scott knew in his heart that it was for his family he was putting up so desperate a struggle. It was them after all, not the Banks, whom he had most wronged by his sanguine anticipations : " Indeed of what use is my fighting unless for the benefit of my children, and should you, which God Almighty forbid, lose your health in earnest, I am sure they might take Abbotsford and everything else for I neither could nor would persevere in the labour which I now go through with joy and pleasure to save it for my family " (*31st October*). What he had written earlier of his friends was true of his family: "It is written that nothing shall flourish under my shadow—the Ballantynes, Terry, Nelson, Weber all came to distress. Nature has written on my brow, Your shade shall be broad but there shall be no protection derived from it to aught you favour." Moreover, at the very time he was thus meditating, he was making unconsciously an enemy (April 1828), an enemy with all the Scottish genius for remembering a slight. Carlyle wrote to him on 13th April, 1828, announcing a gift from Goethe of two medals which he had been commissioned to transmit: " Being in this curious fashion appointed, as it were, Ambassador between two Kings of Poetry, I would willingly discharge my mission with the solemnity that beseems such a business ; and naturally it must flatter my vanity and love of the marvellous to think that by means of a Foreigner whom I have never seen I might now have access to my native sovereign whom I have so often seen in public and so often wished that I had claim to see and know in private and near at hand." That is the elaborate kind of complimentary address which Scott disliked in foreigners : "A Russian Princess Galatzin, too, demands to see me in the heroic vein. Elle voulait traverser les mers pour aller voir S. W. S. and offers me a rendezvous at my hotel. This is precious tomfoolery" (*November*, 1826). But Carlyle's letter is the kind of letter one does not like to write and get no answer to. Scott was in London, depressed about Johnny Lockhart and Terry, dining and breakfasting at innumerable houses : " In this phantasmagorial place the objects of the day come and depart like shadows." Carlyle's letter was forgotten, and a second letter, transmitting the medals in May when Scott was at home, remained also unacknowledged. It is no wonder that Carlyle, a benevolent but not a generous man, never forgot or forgave, as his review of Lockhart's *Life* was to show.

The enormous demand of the booksellers for the first volumes of the *Magnum Opus* which appeared with the prospectus in May 1829 excited the highest hopes in both Cadell and Scott : " After the Court I came round by Cadell who is like Jemmy Taylor

Full of mirth and full of glee,

for which he has good reason having raised the impression of the Magnum to 12000 copies and yet the end is not for the only puzzle now is to satisfy the delivery fast enough." (30*th May*, 1829.) Indeed, the effect on Scott's mind was to revive some of the old sanguine optimism excited in earlier days by the success of *Marmion* and *The Lady of the Lake*, and later by *Waverley* and its successors. It had always produced a certain measure of self-deception, and in the weakening condition of his health and his overwrought brain was to lead to illusion. " I write to send you a copy of the Waverley novels. . . . Their sale is prodigious. If I live a few years it will completely clear my feet of former encumbrances and may perhaps enable me to talk a word to our friend Nicol Milne,

But old ships must expect to get out of commission
Nor again to weigh the anchor with a yo heave ho.

However that may be I shall be happy to die a free man with the world and leave a competent provision for my family " (*To Walter, 2nd June,* 1829). The same letter records that he has suffered from a passing of blood. In January of the year he had noted : " I cannot say I have been happy for the feeling of increasing weakness in my lame leg is a great affliction. I walk now with pain and difficulty at all times and it sinks my soul to think how soon I may be altogether a disabled cripple. I am tedious to my friends and I doubt the sense of it makes me fretful."

Despite work and resolutions Scott's social life remained a full one and his interest in passing events, political and local, keen. The letters of the closing months of 1828 and opening months of 1829 are full of the Burke and Hare murders : " This is a truly horrid business about Burke and his associates. I have been poring at the account in the paper till I am well-nigh blind" (*26th December*, 1828). He breakfasted out and he dined out and attended meetings and funerals and wrote endless letters. It was at a public dinner in February 1827 that the authorship of the Novels was acknowledged. In June 1829 he made his usual annual excursion to Blairadam in Fifeshire, visiting Falkland Castle. But old friends were dropping off, in July " poor Bob Shortreed the companion of many a long ride among the hills in quest of old ballads. He was a merry companion, a good singer and mimic, and full of Scottish drollery.... So glide our friends from us—*Haec poena diu viventibus*. Many recollections die with him and poor Terry", who had died in June. In October he suffered a severer loss, the quondam poacher, his factotum on the Abbotsford estate, Tom Purdie : " I write to tell you the shocking news of poor Tom Purdie's death by which I have been greatly affected.... Poor fellow, there is a heart cold that loved me well, and I am sure thought of my interest more than his own. I have been seldom so much shocked" (*To Laidlaw*, 31*st October*, 1829). " I am so much shocked that I really wish to be quit of the country and safe in town. But there are things to arrange of course all of which used to be left to that poor fellow" (*To Cadell*, 4*th November*).

In February 1830 came the first unmistakable shock of paralysis : " I have laid aside ", he writes on 26th May, " smoking much ; and now, unless tempted by company, rarely take a cigar. I was frightened by a species of fit which I had in February, which took from me my power of speaking. I am told it is from the stomach. It looked woundy like palsy or apoplexy. Well, be it what it will, I can stand it." At Lockhart's suggestion, who wished to distract him from the " exciting and feverish " (see p. 176) composition of novels, he took up the long talked of " Bogles ", and, in the form of letters to his son-in-law, toiled throughout the year at " my infernal demonology—

a task to which my poverty and not my will consents."
To this in the course of the year he added the Essays on
Ballad Poetry, for the *Magnum Opus*, a review for Lockhart
of Southey's *Life of John Bunyan*, and a Fourth Series of
Tales of a Grandfather, the subject French History, to say
nothing of introductions and notes for the *Magnum Opus*.
In June he made his thirteenth and last visit to Fifeshire:
" Our meeting at Blair Adam was cordial, but our numbers diminished." They visited Culross where Sir Robert
Preston, at the age of ninety-five, was repairing " the old
House of Culross, built by the Lord Bruce of Kinloss ", and
" the wise are asking for whose future enjoyment ". They
visited Lochore with an intention of going to church, but
" were let off for there was no sermon, for which I could
not in my heart be sorry ". Later in the same month he
took another " day's relaxation . . . and . . . surveyed the
little village [Prestonpans], where my aunt and I were
lodgers for the sake of sea-bathing, in 1778 I believe ".
The place was full of memories: " I saw the church
where I yawned under the inflictions of a Dr. McCormick,
a name in which dulness seems to have been hereditary. I
saw the Links where I arranged my shells upon the turf,
and swam my little skiffs in the pools . . . my kind aunt . . .
old George Constable, who, I think, dangled after her . . .
Dalgetty, a veteran half-pay lieutenant, who swaggered
his solitary walk on the parade, as he called a little open
space before the same pool . . . Preston . . . the little
garden where I was crammed with gooseberries, and the
fear I had of Blind Harry's spectre of Fawdon showing his
headless trunk at one of the windows ", an early playmate
" a very good-natured pretty girl (my Mary Duff) ". " I
was a mere child, and could feel none of the passion which
Byron alleges, yet the recollection of this good-humoured
companion of my childhood is like that of a morning
dream." They (his companions were the printer and the
publisher) visited the scene of the battle, and Cockenzie
where Cadell was born and where his mother and brother

still resided. But there " the whole day of pleasure was damped by the news of the King's death ".

He returned to Edinburgh to bid farewell to another old friend and companion at the Clerks' table. In 1807 Scott's joyous letters from London to his wife (pp. 92, 95) are saddened at moments by reflections on the ill-health of three friends—George Ellis, Charles Marriott, and Colin Mackenzie. The death of the last seemed as imminent as that of the two former actually was : " Colin Mackenzie has left London at last but not till he had done all that was imprudent in exposing himself to the most bitter easterly winds I ever felt. I parted with him with a deep presentiment of evil & a most solemn though I fear fruitless recommendation to him to go abroad—if he does not—we shall never see him more—& such a blank in my domestic feelings & affections will never, never be filld up " (*30th March*, 1807). " It is a cruel case for me to have taken leave of two such men as Colin Mackenzie & Marriott under circumstances of such a painful nature. . . . I am however convinced that this life is a scene of trial & that early death is in many instances a blessing rather than a misfortune " (*Letters*, XII, p. 107). But Mackenzie had lived, and shared with Scott the daily toil of the Court of Session. It was now that, on 8th July, returning from the Court, Scott called and found him " suffering under a degree of slow palsy, his spirits depressed, and his looks miserable, worse a great deal than when last I saw him. . . . I looked only on the ghost of my friend of many a long day ".

By the end of July the last proof sheets of " the ghosts " were in James's hands, and Scott, in the old way, is writing to Murray, who had backed Lockhart's suggestion and was the publisher, " to draw for the copy money say £700 " (*Letters*, XI, p. 376). And already he was getting ready for, or at work on, *Count Robert of Paris* and *Castle Dangerous* (*Letters*, XI, pp. 373 and 391 with note) ; for the latter Cadell had agreed " to carry to Sir Walter's cash account the sum of £1200 " on 6th July ; and when, in September, as part of the policy of drawing Scott off from the novels, Cadell offers £750 for the *Reliquiae Trottcosienses*—an account of the various curios collected at Abbotsford—Scott stipulates that it shall not "appear till after the publication of Count Robert of Paris" (6*th September*, 1830). In December, however, Ballantyne pronounces himself displeased with the opening chapters of *Count Robert*. It does not open well, he reports to Cadell, and Cadell to Scott, whereas a good opening in Scott's work has always led on to an interesting story—witness *The Talisman* as compared with *The Betrothed*: "I confess I think 24 pages an enormous length for a single conversation, of no great interest perhaps, between Achilles & Hereward." But neither Ballantyne nor Cadell is for abandoning the work, and the end of 1830 and early months of 1831 are given to dictating to Laidlaw: "Wrote on by Mr. Laidlaw's assistance. Things go bobbishly enough ; we have a good deal finished before dinner" (19*th January*, 1831). "I wrote with Laidlaw. It does not work clear ; I do not know why. The plot is, nevertheless, a good plot, and full of expectation" (28*th January*). His description of one day's work is illuminating both for his life at the time and for the light it sheds backwards. " Rose at seven. Dressed before eight, wrote letters, or did any little business till a quarter past nine. Then breakfast. Mr. Laidlaw comes from ten till one. Then take the pony, and ride *quantum mutatus* two or three miles, John Swanston walking by my bridle-rein lest I fall off. Come home about three or four. Then to dinner on a single plain dish and half a tumbler, or by'r lady three-fourths of a tumbler, of whisky and water. Then sit till six o'clock, when enter Mr. Laidlaw again, and work commonly till eight. After this, work usually alone till half-past nine, then sup on porridge and milk, and so to bed. The work is half done. If any [one] asks what time I take to think on the composition, I might say, in one point of view, it was seldom five minutes out of my head the whole day. In another light, it was never the serious subject of consideration at all, for it never occupied my thoughts entirely for five minutes together, except when I was dictating to Mr. Laidlaw." These last two sentences describe, I believe, the manner in which that great creative imagination, now on the wane, had always worked, in the twilight of the conscious and the unconscious. If he can give a name to *Guy Mannering* before *Waverley* is well away, or *The Antiquary* twelve months before it appeared, it was not because these novels were in cold storage, ready at any time to be transcribed by James and released as from a bonded warehouse. That, I am convinced, is a mare's nest. In a way the novel was already written when the idea was once conceived, but that central idea was capable of burgeoning in thick-coming fancies as he roamed with his friends, fancies that brightened and expanded once the pen was in his hand.

On 16th April, 1831 came the severest stroke from which Scott had yet suffered, the beginning of the final phase, and a month later the sentence passed on the last volume of *Count Robert* by printer and publisher, with which and Scott's reaction I have dealt already. Thereafter Scott becomes more and more but a shadow of himself—and he was *not yet sixty*. " If I was born in 1771 ", he writes on 2nd July, 1830, " I shall only be sixty in 1831, and, by the same reasoning, sixty-four in 1835, so I may rough it out, yet be no Sir Robert Preston. At any rate, it is all I have to trust to," *i.e.* if he is to clear himself. It was not to be. The pathetic details of the last months are fully recorded by Lockhart and I do not propose to elaborate them. Lockhart in May accompanied him on an expedition to the West to gather impressions for *Castle Dangerous* and was made acutely aware of the weakening of his extraordinary memory and the quickening of the sensibility which his stoical strength of will had concealed from many, and still does. " High and exalted feelings, indeed, he had never been able to keep concealed, but he had shrunk from exhibiting to human eye the softer and gentler emotions which now trembled to the surface. He strove against it even now, and presently came back from the Lament of the Makers, to his Douglasses, and chanted ... in a sort of deep and glowing, though not distinct recitative, his first favourite among all the ballads,

> 'It was about the Lammas tide,
>   When husbandmen do win their hay,
> That the Doughty Douglas bownde him to ride
>   To England to drive a prey'—

down to the closing stanzas, which again left him in tears,

> 'My wound is deep—I fain would sleep—
>   Take thou the vanguard of the three,
> And hide me beneath the bracken-bush,
>   That grows on yonder lily lee....'"

He had quoted the same stanza when he had thought himself dying in 1819 and " was mentally bequeathing to you my batton "—the baton of the Tory Party in Scotland. And now, as earlier, Scott was profoundly agitated by the course of political events—the ever nearer advent of the Reform Bill. He was terribly anxious to deliver himself of another Malachi Malagrowther letter, or an address to the County, but his draft was set aside. The painful episode in May, when he with other Tories was booed and pelted in Jedburgh, has naturally been much commented on. To me it seems that blame attaches less to either Scott or the poor weavers than to the politicians who were using the mob to promote a reform which for years did mighty little for those whom they had used, merely substituted for the landed gentry the rule of the industrial magnates. In September came Wordsworth, his daughter, and a nephew Charles, afterwards Bishop of St. Andrews and a great champion of the Union of the Churches. " At noon on Thursday we left Abbotsford, and on the morning of that day Sir Walter and I had a serious conversation *tête-à-tête* when he spoke with gratitude of the happy life which upon the whole he had led."

> A trouble, not of clouds, or weeping rain,
> Nor of the setting sun's pathetic light
> Engendered, hangs o'er Eildon's triple height:
> Spirits of Power, assembled there, complain
> For kindred Power departing from their sight.

Wordsworth had never spoken with whole-hearted admiration of Scott's poetry nor of the Waverley Novels. But there was a strong link between both the men and their work. For both the open countryside was the breath of life; and the best work of both had been the interpretation of the mind and heart of common people. The novelist who described the mourning of the Mucklebackits and the character of Jeanie Deans has more essentially in common with the poet of "The Affliction of Margaret" and "Resolution and Independence" than with most of his followers in romantic historical fiction. There are even resemblances between Matthew or the old Cumberland beggar and Edie Ochiltree, different as is the two writers' manner of treatment.

In the year 1818 in which Lockhart made Scott's acquaintance, but somewhat earlier in the year, an American of whom he makes no mention, but who was a man of distinction in his own country as orator and reformer, Edward Everett visited Abbotsford by invitation. Like Washington Irving and others he dwells on the charm of Scott's hospitality and manners, his recurrent Scotticisms as "I mind" for "I remember", the winning grace of Sophia and the bond of sympathy and affection between her and her father; but he also records a saying which recalls Wordsworth, and reveals the strain of deep humanity which underlay Scott's worldliness and Wordsworth's complacent egotism: "Some poor person, as we passed along, expressed himself in terms of warm gratitude to Sir Walter for his kind inquiries after a member of his family who was ill. When we had passed on I made some remark on the strong and apparently sincere language of gratitude ... prompted, as I supposed, by some former and more important acts of kindness on his part. Without particularly replying to the suggestion he said : ' for my part I am more touched by the gratitude than the ingratitude of the poor. We occasionally hear complaints of how thankless men are for favours bestowed upon them ; but when I consider that we are all of the same flesh and blood, it grieves me more to see slight acts of kindness acknowledged with such humility and deep sense of obligation.' " Just so Wordsworth :

> I've heard of hearts unkind kind deeds
> With coldness still returning;
> Alas! the gratitude of men
> Hath oftener left me mourning.

Wordsworth left Abbotsford, impressed by the kindness of young Walter to his father and his patience with his sister Anne who, Wordsworth and his daughter were convinced, was on the verge of a nervous breakdown. Scott himself set out on the next day, and, after a short stay in London and delays at Portsmouth, sailed for Italy in the *Barham*. It was, as Scott said of Colin Mackenzie, the ghost of the man who had been that visited Malta and Naples and Rome. He could revive and converse with those who called, and take a momentary interest in this or that sight, but these took no hold on his memory. To Charles, his poor son, attached to the Embassy at Naples, himself already a victim of rheumatism, nothing gave a greater shock than the discovery of his father's mental condition : " I have been much shocked with the change in papa for although I expected from your letters to find him feeble and speaking with difficulty I was not aware that his mind had been so much affected as it evidently is, also that he is at times sensible of this himself." A great strain was put upon Charles which he bore, I think, with commendable courage. Anne was nervously worn out. She died five months after her father. Walter was also feeling the strain. " Walter does not choose to bear with Anne's temper and she from bad health cannot help saying what would irritate any person ; now I do not answer on these occasions, so we remain good friends " (*Charles to Sophia 3rd Jan.*, 1832). From Naples they moved to Rome where Scott met friends and had intervals of a clearer mind and brighter spirits. Occasionally his old humour shines out as when he tells Laidlaw that the Neapolitan soldiers declare that, except for fighting, they are the equal of the best soldiers in Europe. On 11th May they started for home overland, the news of Goethe's death hastening Scott's decision to return. At Mainz on the Rhine there came to visit him no less a person than Arthur Schopenhauer, and Scott's last letter was an apology for not being able to see him.[1] On the river he

[1] In 1831 Schopenhauer, driven from Berlin by an outbreak of cholera, settled at Frankfort but on account of ill-health moved to Mannheim where he was in residence throughout 1832. Of his familiarity with the work of Scott, though his biographers say little about it, his *World as Will and Idea* bears testimony. Scott illustrated his doctrine that it is from the mother talent is inherited though from the father may come physique and character : " Walter Scott's mother was a poetess and was in communication with the wits of her time, as we learn from the obituary notice in the *Globe* of 24th September 1832. That poems of hers appeared in print in 1789 I find from an article entitled ' Mother-wit ' in the *Blätter für Litterarische Unterhaltung* of 4th October 1841, published by Brockhaus." Scott's novels, too, proved to Schopenhauer that " Dramas and Epics ... always describe only fighting, suffering, tormented men; and every romance is a raree show in which we observe the spasms and convulsions of the agonised human heart. Walter Scott has naively expressed this aesthetic necessity in the conclusion of his novel *Old Mortality*." Finally Scott was, with Swift and others, a proof that what wears out the brain is not old age but " long-continued over-exertion of the intellect or brain ... Goethe remained to the end clear, strong and active-minded because he, who was always a man of the world, and a courtier, never carried on his mental occupations with self-compulsion " (*The World as Will and Idea*. ... Translated by R. B. Haldane, M.A. and John Kemp, M.A. London 1891). Had Schopenhauer lived to see the *Journal* in its entirety his sense of the tragic character of Scott's life would have been deepened ; nor would he have found that Scott's view of life differed greatly from his own : " Life could not be endured were it seen in [its] reality." Scott differed only in his resignation, and his hope for a better life hereafter.

had another shock, and from the time he reached London on 13th June I doubt if he was ever able to speak articulately more than a sentence. That is the impression one gets from the letter written to Skene by William Laidlaw, Scott's entirely faithful and honest friend though a robust Whig, when Scott had been brought to Abbotsford in July: " Your Friend is as helpless and requires to be attended in every respect as an infant of six months old. Of his powerful mind, which as it were shone over the civilised world, there remains only a pale and uncertain glimmering—sometimes though but rarely it blazes out for a brief moment and this makes the melancholy sight more hard to bear. They tell me he is seldom conscious—and he complains greatly and speaks much—and he is generally extremely restless and impatient and they tell me irritable—I have rarely seen him show any such symptoms for he always knows me, seems relieved to see me, holds out his hand and grasps mine and looks in my face and always attempts to speak—often he seems anxious to inquire about or to tell me something but he rarely makes out a sentence and when he finds he cannot make himself understood he lets his head sink, and he remains silent untill I offer to go away when he holds my hand firmly and sometimes entreats me not to go yet" (*Kaeside, 15th August,* 1832).

Lockhart's story of his being sent for alone to the bedside when Scott bade him " be a good man—be virtuous—be religious—be a good man—nothing else will give you any comfort when you come to lie here " is, I fear, a pious myth—a concession to the censorious piety of the Evangelical age, for I find, among the Abbotsford papers now in the National Library, a letter to Lockhart from a lady relative of Scott suggesting some such words : " When you write anything of the last very melancholy weeks at Abbotsford I think it will be most valuable to mention any of the few remarks he uttered when his mind was clear of a religious tendency such as I heard he said occasionally, Oh be virtuous! It is ones only comfort in a dying state! and anything of that kind, for there *are* wicked people who will take a *pleasure* in saying that he was not a religious man; and *proving the contrary will do much good.*" Such death-bed legends are not unheard of even to-day. One was put abroad for a day or two, and then peremptorily denied, regarding the late Lord Balfour. Scott, like many another, was quite unconscious for days before he died: "After about forty hours of stupor he breathed his last," Sophia writes to a friend five days after his death, " for the last fortnight his life was a miracle; every day the doctor took leave saying it was impossible he would outlive the night, and life was only kept in by opiates; his mind never returned for an instant." [1] Gangrene had set in on the 11th September, and on the 21st the shadow of Scott passed away at 1.30 p.m. "Scott is dead," wrote an old political enemy but personal friend, Henry Cockburn. "He expired yesterday. I had been on a visit at Kirklands to Richardson who, I believe, will be one of the executors; and on coming home to-day I saw Abbotsford reposing beside its gentle Tweed, and amidst its fading woods, in the calm splendour of a sweet autumnal day. I was not aware till I reached Edinburgh that all that it then contained of him was his memory and his remains. Scotland never owed so much to one man" (*Journal of Henry Cockburn,* 22nd September, 1832).

[1] *Official Historical Catalogue, Scottish Exhibition, Glasgow,* 1911, p. 106.

EPILOGUE

SCOTT's illness and journey in quest of health meant heavy expenditure, increase of debt, and a difficult outlook for his family, in view of the fact that of his liabilities, so far, eleven shillings in the pound had been paid, leaving another nine shillings to be found, to say nothing of current interest since 1826. Economy had never come easily, even with the best of resolutions, to Sir Walter ; and with the disintegration of his brain the old habit of drawing bills on his publisher, which incoming profits were to clear, revived in a manner that not a little dismayed Cadell. In a letter to the younger Walter of 30th April 1832 he outlined the position with the rather brutal frankness with which he had been in the habit of addressing Constable in the days of their partnership, and James Ballantyne in connection with the printing of later books and the *Magnum Opus*.

"Sir Walter got from his trustees when he left last October - - - £500 0 0
This met his London expenditure and left a considerable balance over. For this balance he drew from Malta. But on getting to Naples he made so great a howling about money that I paid Coutts and Co - - - 300 0 0
His howling however continued so great that I sent him further to Naples - 500 0 0
Here is in all - - - - - 1300 0 0

I had scarcely a doubt from the tenor of his letters that this sum must last for many months to come. What was the surprise therefore of Mr Gibson and myself to get advice from Coutts and Co. of two fresh drafts (our advice was only last Friday) one for £500 and the other for £200 making say £2000 in six months! This is Captain Osbaldistone with a vengeance—of the £2000 the Trustees will only pay £500 so that here is £1500 from me besides £2000 more your father owes me :

Say his debt to me - - - - £3500	0	0
There are many open accounts for which I am constantly dunned—they will I am sure come to - - 700	0	0
There is - - - - - 4200	0	0

of a new debt running on against your father at a speed too which is destruction itself. His whole income just now is about £1200 p.a. his rate of spending you can form some idea of. He writes to me to buy up debts, to buy carriage horses, to buy ponies. *I pay no attention* to these instructions." Cadell then goes on to tell Walter that he has made a practical proposal to Gibson, Factor to Scott's Trustees ; and this proposal is outlined in the letter which is forwarded. He had, he says, approached various of the creditors with proposals to purchase their debts. But the reply of nearly one and all was : " we expect full payment and will not sell." As one of them put it, " knowing the honourable feelings of Sir Walter Scott and that if he lives his whole engagements will ultimately be discharged I am sorry I cannot meet you." That is surely a great compliment to Scott's character and achievement. But Cadell goes on to say that if this is their temper when Scott is ill, what will it be when he dies? They will expect the full interest on the debt. But, he thinks, they might respond to a prompt offer of the whole remaining debt less interest. He suggests therefore a scheme, which he thinks he can carry through with the help of friends, that is, probably, the same relatives as had helped to set him up as Cadell and Co. It will mean that in addition to the sums which are due to the Trust, or will be shortly due, he must find some £17,000 to £23,000. On Scott's return it was clear that there was to be no more work. Lockhart, in order to come with him to Scotland, had to borrow from Blackwood on the promise of a "Noctes" for the Magazine. Cadell advised the brothers to have a proposal ready on the shortest notice. Accordingly in the October following the death of Scott a letter was addressed to the Trustees by Walter, Charles and Lockhart in which, after stating what funds were immediately available, being sufficient to pay a further dividend of 6/- in the £, they undertook to provide the money necessary to make this into a payment of 9/- which with the previous payments would mean that the debt was paid in full, less the current interest since 1826. In return they asked the Trustees and Creditors to surrender the estate of Abbotsford and other properties in their hands, including "the half copyrights of Scott's Novels, and Romances, Poetical Works, and Miscellaneous Prose Works now vested in you". The other half of these were already Cadell's. To this the creditors assented. Cadell found the necessary funds, some £30,000, and in return secured immediately or within a short time full possession of the copyrights. In May 1847 Lockhart writes to Croker : " I have finally settled all Sir Walter's affairs. There remained : debt secured on his lands, £8500 ; to Cadell £16,000 ; and sundries £1000. I have taken the £1000 on myself, and Cadell obliterates the £24,500 on condition of getting the whole remaining copyrights of Scott's Works, and also of the Life. In a year or so thus my son gets Abbotsford burdened only with his aunt's jointure—the surplus income, unless things improve, about £400 a year...." (*The Croker Papers*, III, p. 106).

Scott's *Works* proved a good bargain for Cadell. In 1848 when he was apparently preparing to sell his interest he wrote to a certain M. P. Stoniman, 65 Pater Noster Row, sending him " particulars connected with Sir Walter Scott's works which you thought needful to enable those not minutely acquainted with the never ceasing demand for them to judge of their value as a property". He then gives details of the sales of various sets of the works,— novels, poems, *Napoleon*, etc., etc., and continues " the figures would appear almost incredible—but so it is and during the progress of these doings I have paid Sir Walter Scott's debt and the debt on the estate of Abbotsford " [the debt incurred at Cadell's instance to assist Hurst, Robinson and Co.] " in a word a trifle over £76000 and what is more surprising as I have already said the demand for his work continues—aye, every hour, every minute of the day some one of them is called for, and a better proof I cannot give of this than that while I write to you I am told from home that twenty volumes of the novels, forty eight volumes (edition) of Prose twenty eight volumes (edition) must be reprinted forthwith to keep the market supplied."[1] Thus what to Scott and his family had proved fairy gold swarmed upon Cadell and there solidified. In 1837 Cadell wrote to Laidlaw : " Strange to think that all the Ballantynes and Constable are gone, and I am left alone of those behind the curtain during so many critical years! Born at Cockenzie in East Lothian, educated for business above five years in Glasgow, I came here [to Edinburgh] a raw young man of twenty one in the winter of 1809-10, and have cuckooed all these men out of their nests, firmly seated in which they all were at the time " (Robert Carruthers : *Abbotsford Notanda* appended to Robert Chambers's *Life of Sir Walter Scott*, edition of 1871). " Business is business", and business ethics are business ethics. Yet to an outsider it does seem that it would have been just, at least noble, if Cadell had said : " Of the debt which you have paid £40,000 is a debt for which Constable and I were jointly and individually responsible. I will pay, as part of my debt, to your family the £20,000

---

[1] What Cadell means is that twenty vols. of the edition of the novels in forty-eight vols., and eight vols. of the edition of the Prose Works in twenty-eight vols. are called for.

needed to clear the capital debt and leave to them the profits of the half copyrights and of the *Life*. Even so I am making a good thing of the bargain." One feels at times as if Scott's best friend, had he been left to take his own way, was Abud whose action would have compelled him to a sequestration.

To add anything further to the criticism of Scott and his work is not my intention. The work of few has been examined so thoroughly, so variously judged, from the periodicals of his own day down to our own, or by better qualified judges—Adolphus, Senior, Jeffrey, Hazlitt, Bagehot, Leslie Stephen, and Stephen's gifted daughter, Virginia Woolf. The only criticism of any value now would be one that did not merely record the reaction of this or that individual yesterday or to-day, but one which should endeavour to see the English novel as it was when he began to write and do justice to his special contribution to its development ; secondly, which, taking what Arnold called the personal estimate, would recognise the fitness or unfitness to judge of those to whom it has made appeal from the outset. One might then try to estimate what, with all the changes of fashion and taste which have ensued since Scott's death, bears still the imprint of a great creative genius. The range of his work alone, as poet, editor, historian, critic, essayist, novelist, and the vitality which he communicated to it all, places him to my mind, when all is said about his shortcomings, in a class by himself. Who has covered so many fields with any comparable success in them all?

I would rather, for it has an historical interest, say a word in closing on what all his critics, early and late, just and unjust, have recognised as his most definite limitation. I do not mean the want of passion (in the narrow sense of the word) of which Balzac and Mr. Forster complain, for as a fact many of our greatest English novelists, Fielding, Smollett, Jane Austen, Thackeray, Dickens, have not shone signally in this field. It has been a subordinate interest in their work. In the portrayal of passion the greatest of English novels is *Wuthering Heights*, immeasurably so. Carlyle has stated what I have in view, in his own fashion, when he complains of the absence of any sense of a mission in Scott's work : " Perhaps no literary man of any generation has less value than Scott for the immaterial part of his mission in any sense ; not only for the fantasy called fame with the fantastic miseries attendant thereon ; but also for the spiritual purport of his works, whither it tended, hitherward or thitherward, or had any tendency whatever —except to make money." Elsewhere Carlyle discovers that Shakespeare too had no conscious motive " beyond drawing audiences to the Globe Theatre". Bagehot, in an essay which describes admirably the blend in the novels of romantic imagination and good sense, expresses the same thought when he speaks of Scott's deficiency in " the searching and abstract intellect ", his want of any adequate " treatment of man's religious nature ".

One might traverse to some extent both these statements as they stand. There is more thought than meets the eye in Scott's judgements on life and character and history. So far from being indifferent to the drift and effect of his novels Scott has even sacrificed their romantic interest to his determination to stress the worth of principle, character. Whatever else his heroes are they are always in the last resort men of high principle. Nor is it quite just to say that the creator of Jeanie Deans and the Jewess Rebecca is insensible to the values of moral and religious convictions.

What seems to myself Scott's limitation is rather that in his judgement on characters and on historical epochs he seldom or never transcends the conventional, the accepted. His heroes and heroines have always principle sufficient to preserve them from more than aberrations of feeling, errors of judgement ; but the two characters I have mentioned, Rebecca and Jeanie, are the only persons whom he describes, not only with sympathy, but with a whole-hearted moral approval. Of the historical events which he chooses for the setting of his story his judgement is always that of the good sense and moderated feeling of his own age. He will not take sides out and out with either Jacobite or Hanoverian, Puritan or Cavalier; nor does he attempt to transcend either the prejudices or the conventional judgement of his contemporaries, he makes no effort to attain to a fresh and deeper reading of the events. There was in Scott's mind a dualism which he made no attempt to bridge, of which he was not himself fully conscious. In the novels it shows itself in the contradiction between his romantic sympathies and his sober judgement. He does not surrender himself to the full romance of his story as Dumas does, or as, in a different way and portraying a different aspect of life, does Balzac. Hence the decay of his popularity with boys and young people. What boy can do justice to Scott's masterly portrayal of Louis XI, his clear envisagement of the conflict between the Macchiavellian but patriotic politician and the passionate feudal chivalry of the Duke of Burgundy—the same contrast as Shakespeare has adumbrated between the chivalrous Hotspur, the knight whose watchword is "Honour" and who yet is willing to cut and carve England with Scots and Welshmen, and the Prince whose honour is inseparable from the greatness of his country?

The dualism I have in view pervaded Scott's life as well as his work. I do not refer merely to the contrast between the good sense which pervades everything he wrote from letters to novels and the folly, for it is difficult to give it any other name, of his financial dealings. I am thinking rather of his outlook on life and politics. Mr. Edwin Muir has suggested that a more definite centre might have been given to Scott's work had Scotland been still a nation. I probably do not quite understand the thesis, for I find it difficult to think of national feeling as the inspiration of a literature of any great breadth. Patriotism has a narrowing effect, and acts too potently on the malevolent emotions. The inspiration of Shakespeare's historical plays is national, and in consequence he is as unjust to Joan of Arc and the French as Homer to Hector and the Trojans, or more so. No; the fundamental question to which the French Revolution gave life was social, not national, though the policy of Napoleon lent to national feeling, for a time, the predominance. Scott, like Burns, had imperial as well as national sympathies. He had but to look round, then as now, to see that small nations in Europe exist on sufferance, that Scotland within the British empire enjoyed a more secure freedom than Switzerland or Holland or the states in Italy. He was a Tory, who had, under the influence of the Revolution and the War, identified Toryism with Patriotism. Many of his countrymen, unable to look beyond the word Tory and all the animus that word awakened when we were all, or most of us, enlightened Liberals or Radicals, Mr. Gladstone's most enthusiastic followers, have been unable to forgive him for not welcoming the Reform Bill and the advent of the great doctrine of *laissez faire* which to Macaulay was the promise of Utopia, to Carlyle became anathema: " The haggard despair of Cotton-factory hands, Coal-mine operatives ... in these days is painful to behold; but not so painful to the inner-sense as that brutish, God-forgetting Profit-and-Loss philosophy and Life-theory which we hear jangled on all hands ... as the Ultimate Gospel and candid Plain-English of Man's Life.... *Laissez faire* on the part of the governing Classes, we repeat again and again, will, with whatever difficulty, have to cease; pacific division of the spoil and a world well let alone will no longer suffice. A Do-nothing Guidance and it is a Do-something World." When the rumour of the coming disaster reached Scott, as he sat alone in the small room in 39 Castle Street, he wrote: " Some at least will forgive my transitory wealth on account of the innocence of my intentions and my real wish to do good to the poor." The last words are true.

Though a Tory Scott did wish to do good to the poor. Nor was he the only person who was moved by the same sympathy yet did not feel sure that the good of the poor was to be advanced by the doctrine of *laissez faire*. He saw the source of the evils that were coming, and he indicated some of the means which might be used to alleviate the lot of the victims. To Scott as to Carlyle the main source of the evil was the divorce of any tie between the employer and the labourer but the cash-nexus: "When the machinery was driven by water the Manufacturer had to seek out some sequestered spot where he could obtain a suitable fall of water, and there his workmen formed the inhabitants of a village around him, and he necessarily bestowed some attention, more or less, on their morals and their necessities, had knowledge of their persons and characters, and exercised over them a salutary influence as over men depending on and intimately connected with him and his prospects." It is just such a settlement which Scott describes in *Chronicles of the Canongate*. "This is now quite changed. The manufacturers are transferr'd to great towns where a man may assemble 500 workmen one week and dismiss the next, without having any further connection with them than to receive a week's work for a week's wage, nor any further solicitude about their future fate than if they were so many shuttles." The remedy which he would apply would have shocked Macaulay and the economic Whigs, but time has wrought changes in our views: "There would perhaps be no means so effectual as that (which will never be listened to) of taxing the manufacturers according to the number of hands which they employ on an average and applying the produce in maintaining the manufacturing poor. If it should be alleged that this would injure the manufacturers I would boldly reply ' And why not injure or rather limit speculations the excessive stretch of which has been productive of so much damage to the principals, to the country and to the population whom it has in so many respects demoralised'." But neither Tory nor Whig dreamt of such restrictions on wealth and justice to the poor, though Scott was not the only old Tory who had doubts regarding the benefits of *laissez faire*. In the decade following Scott's death Maginn gathered round him in *Fraser's Magazine* a number of men who would have had the Tory party not be content with stealing the Whigs' clothes, but constitute themselves the guardians of the poor against the cruelties of industrialism and *laissez faire*. Coleridge, Southey, Carlyle, Disraeli, Cobbett were all moved by a spirit which with Disraeli begot Tory Democracy, with Carlyle something like the demand for a Dictatorship of or for the Proletariate. Tory Democracy had this at least in common with socialism, the belief in the necessity of a Government which recognised its duty to govern, and to protect the poor against exploitation. But all this lay far ahead. The country had to pass through the phase which makes Victorian England one of the darkest chapters in our industrial history, an age of Two Nations, the overwhelmingly rich and the degraded poor. Scott had no clear view of the social problem though he felt it in his bones. What I wish to emphasise is this dualism in his mind which he himself hardly suspected or understood. On the one hand his sympathies are feudal and aristocratic. The passing of power from the landed aristocracy which the Reform Bill was to bring seemed to him, like Socialism to the late Lord Rosebery, to be the precursor of " the end of all things ". On the other hand was his real sympathy with the poor. Nor is it quite just to say that Scott saw the poor only as they seem to their worldly betters. Whatever his prejudices his imagination had a wider vision. As Shakespeare set out to satirise the Jew for the amusement of an Elizabethan audience in the mood for a pogrom, and then, in virtue of his divining imagination, could not help seeing the Jew through his own eyes, so Scott is well aware that the poor pass their own judgement on their betters. I have cited one instance from *Chronicles of the Canongate*. There is an equally striking instance in *The Bride of Lammermoor*:

"If Lord Ravenswood protected his people, my friend, while he had the means of doing so I think they might spare his memory."

"Ye are welcome to your ain opinion, sir," said the sexton; "but ye winna persuade me that he did his duty, either to himself or to huz puir dependent creatures, in guidin us the gate he has done—he might hae gien us life-rent tacks of our bits o' houses and yards—and me that's an auld man living in yon miserable cabin, that's fitter for the dead than the quick, and killed wi' rheumatise, and John Smith in my dainty bit mailing, and his window glazen, and a' because Ravenswood guided his gear like a fule."

"It is but too true," said Ravenswood, conscience-stricken, "the penalties of extravagance extend far beyond the prodigal's own suffering."

Scott dreamed, says Lockhart not unjustly, of the feudal system as "a scheme of life so constituted originally, and which his fancy pictured as capable of being revived, as to admit of the kindliest personal contact between (almost) the peasant at the plough and the magnate with revenues rivalling the monarch". If he thought too highly of the rich nobles he was not alone in suspecting that no great and immediate benefit would accrue by the substitution of the power of the ignoble rich. "How beautiful is the benignant rule of Whiggery," wrote Maginn after the great reform was completed, "and the *juste milieu*! Good people of the Trades' Unions, do you not now feel how completely you have been humbugged? When you bellowed for a reform which could not, by any possible chance, be of the slightest advantage to you, you were honoured and cherished as the 'people of England'; when you venture to beg for the remission of a harsh punishment of your own brethren, you are flung forth as something too filthy to be touched; and if you dare to growl you are threatened with the dragoon's sabre or the policeman's bludgeon." But no clear idea of the social problem was consciously woven by Scott into his picture of life in the novels which, like Shakespeare's plays, were written to amuse, not to teach. Scott's contribution to the movement democracywards was unconscious. It lay in what he taught not novelists alone but historians—Carlyle, Macaulay, Motley, Prescott, Thierry, Guizot, Michelet. They learned from him in various degrees not only that history can be made dramatically vivid, but also the importance of the common people who in earlier histories seem hardly to exist. "It would seem, perhaps, absurd to fix upon the most unreflective of writers, Sir Walter Scott, as the chief initiator of a philosophical influence; but I believe there is little doubt that historical humanism in England, as on the Continent, received an epoch-making impulse from his writings." (Bernard Bosanquet: *Growth of Modern Philosophy*.)

My thesis is not, of course, that Scott had been a better novelist had he held this or that particular view of the political and social questions of the day, but that if he had held any view with greater and clearer singleness of mind, had there been less of division between his imagination and his sense of the reality of things, it might or would have lent to his heroes, and not to these alone but to the historical characters, more of intensity and interest. They would have stood more clearly for this or that cause. We should have followed with greater interest the conflicts and development of their inner life. But I venture to think that the same is true in a measure of Shakespeare, though he conceals, or compensates for, the same want of complete clearness as to the inmost significance of the character by his unmatched command of the poetry of passion. We might have been more aware of it if his medium had been the prose novel. What is exactly the central, governing thought in the mind of Brutus, of Hamlet? Macbeth hardly knows what is the source of the turmoil in his breast, and critics are divided about it. Lear knows only what he thinks his daughters ought to feel, and have failed to feel, of love and gratitude—except Cordelia whom he has wronged. That the relation between parent and child has in it the latent possibilities of tragedy without the necessary villainy of a child is beyond the range of his thought, perhaps of Shakespeare's or the mind of his audience. Both writers alike start from a story, traditional or springing from the poet's own inventive faculty, and are content to let the characters come to life as the story develops. The result for Scott is that the characters he draws with most power and distinctness are just those to whom the circumstances of their lives present few problems of thought, whose lives are governed by simple, elemental feelings.

INDEX

Abbot, The, 183, 188, 199, 200, 204, 209, 210
Abbotsford, the poet's home, 104, 110, 113, 115, 136, 148, 151, 152, 162, 165, 170, 181, 186-9, 193, 210, 212-5, 220, 222-7, 229, 230, 252, 257-9, 262, 263, 293, 303, 304
Abercorn, Lady, 100, 109, 112, 192, 236
— Lord, 93-5, 98, 99
Abercromby, George, 20
Abud, Jewish broker, 265, 284, 305
Adolphus, John Leycester, 215
Alvanley, Lady, 225, 227
Anchor Close, the poet's parents' first home, 8, 10
Anne of Geierstein, 278, 280
Antiquary, 128-32, 138, 152, 172, 176, 234, 294
Apology for Tales of Terror, 74
Ashestiel, the poet's home, 89, 104
Ashley, Lord, afterwards Earl of Shaftesbury, 193
Auchindrane, 276

Bagehot, Walter, 306
Baillie, Joanna, 106, 109, 112, 127, 153 n, 158 n, 161, 180, 194, 207, 242, 243
Ballads, 21, 26, 32, 35, 36, 45, 71-82, 291
Ballantyne, James and John, 1, 2, 5, 14, 15, 17, 31, 39, 74, 83-8, 101, 103-6, 108-12, 114-6, 123, 125, 128-33, 135-52, 158-61, 165, 166 n, 171, 173-8, 183, 184, 186, 188, 194, 195, 198, 204, 205 n, 206, 208, 210, 211, 216, 217, 219-22, 229-31, 238-40, 245, 247, 254, 257, 259-62, 270-2, 275, 277 n, 279-81, 288, 293
Bannatyne Club, 215
Barbauld, Mrs., 32

Beacon, The, 195
Belsches, Williamina, 28-32, 34, 36, 39, 41-4, 158, 235, 283
Betrothed, 231, 232, 238-40, 293
Bird, Rev. John, 46, 47, 53, 54, 61
Black Dwarf, 136, 139, 152, 173, 280
Blackwood, William, 124, 132-8, 140, 161, 173, 221, 280
Blackwood's Magazine, 1, 31, 168, 172, 180, 186, 190, 248
Bolton, John, 244
Boswell, Sir Alexander, 195, 259
Bridal of Triermain, 105, 106, 108, 112
Bride of Lammermoor, 171-4, 180, 181
Brönte's *Wuthering Heights*, 306
Buccleuch, Duchess of (formerly Lady Dalkeith), 80, 114, 123
Buccleuch, Duke of, 109, 114, 127, 136, 138, 139, 141, 144, 158 n, 161, 163, 171-3, 180, 263
Bullock, Terry and George, 151
Burns, Robert, 167
Byron, Lady, 161
Byron, Lord, 67, 100-2, 105, 106, 123, 127, 153, 154 n, 167-9, 201, 217, 236, 237, 240, 254, 260, 291

Cadell, Robert, 1, 2, 87, 110, 115, 131, 132, 137, 139-42, 144, 145, 147, 148, 158, 163, 164, 166 n, 171, 173, 176, 183, 205-8, 210, 215, 216, 219-21, 229-31, 240, 242, 253, 254, 256, 257, 259-63, 270-80, 289, 291-4, 301-5
Cadell & Davies, 111
Campbell, Dykes, 2
Canning, George, 91, 92, 227, 244, 250
" Cargill, Josiah," 231
Carlyle, Thomas, 4, 288, 306, 308-10
Carpenter, Charles, 172, 178
— Mrs. Charles, 189, 192
— Charlotte, *see* Scott, Charlotte
Castle Dangerous, 278, 292, 294

315

INDEX

Chalmers, George, 26, 73
Chambers, Robert, 8, 15, 19, 47, 50, 148
Chantrey, Sir Francis Legatt, his busts of Scott, 184, 286
Charpentier, M. and Mme, 47-53
— Margaret Charlotte, *see* Scott, Charlotte
Chronicles of the Canongate, 271, 275, 276, 279, 282-4
Clephane, Margaret, 14, 109, 126, 222
Clerk, William, of Eldin, 19, 26, 29, 30, 35, 43, 235
Cockburn, Henry, 300
Coleridge, John Taylor, 249, 251
— Samuel Taylor, 80, 81, 100, 229, 258 n, 285, 310
Collected works, 271, 276 n, 288, 301
College Wynd, the poet's birthplace, 10
Colquhoun, Archibald Campbell, of Clathick, 63, 197
Compton, Countess of, 225
Constable, Archibald and Co., 1, 39, 68, 83 n-85 n, 86, 96, 104, 105, 108-11, 113-5, 123, 127, 128, 129 n, 131-49, 158, 159, 161, 164, 165, 166 n, 171-3, 175, 176, 178, 180, 183, 184, 186, 187, 203-8, 216, 219-21, 226, 229-31, 232 n, 238, 240, 245, 248, 251, 252 ; their failure, 253-65, 270, 271, 273, 276, 301, 304
Cooper, Fenimore, 285
Count Robert of Paris, 181-3, 278, 280, 292-4
Coutts, Mrs. (Harriet Mellon), 225, 246
Crabbe, George, 109, 112, 196, 268
Craig, James Gibson, 91
Cranstoun, George, 19
— Jane, 20, 32-4, 36 n, 38 n, 63, 158, 235
Croker, John Wilson, 190, 196, 214, 249, 252, 265, 272, 303

Dalkeith, James Skene, Lord, 9, 45, 80, 91, 95, 180
— Lady, *see* Buccleuch, Duchess of

Dance of Death, 127
D'Arblay, Madame, 269
Davy, Sir Humphrey, 187, 194
Demonology and Witchcraft, 5, 6, 230
Dickens, Charles, 147, 150
Disraeli, Benjamin, 249, 250, 252, 310
Doom of Devorgoil, 276
Downshire, Lord, 47, 51 n, 53, 54, 56, 58-66
Dumergue, Antoinette Adelaide, 50
— Charles, 50, 51, 59, 61, 66, 80
— Miss, 151
— Sophia, 59
Dundas, Robert, 11, 45, 92, 93

Edgeworth, Maria, 19, 47, 125, 211-5, 232, 242, 243, 247, 281
— Richard, 48, 51, 53, 211
Edinburgh, fire in, 227 ; the poet's homes in Anchor Close and College Wynd, 8, 10 ; Castle Street, 64, 89, 168, 258, 263, 266, 308 ; George Square, 10, 11, 13
Edinburgh Annual Register, 96, 108, 112, 123, 127, 135, 140
Edinburgh Review, 14, 84, 86, 96, 115, 172
Edmonstone, John James, of Newton, 20
Elliot, William, 7
Ellis, George, 76, 79, 80, 95, 99, 117, 278, 292
Encyclopaedia Britannica, 115, 161, 230
Erskine, Charles, 112, 115
— David, of Cardross, 29
— Mary, 20, 33, 34, 38, 39, 54, 63, 197
— William, 20, 33, 35, 38, 93, 95, 97, 105 n, 106, 176, 197, 198, 248
Essays on Ballad Poetry, 291
Everett, Edward, 296

Fair Maid of Perth, 116, 273, 275, 280, 282
Fairford, Lord, 50, 51
Ferguson, Sir Adam, 26, 54, 73, 170, 223, 224, 228
— the Misses, 257
Field of Waterloo, 127, 129 n, 131
Flaubert's *Salammbo*, 181, 182

INDEX

Forbes, William, 31, 39, 41, 45
Foreign Quarterly, 275
Fortunes of Nigel, 201, 203, 210

George IV's visit to Edinburgh, 196
Gibson, John, 264, 271, 273, 276, 302
Gillies, R. P., 14, 97, 275, 282
Gleig, G. R., his Life of Scott, 2, 9
Goethe, Johann Wolfgang, 201, 202, 288, 298, 298 n
Goetz von Berlichingen, 71, 72
Gordon, George Huntly, 174, 177, 227, 229, 276
Gourgaud, Marshal, 281
Gustavus Vasa, Prince, 193
Guy Mannering, 124-6, 128, 132, 138, 172, 294

Haliburton, Barbara, 7
— Robert, 7, 61
Halidon Hill, 117, 207, 262
Hall, Basil, 32 n
— Captain, 246 ; his Journal, 233
Harold the Dauntless, 127, 129
Haydon, Benjamin Robert, 248, 286
Heart of Midlothian, 138, 163-6, 171-3
Heber, Richard, 74, 78 n, 80, 99, 117, 215, 270
Henderson, T. F., 76, 79
Historical Romances, 204
Hogarth, Catherine, 150
— George, 150
— Miss, 150
Hogg, James, 75, 78, 80, 151, 159, 216
Home, George, 92, 93, 104
House of Aspen, 117
Hughes, Mrs., 224
Hurst, Robinson & Co., 166 n, 205 n, 253, 256, 257, 259-62, 264, 265, 304
Huxley, Colonel, 270

Ireland, Scott's visit to, 241-4
Irving, Washington, 162, 285
Ivanhoe, 166 n, 173-5, 176 n, 181-3, 199-201, 204, 269

Jamieson, Robert, 74, 75
Jobson, Jane, *see* Scott, Jane

Kaeside, 113, 130, 151
Keats, John, 168, 237, 249
Kenilworth, 183, 188, 189, 200, 201, 204, 209, 210, 233
Kerr, Charles, of Abbotrule, 19, 26, 29, 227, 234, 235
Kinnedder, Lord, 197, 198
Knighton, Sir William, 269, 287

Lady of the Lake, 87-9, 99-103, 110, 132
Laidlaw, William, 75, 159, 161, 174, 210, 217, 248, 258, 279, 293, 294, 298, 299, 304
Larreta, Señor Enrique, 182
Lasswade, the poet's cottage at, 64
Lauderdale, Lord, 91
Lawrence, Sir Thomas, his portrait of Scott, 184, 269
Lay of the Last Minstrel, 80, 83, 89, 110 n, 114, 211
Legend of Montrose, 172-4, 176, 202
Lenore, translation of, 32, 35
Leslie, C. R., paints Scott's portrait, 225-7
Letters from Malachi Malagrowther, 265, 281
Lewis, Matthew Gregory, 71, 74
Leyden, John, 74-6
Lives of the British Novelists, 205 n, 218, 230, 245
Llangollen, Ladies of, 244
Lockhart, John Gibson, Scott meets him for the first time, 166-71 ; marries Scott's daughter, 184, 185 ; quarrels with John Scott, 190 ; offered the editorship of *The Quarterly Review*, 248-52 ; borrows from Blackwood, 303 ; his *Noctes Ambrosianae* and *Peter's Letters to his Kinsfolk*, 1, 166, 167 ; settles Scott's affairs, 303 ; his life of Scott, 1, 12, 16, 18 n, 27, 29, 34, 39, 47, 53, 59, 63, 68, 84, 84 n, 86, 101, 117, 124, 126 n, 128, 131, 137, 139, 163, 165, 172-4, 179, 186, 201, 202, 205, 207, 209, 213-7, 235, 241-4, 246, 247, 254, 255, 262, 277 n, 285, 287, 288, 294, 299, 311
— Mrs., *see* Scott, Sophia

Longman, Thomas, and Co., 105, 110, 111, 115, 124, 127, 128, 132, 135, 136, 138-41, 159, 166 n, 175, 176, 221, 265, 268
Lord of Ennerdale, 117
Lord of the Isles, 111-5, 124, 125, 132, 134, 136, 172, 211

Mackenzie, Colin, 195, 292
— Henry, 25, 187
Maginn, William, 310, 311
Makdougall, Ann, of Makerstoun, 6
Malcolm, Sir John, 225
Marmion, 14, 84, 84 n, 86, 89, 166 n
Marriott, Charles, 292
— John, 95
Mathews, Charles, 259
Mellon, Harriet, *see* Coutts, Mrs.
Melville, Henry Dundas, Viscount, 170, 180, 184
Minstrelsy of the Scottish Border, 73, 75, 76, 79, 83, 278
Monastery, The, 116, 174-6, 183, 199, 200, 204, 209
Monmouth and Buccleuch, Ann, Duchess of, 5
Moore, Tom, 246
Morritt, J. B. S., 100, 105, 106, 112, 113, 128, 129 n, 151, 153 n, 158 n, 171, 180, 194, 224, 257 n, 258 n, 269, 281, 285
Murray, John, 83 n-85 n, 112, 124, 127, 132, 134-40, 144, 159, 161, 171, 221, 249-52, 265, 292
— Patrick, of Simprim, 20, 26, 45, 73

Napoleon, Scott's Life of, 240, 245, 264, 266, 268, 272, 274 n, 281, 284
Nicolson, Jane, 46, 51, 53, 56, 59, 61, 65
— Sarah, 46, 51, 53, 151
North, Christopher, *see* Wilson, John
Northcote, James, 286
Novels and Tales, 204

Old Mortality, 137, 139, 154, 158, 161, 163, 173, 202
Owen, Wyrriot, 49, 50

Page, Anne, 223, 224
Paterson, Robert, "Old Mortality", 26
Paul's Letters to his Kinsfolk, 127-9, 131
Peel, Sir Robert, 269, 287
Percy, Bishop, 75, 76; his *Reliques*, 21, 22, 72
Peveril of the Peak, 208, 209, 221 n
Pirate, The, 201, 202, 209
Poetry contained in the Novels, Tales, and Romances of the Author of Waverley, 205
Pope-Hennessey, Dame Una, 105, 232
Prestonpans, Scott stays at, 291
Purdie, Tom, 186, 229

Quarterly Review, 2, 14, 86, 96, 97, 99, 100, 137, 166, 172, 184, 236, 248-51, 275, 278
Quentin Durward, 201, 208-10, 215, 216, 219, 220, 221 n, 234

Redgauntlet, 7, 116, 181, 209, 230-2, 234-6
Reform Bill, 308-11
Reliquiae Trottcosienses, 293
Representative, The, 249-51
Reynolds, Sir Joshua, 286
Richardson, John, 246
Ritchie, David, 153
Ritson, Joseph, 21, 22, 75, 76
Rob Roy, 138, 141, 158, 160, 161, 163, 164, 166 n, 172, 173, 218
Rokeby, 105-8, 110 n, 111, 112, 189
Rose, William Stewart, 93, 95, 187, 194, 226
Rosslyn, Countess, 91
Royal Society of Edinburgh, 24
Rutherford, Ann and John, 7, 183

St. Ronan's Well, 116, 209, 216, 217, 220, 230, 231
Sandyknowe, home of the poet, 7, 10
Savary, Henry, 260
Schopenhauer, Arthur, 298
Scotland, A history of, 134-6, 138, 171, 173, 175, 183, 240, 272

INDEX

Scott, Ann, the poet's mother, 7-9, 11, 60, 183, 298 n
— Anne, the poet's sister, 3, 8 n, 63, 99
— Anne, the poet's daughter, 92, 162, 189, 214, 241, 242, 244, 252, 267, 268, 285, 297, 298
— Barbara, the poet's sister, 8 n
— Charles, the poet's son, 92, 162, 191, 214, 223, 228, 269, 285, 297, 303
— Charlotte (Carpenter or Charpentier), the poet's wife, 46-67, 126, 127, 212, 214, 226, 267
— Daniel, the poet's brother, 8 n, 14, 99, 248, 282
— Hugh, of Harden, later Lord Polwarth, 32
— Jane (Jobson), wife of the poet's son Walter, 68 n, 223, 229, 237, 238, 241, 242
— Jean, the poet's sister, 8 n
— John, the poet's brother, 8 n, 54, 97, 98, 130, 152
— John, a journalist, 128, 190, 217
— Robert, farmer at Sandyknowe, the poet's grandfather, 2, 6, 7, 10
— Robert, the poet's brother, 8 n, 97
— Robert, of Rosebank, the poet's uncle, 7, 83
— Sophia, the poet's daughter and Lockhart's wife, 29, 30, 43, 68 n, 92, 148, 162, 184, 189, 191, 201, 214, 266 n, 285, 296, 300
— Thomas, the poet's brother, 8 n, 14, 28, 98, 99, 104, 109, 110, 152, 178, 210, 211, 242, 248
— Sir Walter, Bart., his ancestry, 2-9; his treatment of the supernatural, 5; his attitude towards religion, 5, 300; lameness caused by infantile paralysis, 10; childhood and education, 10-16; enters his father's office, 14-16; first love, 17; adolescence and reading, 18-25; called to the Bar, 25; political interests, 3, 4, 27, 91, 121, 295, 308-10; volunteering, 28, 45, 183; second love, 28-44; marries Charlotte Carpenter, 46-67, 256; his character, 67-9, 254, 255, 259; Sheriff of Selkirkshire, 71; ballad collecting and ballad translations, 26, 32, 35, 45, 71-82; his connection with the Ballantynes and Constable, 83-9, 103, 107-15, 123, 129, 131-51, 171, 204, 207, 219-22, 253-76; Clerk of the Sessions, 89; visits London, 90-6; his brothers and sisters, 97-9; *The Lady of the Lake*, 99-102; *Rokeby*, 105-8; *Lord of the Isles* and *Waverley*, 111-16; tours the northern and western islands, 113; as prose novelist, 69, 82 n, 116-23, 172, 177, 209, 210, 306, 312; translations of German plays, 117; *Guy Mannering*, 124-6; visits London and Paris, 126, 127; *The Antiquary*, 128-32; his projected History of Scotland, 134-6, 138, 171, 173, 175, 240; *Old Mortality*, *Rob Roy*, *The Black Dwarf*, and *Tales of My Landlord*, 136-41, 152-60, 163-5, 172, 173; attacked by gallstones, 158, 179; *The Bride of Lammermoor*, *The Legend of Montrose*, and *The Monastery*, 171-6, 180, 181, 183, 199; *Ivanhoe*, *The Abbot* and *Kenilworth*, 183, 188, 189, 199-201; a Baronet, 184; greets George IV in Edinburgh, 196; *The Pirate* and *Nigel*, 201-3; *Peveril of the Peak* and *Quentin Durward*, 208, 215, 216; suffers from brain-fag and depression, 209; visited by Maria Edgeworth, 211-5; *St. Ronan's Well*, 216, 217; entertains at Abbotsford, 222-7; *Redgauntlet*, 231, 232, 234-6; his novels were printed before the whole were completed in MS., 232 n; his day's work, 232, 293; *The Betrothed* and *The Talisman*, 238-40; his *Life of Napoleon*, 240,

320 INDEX

Scott, Sir Walter, Bart.—*contd.*
268, 272, 284; visits Ireland, 241-4; meets Canning, Wordsworth, and Southey, 244, 245; *Woodstock*, 245; always ready to help his friends, 248-52, 287; keeps a journal, 254; financial collapse, 253-65; works to pay his creditors, 261, 264, 265, 270-94; *Woodstock*, 264-6; the death of his wife, 267; dines with the King, 269; an attack of paralysis, 290; his mental condition, 297; goes to Italy, 297; a further attack of paralysis, 299; his death, 300; a scheme to pay off his debts, 301-5; his limitation as a novelist, 306, 312; the dualism in his life and his work, 307, 310; his attitude towards the poor, 308-12
— Walter, of Raeburn, the poet's great-great-grandfather, 5
— Walter, " Beardie," the poet's great-grandfather, 5, 6, 196 *n*
— Walter, son of " Beardie ", 6
— Walter, son of Sir William Scott of Harden, 6
— Walter, Writer to the Signet, the poet's father, 2, 7, 8, 58, 66
— Walter, the poet's brother, 8 *n*
— Walter, the poet's son, 68 *n*, 92, 189, 192, 214, 223, 224, 227, 228, 237, 239, 241, 242, 257 *n*, 287, 297, 298, 301-3
— Walter, the poet's nephew, 189, 223
— Sir William of Harden, 6
— William, the poet's cousin, 29
Sentinel, The, 195
Seward, Anna, 94, 103
Shakespeare, William, 2, 3, 12, 21, 119, 120, 154, 207, 217, 259, 286, 306-8, 310, 312
Sharpe, Charles Kirkpatrick, 79, 80
Shelley, Percy Bysshe, 67, 168, 237
Shortreed, Robert, 20, 26, 59, 73, 290

Siege of Malta, 12
Sir Tristrem, 76, 79, 203
Skene, James, *see* Dalkeith, Lord
Southey, Robert, 100-2, 112, 113, 242, 244, 245, 248, 252, 255, 310
Stewart, Professor Dugald, 16, 23, 35, 39, 91, 115, 212
Stoniman, M. P., 303
Strachey, Giles Lytton, 2
Strutt's *Queenhoo Hall,* 117-19
Stuart, Lady Louisa, 80, 128, 129 *n*, 134 *n*, 153, 174, 198, 201, 202, 224, 239, 283
Stuart of Dunearn, 195, 217
Swinton, Ann and Sir John, 7
Swinton, John of Swinton, 5

Tales of a Grandfather, 136, 272-4, 278, 284, 291
Tales of My Landlord, 137-40, 143, 152, 153 *n*, 161, 163, 165, 166 *n*, 173, 231
Tales of the Crusaders, 231, 232, 238, 239, 247
Talisman, The, 238, 239, 293
Terry, Daniel, 113, 225, 229, 231, 232 *n*, 287, 288, 290
Thomas the Rhymer, 117
Thomson, George, 113, 248
— Thomas, 38, 75
Todd, Colonel Clarke, 7
Turner, Joseph M. W., 277

Victoria, Queen, 287
Vision of Don Roderick, 104

Wales, Prince and Princess of, 93-5
Walker, James, 26
Waverley, 84 *n*, 89, 111-22, 124, 146, 172, 176, 202, 294
Wilkie, David, 162
Wilson, John, " Christopher North ", 184-6
Woodstock, 245, 264-6, 274 *n*, 284
Wordsworth, William, 67, 68, 94, 102, 167, 237, 244, 245, 285, 295-7